£3.49

'COUNTESS DRACULA'

The life and times of the Blood Countess,
Elisabeth Báthory

Tony Thorne

BLOOMSBURY

For Françoise, Cécile and Mathilde. Girls who died.

First published in 1997 by
Bloomsbury Publishing plc
38 Soho Square
London, W1V 5DF

Copyright © 1997 Tony Thorne

The moral right of the author has been asserted

A copy of the CIP entry for this book
is available from the British Library

ISBN 0 7475 2900 0

10 9 8 7 6 5 4 3 2 1

Typeset by Hewer Text Composition Services, Edinburgh
Printed in Great Britain by Clays Ltd, St Ives plc

Contents

MORAVIA

SILESIA

KING

O

HUNG

Bytča

R. Vah

Čachtice

R. Danube

Vienna   Devín   Bratislava

AUSTRIA

Németkereszt úr

Léka   Buda   Pest

Sárvár

Csáktornya

Lake Balaton

TURKI

Mohács

R. Drava   OCCUP

CROATIA

R. Sava

ZON

Adriatic

Sea   SER

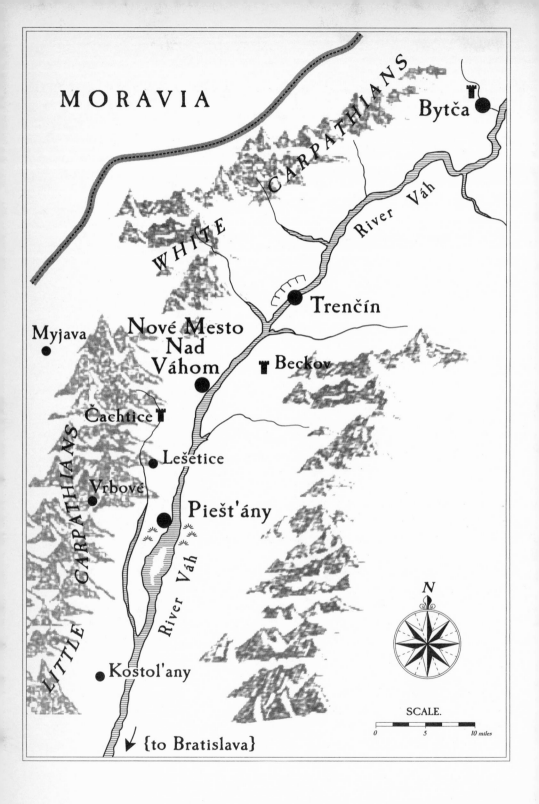

Notes on Pronunciation

Hungarian	Slovak/Croatian	English equivalent
a		*o* as in hot
cs	č	*ch* as in cheese
cz	c	*ts* as in hits
	ć	between *ch* as in cheap and *sh* as in sheep
gy		*d* as in British duke
j	j	*y* as in yes
ly		*y* as in yes
ó	ó	*aw* as in British awful
s	š	*sh* as in sheep
sz		*s* as in savage
zs	ž	*s* as in pleasure
th	th	*t* as in table
ö		*ir* as in British girl
ő		as above, with lips pursed
ü		*ue* as in due
ű		as above, with lips pursed

an accent ´ on a vowel lengthens that syllable, so Báthory = *baah*-tory

The Báthory Dynasty

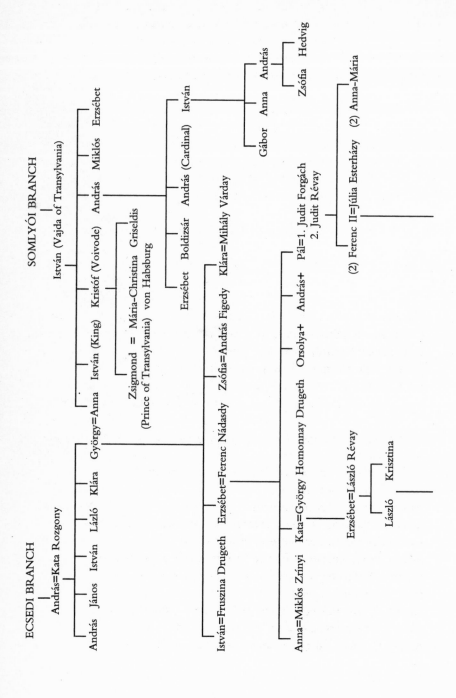

Dramatis Personae

Countess Erzsébet (Elisabeth) Báthory
Count Ferenc (Francis) Nádasdy, her husband
Lady Anna Nádasdy, her elder daughter
Lady Katalin (Kate) Nádasdy, her younger daughter
Lord Pál (Paul) Nádasdy, her son
Count Miklós (Nicholas) Zrínyi, her son-in-law, husband to Lady
  Anna
Count György (George) Homonnay Drugeth, her son-in-law, husband
  to Lady Kate
Gábor Báthory, her nephew, Prince of Transylvania
Anna Báthory, her niece
Anna Darvulia, her confidential servant
Dorottya Szentes, known as Dorkó, her confidential servant
Ilona (Helena) Jó, her confidential servant
János Újváry, known as Ficzkó, her manservant and factotum
Katalin (Katherine) Benecká or Beniczky, her servant
Erzsi Majorosné, a witch
Count György (George) Thurzó, Palatine of Hungary
Countess Erzsébet (Elisabeth) Czobor, his wife
Rudolf II, Holy Roman Emperor and King of Hungary

Matthias II, brother and successor to the above
Sir Imre Megyery, tutor to Paul Nádasdy

A note on Hungarian proper names
In Hungary – then and now – names are given in reverse order, so
Báthory Erzsébet. In this text names are given in 'English' order and
the Christian names of the main protagonists have been anglicized.
The family name ending *-y* or *-i* can be the equivalent of the French
de or the German *von* when attached to a place-name; the ending *-ffy*
originally signified *son of*, and *-falva (of) the village of*. Given the ethnic
mixture in eastern–central Europe there are many cases of non-Magyar
names which can be represented in a Hungarian spelling or in their
original form. Where it is probable that the bearer of the name did
not have Hungarian as their first language, the Slovak, Croatian, etc.
form has been used here.

Preface

During the 1980s a band of young musicians (operating in the hinterlands of the Goth, Industrial and Death-Metal genres) in their search for an arresting name with exotic and sinister associations chose to call themselves *Bathory*. The group has since disappeared and its leader, the reclusive Quorthon, gone to ground. Since 1991 horror fans have been able to subscribe to a fanzine dedicated to the macabre, published in Topeka, Kansas. Its name is *Bathory Palace*.[1] In 1993 in Sunderland in the northeast of England a young vagrant raped and almost killed a fifteen-year-old schoolgirl, attempting during the attack to drink the blood from his victim's wounds. At his trial police claimed that crime had been inspired by Malcolm Foster's obsession with the sixteenth-century Hungarian noblewoman who was renowned for murdering female virgins and using their blood to preserve her beauty and who was sometimes referred to as 'Countess Dracula'.[2] A year earlier, a radically different reading of the same historical personage had inspired a young Dutch artist to change her Christian name legally to the Hungarian *Erzsébet*, to pluck her eyebrows and hairline to resemble more closely the images of her heroine and to appear in her own installations and at social gatherings in the costumes that her muse had once worn.

At the time of writing the most eminent movie-makers in Prague and Bratislava are trying to raise the funds to film a pre-war novel (Nižňansky's *Lady of Čachtice*) based on the life of this same Countess Báthory – Meryl Streep is current favourite to play the title role – but in the meantime the anti-heroine is already on her way, like Nosferatu on his plague ship, heading westwards from her European home towards Hollywood where new patrons are waiting to reinvent her and exhibit her to a wider world. In the centenary year of that one dimensional fictional villain, Bram Stoker's Transylvanian Count, Elizabeth Báthory, the woman caricatured in English as 'Countess Dracula', is an icon whose hour has come around.

Nowadays the standard biography in English resembles the middle-class novel with its use of an omniscient narrator telling a story woven seamlessly from unseen earlier histories and from the results of library researches. If the subject is a figure from English history, an Elisabethan grandee, for instance (Elisabeth Báthory was a contemporary of her royal English namesake and of Shakespeare), the wealth of original documents that survive, together with the commentaries of successive generations of experts, will give a modern writer a head start. In the case of a Hungarian of the sixteenth or seventeenth centuries, even one of the very highest rank, the chances of retrieving sufficient material for a comprehensive treatment are very remote indeed. The archive papers are scattered and incomplete, many collections are still unsorted and inaccessible following the turbulence of the last hundred years. In Elisabeth's own day Hungarian nobles very rarely knowingly destroyed documents but many were lost in the upheavals such as the aftermath of the Rákóczi rebellion in the eighteenth century when the Habsburgs left many Hungarian castles and manor houses in ruins.

This book, the first to attempt to reconstruct and deconstruct Countess Dracula in all her many incarnations, is offered simultaneously to the vampire enthusiast, the armchair time-traveller, the amateur detective and the simply curious; it is not designed primarily for an academic readership, although it is hoped that scholars will approve of it. The intention is to gather together as many as possible of the fragments of information that remain, assemble them into a rough mosaic and see if a pattern or a picture emerges. Such a book, with its mix of history, digression, anecdote and opinion, is more likely to resemble not a twentieth-century novel, but an eighteenth-century picaresque or an amateur travelogue of the nineteenth.

Preface

To do justice to a being who is not simply ambivalent but multiple it seems best to begin by letting the past speak for itself. For this reason trial transcripts, letters, chronicles and contemporary opinions are reproduced here in something like their original form, often at length, enjoying the same status as authorial insights and perhaps helping the reader to come to some conclusions uncoerced. The reader will have to trust the writer in one respect; none of the important material relating to the Countess exists in the original in English, so almost every word has been subject to the added intervention of the translator. In another attempt at preserving authenticity, all sources have been translated expressly for this book, most of them for the first time. For the sake of coherence some concessions have been made to English style, but where strange formulations occur, these are (it is hoped) an approximation of those voices from the past as they were first recorded. Sources are given in the chapter end-notes and in the bibliography, but anyone requiring more detailed references is invited to contact the author, who will be glad to provide them if he can. Documents are reproduced with the permission of the institutions where they are held. All translations are the responsibility of the author: his gratitude to those who helped him is expressed in the acknowledgements at the end of the book.

TT. London, 1997

Báthory Erzsébet.

INTRODUCTION

I could a tale unfold whose lightest word
Would harrow up thy soul, freeze thy young blood,
Make thy two eyes, like stars, start from their spheres . . .

William Shakespeare, *Hamlet*

In the years before she killed herself the Argentine surrealist Alejandra Pizarnik wrote dozens of tiny, fragmentary poems, or perhaps one great poem with many interruptions, a series of messages of anguish, delirium and violence, all seemingly dispatched from the edge of a private nightmare.[1] She also wrote one short story, in the style of the *ficciones* of Jorge Luis Borges; the piece, which was written in the late 1960s, was entitled 'Acerca de la Condesa Sangrienta' – 'Concerning the Bloody Countess'.

In this narrative, really a series of vignettes, Alejandra Pizarnik tells the story of a European aristocrat who rules a private, hidden world of torture chambers inside her mediaeval castle. Within this underground kingdom the Lady gives herself up to the passions of endless cruelty, watching from her throne as her silent crones whip, burn, cut and pierce the bodies of a procession of helpless peasant girls

1

and seamstresses. Sometimes the beautiful and deranged Countess would simply sit and stare ecstatically, occasionally erupting in peals of demonic laughter or torrents of blasphemy; at other times she would take part in the torment herself, stabbing the girls with needles or pinching their flesh with silver tongs, placing red-hot spoons and irons on the skin of their arms and the soles of their feet, and when she was exhausted or prostrate with illness, reaching from her bed to bite them.

One episode – 'The Lethal Cage' – tells of a refinement in the method of torture used by the Lady and her assistants. This involves an iron cage lined with knives and decorated with sharpened blades which can be raised towards the roof of the stone chamber by a pulley. A naked maiden is shut into the cage by one of the old women and is lifted ceremonially into the empty air: 'The Lady of These Ruins appears, a sleepwalker in white. Slowly and silently she sits upon a footstool placed beneath the contraption . . .' The servant-woman, Dorkó, taunts the cowering girl from below with the glowing end of a heated poker. When the terrified victim recoils, she is pierced by the blades, 'while her blood falls upon the pale woman who dispassionately receives it, her eyes fixed on nothing, as in a daze. When the Lady recovers from the trance, she slowly leaves the room. There have been two transformations: her white dress is now red, and where a girl once stood a corpse now lies.'[2]

Pizarnik took her black fairytale, abridged but almost unchanged, together with its title from La Comtesse Sanglante, a work published in Paris in 1962 by another surrealist, Valentine Penrose, the first wife of the English painter and critic, Roland Penrose, and a friend of Pablo Picasso. In Penrose's 200 pages, which purport to be a work of history but read as a sustained hallucination, the Countess Elisabeth Báthory is situated in time and place: the end of the sixteenth century and Hungary. She is a being with a past and a future, a family, and a role in the world, who gradually allows her madness, coupled with her absolute power over her subjects, to transform her into an implacable monster: 'Foul stenches did not revolt her; the cellars of her castle stank of corpses, though lit by a lamp of burning oil of jasmine, her room . . . reeked of spilled blood.' Like those ascetic sectarians of the universal Mother, who kept their hands impregnated with the smell of rotting skulls which the Ganges sometimes throws up upon its banks, she did not shrink from the odour of death . . .[3]

Valentine Penrose also presents a series of cameos reminiscent of dark fairytales, many of which she adapted like much else in her book from a nineteenth-century source in the German language. This was one of the most widely quoted of the studies of the Báthory case, and the origin of the grim sobriquet which has stuck to Lady Elisabeth ever since it appeared: *Die Blutgräfin* – 'The Blood Countess'. The work was published in Breslau in 1894 and its full title was *Die Blutgräfin (Elisabeth Báthory): Ein Sitten und Charakterbild* ('A Study of Character and Behaviour'). The author was R. A. von Elsberg, actually the pen-name of the Austrian gentleman–essayist Ferdinand Strobl von Ravelsberg. Von Elsberg emphasises Elisabeth's yearnings after her husband's death:

> She was still a woman desired, and *lebenslustig* [with a desire for life], surrounded by young lords. Once it was that she was riding to the castle accompanied by one of her ardent lovers and they passed by a *mütterchen* [little old lady] who was standing there on the wayside. 'How would you feel if I commanded you to kiss this woman?', the Lady asked her swain. 'Brrr!' he answered with a grimace. And she was struck with terror in the depths of her soul, for it would happen to her as well, just a short time would pass and she would turn from a desirable and celebrated beauty, whose kisses were the dream of every young gentleman, to an ugly and neglected old woman.

The Grand Guignol atmosphere and hyperbole of Valentine Penrose's work, but not its quirkily obsessive charm, were reheated for the French market with Maurice Périsset's *Comtesse de Sang*, published in Paris in 1975. Périsset recounts a formative episode from the same Countess's childhood (she was born in 1560), an incident that taught the highly strung young girl how the power of life and death could be exercised with impunity over her social inferiors, and how snuffing out their worthless lives could be both exemplary and entertaining. The gypsies on her family demesnes in eastern Hungary were lower in status even than the Slav and Magyar serfs, eking out a living by burning wood for charcoal, mending pots and pans, or selling rotting horseflesh. One of these outcasts was suspected of selling his daughter to the Turks for cash, and was dragged before the local justices and condemned. The pubescent heiress was taken from the manor-house by her parents, or, some say, escaped from her tutor's supervision, to witness the execution. In a ritual inspired by the pre-Christian nomadic culture of the Great Plain, a horse was disembowelled and the gypsy forced into its stomach, which was then sewn up, leaving him to die slowly inside the putrefying carcass. The young girl, at first repelled by the scene, is finally overcome by the black humour of it, and gives herself up to helpless laughter.

These same tableaux appear in one form or another in most of the literature which has grown up around the persona of the Bloody Hungarian Countess, but there is another scene, essential to her mythos, which is present in all the accounts. This was introduced for the first time to the wider English-speaking readership, or so later commentators have invariably believed, by the author of that rousing Victorian hymn 'Onward Christian Soldiers', the Reverend Sabine Baring-Gould, in his *Book of Were-wolves* published in London in 1865. But, quite apart from the many entries in continental reference works which had appeared by the 1840s and which would have been accessible to the educated Englishman, there was another publication, rediscovered by this author, which more elegantly set out the essence of the Báthory myth in the English language as early as 1839. John Paget's travelogue, long out of print, contains the following passage:

Elisabeth was of a severe and cruel disposition, and her hand-maidens led no joyous life. Slight faults are said to have been punished by most merciless tortures. One day, as the lady of Csejta was adorning at her mirror those charms which that faithful monitor told her were fast waning, she gave way to her ungovernable temper, excited, perhaps by the mirror's unwelcome hint, and struck her unoffending maid with such force in the face as to draw blood. As she washed from her hand the stain, she fancied that the part which the blood had touched grew whiter, softer, and, as it were, more young. Imbued with the dreams of the age, she believed that *accident* had revealed to her what so many philosophers had wasted years to discover – that in a maiden's blood she possessed the *elixir vitae*, the source of never failing youth and beauty. Remorseless by nature, and now urged on by that worst of woman's weaknesses, vanity, no sooner did the thought flash across her brain than her resolution was taken; the life of her luckless handmaiden seemed as nought compared with the rich boon her murder promised to secure.[4]

This is the nub, the kernel of the fable, which is shared by all the histories, the novelisations, the plays and poems and operas that took Elisabeth Báthory as their inspiration. Paget continues: 'Not satisfied with the first essay, at different intervals, by the aid of . . . accomplices and [a] secret passage, no less than three hundred handmaidens were sacrificed at the shrine of vanity and superstition.'[5]

An image of the Lady of the Manor, seated in her marble bath and washing her white breasts and shoulders in blood, is the focal-point in the Paris-based Polish director Walerian Borowczyk's portmanteau film, *Contes Immoraux* ('Immoral Tales') made in 1974.[6] Countess Elisabeth Báthory is played by the fashion designer and socialite Paloma Picasso, daughter of the painter. The juxtaposition of crass soft pornography, action which veers between living sculpture and bedroom farce, and a poetic, surrealist vision of fetishistic beauty is typical of Borowczyk and evokes a quintessentially eastern – now we should say central – European atmosphere: the claustrophobia of landlocked places and the irruption of tragedy into slow, soporific lives.

A peculiarly French tradition of the avant-garde which appropriates historical figures for a cult of sin and erotic excess lies behind the work of Penrose, Pizarnik, Borowczyk who was in exile in Paris and the several operas and plays produced in the 1970s and 1980s which portrayed Elisabeth Báthory as a symbol of tragic, almost heroic, abandon. This tradition is epitomised by the writings of Georges Bataille, high-priest of transgression and promoter of an aesthetic of the morbid and the pornographic, coiner of slogans such as 'eroticism is the affirmation of life, even unto death'. Bataille writes of Báthory as one of his *outrés et dépensés* exemplars of redemption through the practice of evil in works such as *Les Larmes d'Éros* ('The Tears of Eros'). Her most memorable, indeed only, appearance under her own name in the English-speaking cinema was in a film which was to become a staple of late-night horror festivals and celebrations of kitsch cinema. It was this film, the 1970 production *Countess Dracula*, that introduced the nickname by which Elisabeth Báthory is often known in the English-speaking world.[7] The film was firmly fixed within the popular horror genre for which Hammer films were known: the introduction of a female vampire was a logical progression from the standard plots based on variations of the Dracula, Frankenstein, werewolf and mummy clichés which Hammer had reinterpreted *ad nauseam*.

Countess Dracula was produced and directed by Alexander Paal and

Peter Sasdy, both expatriate Hungarians. This concept was credited to the Hungarian writer Gabriel Ronay, who later produced a book, *The Truth about Dracula*, which claimed that Countess Báthory had indeed been a living vampire and the precursor of Bram Stoker's Count, but that the drinking of human blood and the bathing in the blood of virgins had been thought too shocking and had been removed from the official evidence given against her in her lifetime (hardly a credible thesis given the horrors that were recorded).[8] Despite its originators' nationality there is no sense in the film of the primary colours of the hot Hungarian landscape in summer, nor of the black-and-white Slovak winter when an iron cold settles on the stark forests and mute villages. The sense of life as a gallop and a dance, punctuated with moments of passionate melancholy, that can sometimes still be felt in Hungary is missing.

At least 320 films with a vampire theme were released between 1920 and 1990. Strangely, for a medium and a genre that have thrived on exaggeration, the handful of horror films which have been based on the legend of Elisabeth Báthory have shied away from confronting the enormity of her wickedness. A straightforward dramatisation of the crimes alleged against her in her lifetime – the murder of more than 600 women, genital mutilation, cannibalism – would entail a bloodbath – figuratively and literally – that would stretch the tolerance of the most liberal of end-of-century censors and risk unsettling even the most hardened *aficionado* of splatter-movies.

Of the films based on Countess Báthory's career only Peter Sasdy's made the explicit link with 'Dracula', borrowing the name for purely commercial reasons which had nothing to do with the plot. Nevertheless, the idea that the Irishman Bram Stoker's fictional Count Dracula was indeed based to a large extent on the personality of Elisabeth has been promoted by Raymond McNally, the American author who, sometimes writing with the Romanian Radu Florescu, has contributed a whole series of books and articles to recent vampire literature. After producing a biography of the historical Dracula, Vlad Tepes 'the Impaler', McNally briefly visited Austria and the then Czechoslovakia and wrote *Dracula Was a Woman*, subtitled *In Search of the Blood Countess of Transylvania*, (1983) which provided a brief summary of the career of Countess Báthory together with a long vampire-related bibliography and filmography.

McNally points out that there are several elements in Stoker's novel (first published in 1897) which cannot be directly inspired by Vlad: Stoker's vampire is one of the Székely people of Transylvania, ethnically Magyar not Wallachian; he is a count rather than a prince, and – perhaps most importantly – he enhances his youthfulness by drinking human blood, a detail not found in any of the other sources known to have been consulted by Stoker. The difficulty in confirming any such connection is that Bram Stoker kept copious notes during the long gestation period that his novel went through, and although it is known that he met the Hungarian Ármin Vambéry, an expert on his country's history, there was no mention at all of Countess Báthory in those notes. It is certain, however, that Stoker was familiar with Baring-Gould's *Book of Were-wolves*, quoted above, but had he been considering writing about a vampire *femme fatale* with strongly sapphic tendencies, Stoker need have looked no further back than 1871, to Carmilla, the heroine of the novella of the same name published by J. Sheridan le Fanu, another Victorian author of Irish blood.[9]

From folklore and anthropological studies le Fanu took the notion of an unquiet soul who returns to earth in human or animal form to drain the life gradually from its mortal victims. In his tale, set in the Styrian region of Austria, an undead countess, Carmilla Karnstein, befriends the heroine Laura, who, after half-remembered nocturnal visits from her strange acquaintance, finds herself wasting away. Le Fanu nowhere acknowledged the Báthory legends as the source of his work, and he need not have known of them firsthand to have introduced the device of a female aristocrat as villain; the concept had been rehearsed in Tieck's *Swanhilda*, Hoffmann's *Aurelia* and Poe's *Berenice* among others. But the setting of the story in the lands of the Habsburg Empire may be significant, for it was there that the legends of the historical Countess Báthory had become embedded in folklore.

Thus it does seem likely that Elisabeth had infiltrated the literary consciousness of horror writers in English but was not acknowledged. Why was she herself not celebrated in Victorian fiction? European neighbours have found it difficult to appreciate the extent of a puritanism in Victorian society (even allowing for its seamier underworld) which lingered well into the 1960s. Any more than a hint of lesbianism, for example, let alone unnatural love coupled with female sadism, was a taboo until recently; and many people have found blood-drinking distasteful and blood-bathing even more so. One hundred years ago for a writer like Stoker, the idea of choosing as a heroine a blood-obsessed lesbian mass-murderess would have been a short cut to literary obscurity.

The first and last appearance of any Báthory in English literature was the invention of the fictional 'Bethlen Báthory' – an amalgam of Elisabeth Báthory's nephew Prince Gábor and his successor, Gábor Bethlen, by Coleridge for his play *Zápolya* (his least successful work), which in its risibly confused version of Hungarian history – the historical tyrant King John Zápolya[10] is transformed into Báthory's mother – is characteristic of the cavalier way in which Hungary's history has been toyed with by outsiders when they have bothered to consider it at all.[11]

To locate and make sense of Elisabeth Báthory is not going to be an easy task. Looking for her demands an imaginative displacement in space and time, to a part of Europe which, almost a century after the dissolution of the Austro-Hungarian Empire and half a decade on from the end of communism, is still largely unknown or misunderstood, and to a time which forms a precarious bridge between our own post-Enlightenment reality – difficult enough to negotiate if we look back more than a generation or two – and the almost unknowable mediaeval world which went before.

During the long years of the Turkish wars Hungary was a place where only a handful of mercenaries and adventurers from the rest of Europe cared or dared to go. Captain John Smith, the husband of Pocahontas, fought there against the infidel, as did several of the Devonian 'gentlemen of the West' in Walter Ralegh's circle.[12] News of Magyar heroism and rumours of Byzantine excesses committed inside the ramparts of mysterious Transylvania filtered back to London and Paris by way of Constantinople, and when the Turks withdrew at the end of the seventeenth century there was an intense curiosity, especially in neighbouring Austria and Italy, about what really lay in these once forbidden territories on the ill-defined eastern fringes of the Christian world.

Vampire fiction has invariably been refracted to us through a Germanic lens – its dramas have been set among dank forests, brooding, cold fortresses, but Elisabeth Báthory's history was played out not to the sound of groaning pipe-organs and beer-songs, but in a region where cimbalom and cithare music hangs in the warm air.

The Scot William Lithgow records several times his wonder at the late-summer landscape of Hungary in 1616: '. . . Hungary . . . may be termed the granary of Ceres, the garden of Bacchus, the pasturage of Pan, and the richest beauty of Sylvan; for I found the wheat here growing higher than my head, the vines overlooking the trees, the grass justling with my knees, and the high sprung woods threatening the clouds.'[13] Other later travellers from Britain and France indulged their prejudices and frequently complained about the bad conditions of the roads in Hungary, the ferocious aspect of the people, and the discomfort suffered in the inns and taverns which they were forced to patronise.[14]

It has always been the language of Hungary, sharing five or six words with Finnish but otherwise unrelated to any other European tongue, which has both symbolised and enshrined the separateness of its people.[15] Some of Hungary's neighbours had a deeply ambivalent appreciation of the cadences of the Magyar language. The ardent Romanian nationalist mystic Emil Cioran wrote:

> Although I have known only its curses, I like the Magyars' language infinitely, I cannot have enough of its silence, it enchants me and horrifies me, I surrender to its charm and its terror, to all its words concocted from nectar and cyanide, which so properly match what one's death agony demands. We should all sigh out our existence with a Hungarian word; otherwise it is not worth dying.[16]

From the earliest days, visitors from the west returned with proverbial tales from the great store of anecdotes that already existed to illustrate the exotic customs and uninhibited ways of the Magyars. At the end of the sixteenth century the Frenchman Fumée told the tale of 'a certaine tayler of Varadin' who surprised his young wife in bed with one of his closest friends. The enraged cuckold, egged on by the townspeople, dragged his wife to the town square, where according to local custom he should execute her himself with a sabre. So piteous were the doomed girl's pleas to be allowed to live that the jilted husband thought again, then decided to forgive her. The onlookers had also been won over by his wife's display and applauded his merciful action. It so happened, Fumée went on, that not long after these events, the wife found her husband in the act of copulating with 'a common wench'. The proceedings were repeated: the man was taken to the market square, the wife made ready to strike off his head, and the husband pleaded movingly for mercy. The watching crowd was poised to praise the woman for her forbearance, but she brushed aside the tailor's promises and coolly beheaded him. Just a piece of colourful folklore, but the coming together of bravura and cruelty, the sense of a grim delight in mischief (although English has no word for it and has to borrow *Schadenfreude* from German, Hungarian expresses the notion by its own *káröröm*), will be encountered again and again in the search for Countess Báthory and the spirit of her time.

It is unfashionable now to talk of a 'national character', nevertheless, the modern traveller to east-central Europe, if she or he stays long enough, will experience the peculiar mixture of giddiness and introspection ('one eye weeping while the other smiles') which characterises the Magyars, and the wistful warm-heartedness behind the stoic countenances of the Slovaks. And it was Slovakia, although the region was then without a name and its people without a voice, that was the setting for Elisabeth Báthory's eventual downfall.

In the Czechoslovakia that came into being in 1918 and later, from 1993, in the new Slovak state, Countess Báthory has had relatively little importance as a historical reality; few scholars have paid her serious attention, although her castle in Čachtice and the village below it have often featured in folktales and songs. An older generation of Slovaks were aware of the atrocities alleged against Bátorička ('Little Báthory') through short stories and articles dating from the turn of the century.

She is known today mainly from character sketches in periodicals and the semi-fictional romance *Čachtická Pani* (*Lady of Čachtice*), a melodrama by the journalist Jožo Nižňanský which was first serialised in the Czechoslovak newspaper *A–Z* in the 1930s.[17] This work, which was later published as a 600-page novel, is the one certified bestseller among the middle-European dramatisations of the Báthory affair, a title still unknown outside the Slovak and Czech republics, where it has been in print since 1932 and has sold nearly three million copies. Nižňanský carefully studied the texts relating to the historical Countess Báthory and juxtaposed in his pages real characters with fictional creations to stage a struggle between good and evil reminiscent of the adventure novels of Walter Scott.

The late-twentieth-century versions of Nižňanský's romance of the 1930s are two novels in English pitched squarely at the vampire and fantasy market, published, one in Britain and one in the United States, in 1994 and 1995 respectively. *The Blood Countess* by the Romanian–American author Andrei Codrescu intersperses buggery, sadism and masturbation with evocations of sixteenth-century pageantry and manifestations of Elisabeth's baleful power in the present day, as when a Hungarian professor of history called Lilly Hangress (based on one of the Countess's real biographers, Dr Katalin Péter) is suddenly possessed by Elisabeth Báthory's restless spirit and orates in her voice: 'Mass slaughters of peasants, the cyclical devastations of the Black Death, the unending battles, made my world an unsteady island on a sea of blood. There was literally and metaphorically no place for me to step without stepping in blood . . . Given this red liquid medium in which I spent my life, it would have been surprising if I *didn't* bathe in blood.'[18]

As for the British novel, *Blood Ritual* by Frances Gordon, the blurb introduces its heroine and sets the tone: 'She was dazzlingly beautiful, prodigiously cruel and possessed of a consuming vanity which led her to worship strange and dark gods. Her blood descendants still live on deep within the Carpathian mountains and are determined Elisabeth's line should not die . . .'[19]

Both novels used the opening up of eastern Europe and the political turmoil there as a backdrop for the sort of neo-gothic fantasy that the American vampire authoress Anne Rice had pioneered (Gordon's book actually advertised itself as being 'in the great tradition of Anne Rice'). But neither conveys any sense of place; both play idly with the notion of a supernatural malignancy crossing from past to present. Otherwise they rely on easy thrills and contrived tensions.

Outside these works and the neat, finite references in anthologies and encyclopaedias of horror – 'armed with her special flesh-tearing silver pincers, a manual of tortures her husband had used when fighting the Turks and a taste for flagellation learned from her aunt, she set out to indulge herself and while away the lonely hours . . .'[20] – Countess Dracula's is a name to conjure with, but not much more. After all, the repressions and tensions which made the vampire a potent symbol for the nineteenth-century consciousness no longer obtain. But vampires are surprisingly still with us, thriving in our popular culture: the Victorian gothic has become the amoral soap opera of Anne Rice. In fact, we can all be vampires now; we crave longevity, immortality, and it is offered in the form of cosmetic surgery and cryogenics. In the wealthier suburbs of Los Angeles and Sydney mummification is back in vogue. We can enjoy vicariously the catharsis of bloodletting that for our ancestors was viscerally real, watching our videos as the helpless doll-victims – college co-eds now rather than chambermaids or seamstresses – are racked, mutilated and bled, just as *she* is said to have watched.

The opportunity to explore the myth and reality of 'Countess Dracula' for the first time is an irresistible one for a writer. The persona of the Blood Countess is almost too rich in significance. She is two Jungian archetypes – the wicked stepmother and the fatal seductress – in one. She embodies so many modish end-of-century themes – she is an alleged murderess (in the 1950s and 1960s murderers were the outsiders, the supreme existentialists; now they are serial killers, the ultimate consumers), a vampire, a woman wielding power in a man's world, and she is also from far away in time and place, so the Báthory biographer can fantasise that he is an early anthropologist, opening up new territory – in this case the forgotten eastern half of the European continent and the communities of 400 years ago.

It is not true, as the American authors McNally and Codrescu have written at different times, that the Hungarian authorities or the country's academic establishment have conspired to hush up the case of Countess Elisabeth Báthory. What is true is that she has been marginalised in her country's history and that, not surprisingly, Hungarians have not celebrated the memory of what may be their most monstrous forebear. Her picture does not hang in the National Gallery in Budapest next to the heroes of the Turkish wars and the struggle for independence, but is stored underground in darkness.

How did an heiress from an ancient and noble line come to stand accused by history of presiding over cannibal feasts, the application of systematic and imaginative torture and the extermination of maidens in their hundreds, all in the cause of cosmetic rejuvenation, stalking the labyrinths of the European imagination, her hands dripping with blood, part Morgan le Fay, part Lady Macbeth, part Morticia Addams?

CHAPTER ONE

An Incident at Midwinter

Beate Ungheria! se non si lascia
Piu malmenare.
(Blessed Hungary! If she no longer allows herself to be mistreated.)

Dante, *La Divina Commedia, Il Paradiso*

The landscapes of Greater Hungary ~ Čachtice today ~ an incident at midwinter ~ George Dózsa's peasant crusade ~ perpetual servitude ~ the Battle of Mohács and the Turkish occupation ~ nationality and identity ~ Transylvania ~ the Fifteen-Year War against the Turks ~ noble courts and their inhabitants ~ Rudolf II, the imperial recluse ~ along the Váh valley to Bytča ~ a mysterious correspondence

Borders in this part of the world have always been impermanent things; mountains and rivers have been the points of reference by which the inhabitants negotiated their worlds. The Danube, the greatest river west of the Volga, flows due east on its way to the Black Sea through the old Habsburg capital Vienna, now all triumphal arches and eagles, and curves gently southward a few miles further on to pass by Bratislava, whose foursquare, mournful castle guards the old walled and tiled city in its shadow. Today the other bank of the river, where the ferry used to embark, opposite the castle, is almost deserted, but the meadows that lie beyond have been covered by a giant complex of hundreds of panelled concrete tower-blocks; a showpiece megalopolis without a heart from the last years of socialist Slovakia. Barely a hundred kilometres downstream the green–brown river abruptly turns due south and passes between gorges, past miles of willow and poplar and shingle beaches to where the twin cities of Hungary's capital stand, located, according to the latest satellite mapping, in the real geographical centre of the continent, so that the green hills of Buda, the ancient limit of the Roman Empire, lie in western Europe and the busy, noisy, dusty conurbation of Pest in the east.

In the sixteenth and seventeenth centuries the highlands were yet more densely covered in forest and the flat lands dotted with thickets and copses. Cross-country travel was almost impossible where creeks and marshes lay, and hard going even on the uncertain roads and bridges which were subject to flash floods, subsidence, rock-falls and the attentions of armed beggars and rogue soldiers. When a great lady or her lord pictured their homeland in their minds, they must have formed a vision of something like a green sea – dark green in the forested north, lighter green on the southern plains – from which rose islands of sunlit yellow, the citadels in which they lived (the *vár*, the castle above; the manor-house, the *kastély*, below), and which made a series of stepping stones connecting the little centres of power and civilisation, outside which were only nameless, powerless beings toiling in the fields and vineyards, gathering wood or tending their animals.

Here at the outset of the sixteenth century was a Greater Hungary, a kingdom more than twice the size of the present Hungarian state. Rising in the south, the Leitha formed its eastern border with the German-speaking Imperial provinces, while flowing into the Danube from the north were the rivers which dissected the old territory of Upper Hungary and delimited the administrative districts: the Váh, the Nitra and most importantly the Tisza (which for the court effectively separated the governable from the barely governable territories in those days). Mountains, too, were actual and symbolic barriers, the western Carpathians marking off Moravia, the Fatras and Tatras separating the prosperous west from the impoverished and troublesome eastern counties, and – a frontier at once natural, psychic and political – the high passes leading to the plateau of Transylvania.

Only a century ago Ferenc Baumgarten, an antiquarian and essayist who lived in Pest, wrote that as one entered Hungary from Austria the landscape subtly changed and the hills began to resemble reclining camels – the first intimation of the east. According to another writer, Hamvas, Hungary was the place where the five *genii loci* of Europe converged: the spirit of the northern forests which pervades an area from Scandinavia to Poland also penetrated the Slavonic lands of the former Upper Hungary. South-west and south of Lake Balaton, where a landscape of vine-covered hills and sleepy villages stretches through Croatia towards the Adriatic, there is an almost Mediterranean atmosphere. Far to the east in present-day Romania lay Erdély – Transylvania – which preserved among its strange mix of peoples a sort of post-Byzantine spirit. The towns of Györ and Sopron, where the German language could be heard, and Sárvár, where visitors from the Netherlands and Italy were entertained, represented the spirit of the west, while the Great Plain was where the endless grass-steppes of the Eurasian east spilled over into Europe proper.[1]

John Paget travelled through the region in 1836. He reported in detail on the topography, the history and the legends of the Waag (Váh) valley, drawing upon the work *Erzahlungen, Sagen und Legenden aus Ungarns Vorzeit* by Freyherr von Mednyansky, published in 1829.

> About two hours from Pistjan [Piešt'ány] (that is, by the road our peasant coachman took us, across the ploughed fields) lies the castle of Csejta [Čachtice], a place so celebrated in the history of the horrible, that we willingly deviated a few miles from our track to visit it. I know not why, but one always feels less incredulous of the marvellous when one has visited the scene of action and made oneself at home in the whereabouts of dark deeds – as though stone walls had not only the ears so often attributed to them, but tongues also to testify to the things they had witnessed. The history of Csejta, however, requires no such aid to prove its credibility; legal documents exist to attest its truth.[2]

Paget's Csejta or Csejthe, where the Danube Lowlands meet the Little Carpathian chain, then two or three days' journey on horseback from the capital Bratislava, is now the small Slovakian town of Čachtice.

The highlands, the Lesser Carpathians and the White Carpathians with which they merge here, are not the rugged peaks of vampire fiction but a broken line of tall steep-sided hills covered with woods of conifers and oaks either side of the broad valley (about a mile and a half wide) of the River Váh, which has been likened to the Rhine, but is narrower and more sedate, about the size of the Thames as it approaches London. The countryside is still relatively unpopulated, with long stretches of open field or forest isolating the communities strung along the river. The topography that Elisabeth Báthory knew is still visible and has not yet been effaced by the carparks and hypermarkets which will eventually follow capitalism across the borders.

Nowadays at Hallowe'en in Čachtice, the local people trundle carts full of flowers up the main street, past the late-seventeenth-century manor-house and the old locked church with its defensive stone wall and onion-domed tower, to gather in the newer Catholic cemetery where they place the flowers carefully on their family graves and light small candles which they arrange on the gravel between the individual plots. By dusk the cemetery will be lit with scores of flickering candleflames and the flashlights of families picking their way between the black marble tombstones.

> The ruins of a once strong castle still remain on the summit of a hill which can be ascended only on one side; for, like many old Hungarian castles, Csejta is built on a limestone rock, forming an abrupt precipice on three sides ... The castle, though once strong ... is now fast falling into decay. It is loosely built of unhewn stone, held together by mortar, and crumbles away with every shower and blast.[3]

One hundred and sixty years after Paget passed through, the late-October weather was mild and misty and away from the town centre, three kilometres along the track that rises gently past the single-storey gypsy houses and through the woods, the open hillside beneath the white stone ruins of Čachtice castle still smelled of herbs, damp grass and leaves and the last wild flowers. There was a benign quietness around the place, no sound carried up from the few houses down in the valley and the surrounding woods muffled any noises made by woodcutters or late-season hikers: 'About the year 1610, this castle was the residence of Elisabeth Báthori, sister to the King of Poland

[sic], and wife of a rich and powerful magnate. Like most ladies of her day, she was surrounded by a troop of young persons, generally the daughters of poor but noble parents, who lived in honourable servitude, in return for which their education was cared for, and their dowry secured.'[4]

By December the weather in this part of the Lesser Carpathians will be harsher, even in a good year. On the lines of steep hills along the valley of the Váh river, snaking north along the Moravian–Slovak border, there will be snow on the black pines, the air will be still and dry and freezing and there will be ice at the river's edges. The year 1610 was not a good one. There had been a heavier than usual snowfall and it was exceptionally cold.

At around seven o'clock in the frozen evening of 29 December 1610, a detachment of soldiers, some on foot and some on horseback, led by a group of mounted gentlemen muffled in fur-trimmed cloaks and feathered hats of bear or wolf skin, advanced as quietly as they could in the darkness up the slight incline of the wide village square towards the church on the hillock at the top. One party had already left the road leading into the village to follow one of the forest paths up to the castle which they knew stood hidden by trees on the hilltop above them. Behind a series of stone walls just next to the church on the high ground there were lights showing at the windows of the manor-house. Outside, one or two watchmen stamped their feet on the cold stones of the courtyard and tugged on the leashes of the great white native dogs, placid Komondors or savage Kuvasz, both bigger and more powerful than giant mastiffs, that guarded the house.

Inside the manor, attendants were serving the evening meal to the lady of the house and a small group of companions seated around the long dining table. The gentlewomen of the court usually ate beside their mistress, together with noble guests, while the senior servants, stewards and bailiffs were allowed to dine in the same hall at a separate table. Although the decoration of the walls and floors of the place was simple by the standards of France or Italy – some Flemish tapestries, Turkish carpets, several large polished wooden chests with ornate Asiatic metalwork locks – the plates and goblets on the table were all of silver and the food was rich. The smell of the highly spiced dishes mingled with the acrid perfume of the wood fires and candlesmoke. Set into thick white walls above the diners were brightly coloured tiles and gothic angels in stone.[5]

Perhaps the guards were quietly surrounded and ordered to keep silent at the point of a sword, or perhaps they had already been tipped off to stand aside. Whatever the case, the soldiers burst open the heavy wooden doors and irrupted into the building, rushing down corridors into all the halls, chambers and annexes of the great house and hustling the astonished servants together. The gentlemen then made their way inside to confront those who had been interrupted in the middle of their meal. In the meantime, in the little houses around the square, there would have been panic. The country was no longer at war and this region was far from the Turkish front-line, but attacks by armed bands of brigands were common, and there had been rumours of uprisings in the air for some months. The soldiers probably went from house to house to reassure the people huddled inside that they had nothing to fear: the intruder in their midst was the Lord Palatine, the Habsburg Emperor's representative, the Viceroy of Hungary himself, Count George Thurzó.

The words that passed in that climactic moment between two autocrats – Count Thurzó, black-eyed, black-bearded and glowering, and the imperious, pale fifty-year-old woman dressed in satin, lace and velvet who was seated at the head of the table – were not recorded. She knew well the features of the man who confronted her, and she would have recognised several of his companions; the faces belonged to attendants she had last seen in the company of her own daughters' husbands and her young son's tutor. Peering nervously over their shoulders were some she knew much better, for only moments before they had been rushing to carry out her commands there in her own home. Once the building had been secured, a handful of the Lady's retainers were hustled away to be questioned and the woman herself was taken out of the house under armed escort. The official records state that she was removed instantly up to the high castle, but at the turn of the twentieth century the local people were still pointing out to visitors one of the long low barn-like houses belonging to the wealthier villagers in which, they said, the proud Countess had been confined for the night.[6]

The servants who had been singled out were bundled out of sight, but perhaps not quite out of earshot of their fellow domestics and, shut somewhere in the extensive cellars or the outbuildings, were put to torture by their captors. While the rest of the household held its breath, the soldiers took torches, lit bonfires and began digging in the frozen earth of the manor grounds. A strong guard was posted around Čachtice while the leaders of the raiding party rode to spend the night in the nearest suitable lodgings in the little town of Vág Újhely (today Nové Mesto nad Váhom) close by.

Some time the following day, the penultimate day of the year, Count Thurzó ordered the members of the Lady's household and her guests to come together, assembled his own entourage and summoned people from the village and the nearby hamlets. Only the lady of the house herself was missing. In front of the estate managers, bookkeepers, watchmen, shepherds and scullery-maids he arranged an exhibition, a macabre tableau consisting of the naked, well-preserved corpse of a young woman, still showing traces of the soil from which she had been exhumed and of lacerations and bruising on her blue–white skin. There were other blemishes which might have been burns, and the marks of ropes were visible on her wrists. Also there on display before them was another girl who was still alive but suffering from grievous injuries; deep suppurating wounds to her back and buttocks were pointed out to the onlookers.

Thurzó addressed his audience and informed them that he had surprised the Countess Elisabeth Báthory, Lady Nádasdy, in the very act of murder. He knew, he thundered, that the innocent maidservant who had died at her hands was only one of many, and that the butchery which they could now see with their own eyes had been practised for years. Yet more victims had been found in the house awaiting torture, he told them, and in his capacity as the highest legal authority in the Kingdom of Hungary, he, the Lord Palatine, had decided then and there to pass sentence on the perpetrator of these outrages against the female sex. He had put her 'between stones' and she would remain imprisoned in her own castle above the village in perpetuity.

The Palatine's claim – that he had stumbled on the Countess at the very moment of dispatching a helpless servant-girl – became a staple of the legend of Elisabeth Báthory, turned into a set-piece by a succession of chroniclers.[7] In the inter-war years of our own century, the Czechoslovak journalist Jožo Nižňanský imagined for his readers the scene as Count Thurzó forced his way into Elisabeth's secret inner chamber:

> The Palatine turned the handle and swiftly opened the door. He was stopped motionless in his tracks. The first sight to greet him was

Elisabeth Báthory herself, her face and arms with rolled-up sleeves were covered in blood. Bloodstains darkened her clothing. Her outrageous screeching against a background of demonic laughter curdled his blood. Dóra and Helena stood beside her, all three guffawing as if demented.[8]

The guards who escorted their noble prisoner from the village to the castle would have been careful to treat her with the courtesy which her rank demanded. She could not be manhandled. While the condemned woman was being allowed to walk unmolested into her detention, her assistants were undergoing the same cruelties that she and they stood accused of. The excruciating agonies that those servants experienced were no less keenly felt than they would be today, but for inhabitants of modern Europe physical suffering has become something exceptional, unexpected, and not the horribly familiar companion of everyday existence that it was for Countess Báthory's contemporaries.

Unless it is understood that a culture of cruelty – not violence, but deliberate cruelty – was endemic in the era that has come to be known as the early modern, the Báthory story cannot be unravelled. The celebration of this culture was something common to all of Europe at that time and its practice had been embedded in Hungarian life, almost institutionalised, since the atrocities suffered by the peasantry in the early sixteenth century. Treacherous, rapacious nobles brutalised their own countrymen for short-term advantage and ignored the long-term effects on the prosperity and vitality of the whole nation. Many of the poor of Hungary became quite indifferent to the threat from the invading Turks and were disinclined to take up arms to defend their feudal masters' privileges.

In 1514 the peasants of Hungary (then still an independent kingdom) were ordered to gather together to assemble a mighty army to fight the Turks. When the country's leaders saw what they had created – a vast and discontented horde intent on homicide and plunder – they panicked, dissolved the army and tried so send them back to their homes. Told by the man appointed to lead them, the squire George Dózsa, that their lords were afraid to fight and were abandoning the country to the infidel, the soldiers rose *en masse* for the first and last time against their feudal oppressors. The nation's crises were usually decided in the east, and it was in Temesvár (Timişoara in Romania today) that the peasant revolt was crushed. As the writer Pálóczy-Horràth imagined it in 1944:

> Our lords prepared a spectacular end for the King of the Peasants. While they had an iron throne and crown made for Dózsa, his imprisoned footsoldiers were not given anything to eat for two weeks. Many perished. But some were still alive, half-mad with hunger when, on July 20 1514, our nobles instructed the gypsy executioners to make a big fire under the iron throne until it was white-hot. They had the white-hot iron crown for the Peasant King ready also. Then they placed our leader on the white-hot iron throne, put the white-hot iron crown on his head and forced his soldiers to eat his roasted flesh.[9]

In the same year that Dózsa's revolt was suppressed, a noble expert in law, Stephen Werböczy, drew up a legal code known as the *Tripartitum*, which enshrined and confirmed the privileges of the nobility and decreed perpetual serfdom for the peasant populace. The feudal system which it consolidated remained in force in Hungary until 1848. The new code chose to see the peasants' affrontery as a sin against the divinely ordained right to rule. It declared: 'The memory and punishment of their treachery must be visited on their descendants, so that all mankind should know what a sin it is to rise against the lords. Therefore in this country all the peasants have lost their liberty by which they may move wherever they will. They are placed under eternal servitude to their landlords.'[10]

Both the higher nobility and the lesser gentry were exempt from all taxes and their absolute power as landlords was guaranteed by force. Serfs were tied to their masters' lands, paid in cash or kind according to the whim of the lord in question, forced to pay tithes, give fifty days' unpaid labour in every year and forbidden to own firearms. They could be judged and condemned even to death by their landlords according to the mediaeval *pallos jog* – the right of the sword – which in theory remained in force until well into the eighteenth century. Refusal to serve was viewed as an act of sedition and the poor were made to sign declarations of obedience whereby they forfeited their right to travel.

The privileges which the aristocrats were to enjoy were set out clearly in the codex, but exactly what their obligations were towards their fellow-citizens, and how they would be punished if they transgressed was not made explicit, even in the case of the murder of a servant by their master – or mistress. Social rank counted above all other considerations in all circumstances: even an act of rebellion against the legitimate ruler was treated quite differently when the rebels were of noble blood. When John Zápolya defeated the forces of two rival barons, Balassi and Majláth, who were trying to unseat him in Transylvania, he ceremonially returned their swords to them and pardoned them both, together with all their followers, who were allowed to rejoin their families unharmed.

The pleasures that the citizens of Hungary enjoyed during those years of the early sixteenth century must have been all the more intense for being so few and so fleeting; peasants and soldiers sleeping in the fields in the long soporific summer afternoons, dancing arm in arm to pipes and viols outside the itinerant wine-seller's tent, while in their strongholds the great families feasted, prayed, arranged their children's marriages and drilled their private armies. No sooner had the national trauma of the Dózsa revolt begun to dissipate than dynastic power struggles and the looming threat of occupation by the Turkish empire combined to throw the Kingdom into turmoil once again.

The name of the small riverside settlement in the south where the most devastating defeat in Hungary's history took place has entered the language as a byword for disaster: it is a staple of modern black humour that a man whose whole family has been wiped out in an accident can be consoled by the set phrase, 'Don't forget, we lost even more at Mohács.' Ulászló's successor, the young King Lajos or Louis II, had not been on his throne long before the Grand Turk, Suleyman, known as the Magnificent, mounted a massive offensive, breaking out of the Balkans and overwhelming the Serbs, who were holding the frontier of Christian Europe, and pushing inexorably towards Vienna. The unpopular King first staged a spectacle for his subjects in his capital; a model of the coffin of the Prophet Mohammed was put on display, suspended as if by Islamic magic 'between heaven and earth', before being set ablaze in front of an exultant crowd. Then, surrounded by foreign counsellors and accompanied by his bishops, the Magyar nobles and mercenary commanders, the King led an ill-disciplined collection of 27,000 quarrelsome and dispirited troops, cumbersome heavy cavalry in the vanguard, out into the field to stop the Ottoman advance. He confronted the Turks at Mohács in the south of the kingdom in August 1526, but a pitched battle turned into an ignominious rout and Louis and 20,000 troops, including many leading churchmen and 500 of Hungary's nobles, died as they fled the battlefield in panic. The Turks sacked the capital of Buda and left a landscape scattered with corpses and burned-out towns and villages before regrouping.[11]

A former nation defeated and paralysed by internal rivalries allowed the Ottomans to consolidate their position for a planned penetration further west. Their ultimate prize was the city of Vienna, from which they could dominate most of Christian Europe, but to ensure their supply-lines from Constantinople they had to pacify the entire turbulent region in between, a task they never fully completed.

Louis II was succeeded by King John Zápolya and there was a standoff until his death in 1541, whereupon the Habsburgs by dynastic agreement inherited the crown and took control of the west and north of the country. The Turks under Sultan Suleyman the Magnificent laid waste the central zone and fifteen years later retook the capital Buda. They occupied the whole of the south-central territories of Hungary, splitting off the eastern region, in which they installed Zápolya's son as puppet prince. This disputed zone, known as Transylvania, was formally constituted in 1568 as a semi-autonomous principality owing allegiance to the Sultan in Constantinople. The defeat at Mohács was not only a psychic wound that stayed fresh for nearly two centuries, it was a strategic catastrophe which allowed the Austrian Habsburgs and the Turks to carve up the ancient Kingdom of Hungary. It is an interesting question whether, had Dózsa's followers been given back their rights and incentives to honour their national heritage, the army facing the Turks at Mohács might have been 300,000 strong and united, instead of 27,000 and indecisive.

For 150 years after this, Hungary remained a divided and unstable entity, under constant threat of invasion from the Turks and from the Habsburgs, who needed Hungary (and coveted Transylvania) as a buffer against the Ottomans, but resented the independence of its powerful aristocracy. With open war or undeclared raids a constant threat in the south and east, the aristocrats of the Kingdom of Hungary remained west of Lake Balaton, on which their fleet rode at anchor beneath the castle of Szigliget, in permanent standoff against the Turkish ships whose topsails and pennants could be seen at the other end of the lake. The great families (sixteen of them owned more than half the surface of Hungary) fortified their palaces and moved in summer from the hot dry flatlands of the little Hungarian plain to the cooler uplands just south of the Danube, or across the river where Čachtice and Bytča can be found in present-day Slovakia.

The political manoeuvring inside the country throughout the years which followed defeat and partition was based on a tension between the 'Habsburg Party' – a faction within the aristocracy who thought that the power of the Austrian empire offered the best chance of reuniting Hungary, and the 'Transylvanian Party' – those who sided with the Transylvanian Prince and sometimes even with the Turks in the hope that this would bring about a new independence. These distinctions were never clear-cut, especially in that everyone concerned was aware of the tactical and emotional importance of Transylvania to the Magyar peoples. Even Count George Thurzó – known all his life as a Habsburg man – secretly nursed an ambition to rule there.

The sense of post-Mohács Hungary as a land deserted by God and good fortune was shared by foreign observers and Hungarians alike. The sixteenth century was a turbulent time for most European countries, with the religious upheaval of the Reformation and the fragmenting into competing beliefs and sects that followed. Then at the end of the century on the continent the Counter-Reformation began to build up momentum. The certainties and structures of mediaeval society were transformed under the influence of humanist intellectuals, and, while the European mind was struggling to cope with these changes, the European body was prey to epidemics. The age was brutal, but full of contrasts; feuds were commonplace, though mediated by codes. There was near-anarchy at times in the political sphere and economic and social progress stopped completely, but poetry flourished.

All of Europe was infected with cruelty, conspiracy and neurosis, but Hungary was in a more dangerously ambiguous state. Its traditions and institutions were still seemingly intact, but operating in an amputated portion of the old nation, threatened on the frontiers by anarchy, beyond the frontiers by hostile aliens, and alternately mocked, threatened and enchanted by the 'fairy garden' of Transylvania, with its febrile vitality and its own geographical integrity. Within the remains of the Kingdom loyalties were divided and allegiances uncertain and shifting: as the people lamented, the Protestant and Catholic propagandists each blamed the other for the tragedies which afflicted their nation.

In the occupied zone, the Turkish Vilayat, ruled from Buda, the

Magyar peasants who had not fled their villages were forced to pay tithes to the local agents of Constantinople, but in some ways they were better off than those who lived in 'free' Hungary, who were bound to their masters' land and had to submit to the hated *robot* system of forced labour. As rights and conditions for commoners slowly improved in England, the Low Countries and Germany, the lot of the three and a half million Hungarians and the 600,000 in Transylvania became worse. The manor estates of the great noble families were enlarged and the aristocracy took up trading in cattle, horses, wheat, wine, cloth and even metals, hoarding when prices were low and virtually crippling the peasant markets and the economies of the towns. Although the senior nobility could have nearly all necessities made on the estates – furniture, clothing, weapons, ornaments and jewellery – and to command their local economies, forcing innkeepers to sell only their wines, for example, the smaller feudal landlords often ran short of cash, and had to resort to moneylenders or pawnbrokers. The senior nobles oppressed the lesser nobles by using litigation, trickery or force to take over their properties and at the same time they enclosed common land: the local records show how the family of Count Thomas Nádasdy (later to be Elisabeth Báthory's father-in-law), who already owned nearly a score of farms in the region, forcibly attached to their estates land belonging to peasants around Čachtice in 1569. To make matters worse for the great majority who depended on the earth for their livelihood, there was a series of poor harvests in the years after 1570 and some landowners reacted by increasing their demand for forced labour from their serfs from one to two or three days in every week; others like Countess Báthory herself later excused her villagers from the labour requirement, but replaced it with high taxes to be collected in the form of cash or wine. Many poor communities, after protesting to the authorities that their lives had become intolerable, staged local insurrections and suffered the terrible consequences. The peasants of Čachtice did not take up arms against their landlord, but did later lodge two formal complaints in Vienna against Count Francis Nádasdy and his wife which were, like all the others, listened to impassively by Rudolf II's officials and then forgotten.[12]

Hungarian did not mean Magyar, but a citizen of the ancient territory of Hungaria or Pannonia, which had first been delineated by the Romans. Hungary and its offshoot, Transylvania, were said to be two *patriae* and one nation. This is because they had been constituted on the same legal basis and had the same common law, judicial traditions and rights towards the King. Legal and religious identity always took precedence over ethnic identity. The other feature of early modern Hungary that is difficult for citizens of modern western nation-states to grasp is its multilingual and multinational nature. In this the Kingdom of Hungary resembled the Habsburg Empire, which was made up of over a thousand separate territories, and in which the emperors themselves never explicitly identified with any particular nationality. Within Hungary there were cities and towns where the German language and customs predominated – among them modern Bratislava (then known as Pressburg in German, Pozsony in Hungarian and Prešporok to the Slovaks living around it), Sopron and Szepesség – and villages where the main language spoken was Slovak or Croatian, not to mention the mobile population of an unknown number of Romany-speaking gypsies.

The senior aristocracy who served the Austrian court were themselves of mixed origins: the Wallensteins and Zerotins were from Bohemia, the Zrínyis, the Pethös, the Keglevichs and the Kollonichs were Croatian; the Drágffys, to whom Elisabeth Báthory was related, were probably of Romanian blood. The Drágffys' name means 'sons of the dragon', referring to the order of knighthood formed to fight the Turks from which Vlad Tepes, the historical Dracula ('little dragon'), took his nickname. Elisabeth Báthory's son-in-law Nicholas Zrínyi was the scion of the Croatian Zrinski warlords, and the Thurzó and Drugeth families likewise bore non-Magyar names. The lords and sometimes the ladies were fluent in several languages; George Thurzó wrote in Latin and classical Greek and, as well as his Hungarian mother tongue, spoke German and Slovak.

It is normal today in a spirit of rapprochement to gloss over the ethnic tensions between the Hungarians, those who oppressed them and those who they in turn oppressed. In the past these divisions were rarely referred to, and such matters are difficult to investigate, since most correspondence was carried on in Hungarian or in the Latin lingua franca, whatever language was spoken privately. Nevertheless, tensions were undoubtedly present, particularly in those parts of the kingdom such as the Nádasdy–Báthory territories in Nitra county where Magyars ruled over native Slavs, just as the Norman barons in England had ruled over their Saxon serfs, whose language they disdained and whose thoughts were hidden to them. Elisabeth Báthory was highly educated and knew Latin, some Greek and some German, but had been brought up in the parts of the Kingdom where only Hungarian was spoken. Whether or not one should learn the Tót (Slovak) or Horvát (Croatian) languages of the subject peoples was a matter debated in handbooks of aristocratic etiquette; the consensus among sophisticates was that it was not necessary.[13] So, unlike the priests who preached in the church beside her mansion, the Countess could not communicate with the humbler inhabitants of her Čachtice estates and surrounded herself with Hungarian-speaking servants brought from the western parts of the country.

The ethnic mix in Transylvania was more complicated and more volatile: officially the principality was said to consist of the three *nationes*, Magyars, Saxons and Székelys. The Székelys were the descendants of a warrior caste who were ethnically identical to the Magyars, but who had been settled in those regions hundreds of years before to guard its frontiers. The German-speaking Saxons were farmers and merchants who had migrated east in the twelfth and thirteenth centuries and now lived according to their own laws in a number of autonomous cities. They had the right to forbid the Prince from entering their territories. Of the Romanians almost nothing is written, and some Hungarian historians claim that there were few of them living within Transylvania at that time. (It was not until 1918 that the region became part of Romania.) But there were certainly serfs of Romanian, Wallachian and Moldavian origin, following the Orthodox faith, which was not officially recognised – the faiths that were accepted were Catholicism, Lutheranism, Calvinism and Unitarianism – as well as the gypsies, living without a voice under Magyar rule and Turkish suzerainty.

In the English language 'Transylvania' has come to signify one thing only: the home of the Vampire of popular repute. The real Transylvania – the Romans' 'land beyond the forest', the Germans' and Slavs' Siebenburgen or Sedmohrádsky, 'land of the seven castles' – in those regions a byword for enchantment, bloody intrigue and almost permanent political chaos, was in Elisabeth Báthory's day a nominal vassal of the Turkish Sultan. Transylvania's instability extended across its mutable borders: between eastern Hungary and Transylvania was a disputed strip, the Partium, whose borders changed according to the tides of war: the townsfolk of Debrecen in the Partium had to pay taxes simultaneously to the Habsburg Emperor, the Hungarian crown and the Turkish Pasha of Buda, and to keep a wary eye on the tactics of whoever had managed to secure the Transylvanian throne. It was just west of the Partium, still within the Kingdom of Hungary, that the Báthorys' ancestral seats of Nyirbátor and Ecsed were to be found. Modern guidebooks in English have followed the American author McNally in referring to Elisabeth as the Blood Countess 'of Transylvania' and asserting that her palace at Ecsed and the castle of Čachtice once lay within that principality's borders, an idea that any citizen of the region will see as ludicrous – the old frontier at its closest was well to the east of the former and hundreds of kilometres from the latter. Despite her dynasty's long links with Transylvania, there is no proof that Elisabeth ever set foot inside the country; indeed, she discouraged her husband from accepting office there.

For all of its troubled existence, Transylvania played a crucial role in the history – and the psyche – of Hungarians. When it was created, this last remnant of old Hungary had no clear political status. At first it went unrecognised by other nations, but eventually the former voivodeship where the Báthorys, although they possessed very little land there, had traditionally held sway, imprinted itself on the minds of early modern Europe as a real political entity.[14] In the late sixteenth and early seventeenth centuries many Hungarian aristocrats secretly looked to the Prince of Transylvania to re-create a Greater Hungary free of Habsburg and Turkish domination, while the lesser nobility in Hungary welcomed the Prince's support in their resistance to the Habsburgs and their attempts to escape the oppression of their own social superiors. The princely succession which the Turks had intended to be hereditary became elective with the end of the Zápolya line, and every change of ruler meant a new outbreak of conspiracies and attempted coups. In fact any real attempts to reunite Transylvania with the mother-country would certainly have been scuppered by Constantinople, which later rebuffed Prince Gábor Bethlen with the assurance, 'We shall never cede Transylvania to Hungary, for Transylvania was invented by Sultan Suleyman.'[15]

As for the Turks, they were characterised as lions or devils by their Christian foes, and Turkish domestic culture had little effect on the Protestant aristocracy's habits. When Turks sent dresses as gifts, they were not worn, but made into bedcovers or sheets, even in Transylvania; only the cultivation and arrangement of flowers and fruit and the making of coffee, for example, were openly adopted. The fact that Turks were infidels precluded any serious attention to their way of life, although among some of those who saw the Turks at close quarters, on the battlefied or on diplomatic missions, there was a sort of mutual respect which even developed into friendship in the case of refugees like Bocskai and Bethlen, who were given sanctuary in the Ottoman court. Long after the Ottomans had been expelled, many Hungarian patriots admitted to a 'Turkish-nostalgia'). If the Hungarian knights wore green into battle to mock their enemy's sacred colour, they did not desecrate the Turkish graves on Hungarian territory. In the truces between battles, tournaments were organised in which the two sides jousted and duelled according to chivalrous rules; this did not prevent both armies from using terror tactics against one another during the many sieges; the exhibiting of heads and displays of mass-impaling beneath the walls of the besieged castle or city were common.

Where the values of the battlefield prevailed, it is not surprising that the adversaries came to mirror one another, each adapting the other's accoutrements, especially weapons and horse-furniture. The Hungarians were resolutely, bravely Christian, but when today we look at the decorated ivory sabre-handles displayed in Sárvár castle which depict the Hungarian light horse soldiers, the Hussars, fighting with their counterparts, the Turkish Janissaries, it is difficult for us to tell one from the other. The German-speaking soldiers who periodically occupied parts of Hungary during the territorial struggles showed the same wilful ignorance and were hated by the natives for their chauvinism as well as their habitual cruelty. They considered that the Hungarians and Turks were one and the same, and when they reconquered a piece of land and were petitioned by the Magyar owners for its return, dismissed them with the stock response, 'Go back to Scythia!' (In classical writings Scythia was the homeland, north of the Black Sea, of warlike barbarian nomads known for their savagery.) Many many years before, during their nomadic wanderings on the plains of western Asia, the Magyar and the Turkic cultures had indeed come into intimate contact; there were still affinities between the two languages which made the learning easy. A number of Hungarian officers (possibly including Countess Báthory's husband, Lord Francis Nádasdy) spoke some Turkish, and Turkish officers wrote letters in Hungarian. Not only did the nobles vie to mount recitals by captured Turkish musicians, but Hungary's foremost romantic poet, Bálint Balassi, had his verses arranged for Turkish music.

★   ★   ★

After more than a decade of uneasy standoff punctuated by local raids, sieges of border strongholds, advances and withdrawals, full-scale war between Christians and Moslems broke out again in 1591. The fifteen-year conflict, known as the Great Turkish War, was sparked by the Serbs, specifically the lawless *uskok* refugees who haunted the border areas; on the Turkish side, illicit raids were launched across the frontier by marauders known as *akinci*. But the fighting soon became generalised, the eastern and western powers locked into an inconclusive but bloody series of campaigns, and war became the *raison d'être* for another generation of men and boys.[16] The picture of the period of the Turkish wars which has been sustained by Hungarian fiction since the nineteenth century is typified by Géza Gárdonyi's novel, *Eclipse of the Crescent Moon*, first published in 1899, in which the dusty summer landscapes are crisscrossed by soldiers, their beards waxed and white with badger grease, travelling as best they can on one or even two wooden legs, missing an arm, a nose, ears. The whole book is pervaded by a kind of jauntiness in the midst of carnage.

It was perhaps the disappearance of the royal court, even more than the territorial losses, that had the most devastating effect on Hungarian society in that period. When Buda fell to the Turks in 1556, the country lost its administrative centre and its cultural and historical heart. The Habsburgs allowed the Hungarians to set up a new capital where the Diet sat at Pozsony, the present-day Bratislava, only a few miles from Vienna. They also maintained a royal court of Hungary as a place for ceremonies, retaining official posts and awarding titles, but all under their patronage. In return for the cosmopolitan culture which the Habsburg court embodied, the Hungarians lost most of their independence. While the alien King ruled from Vienna, it was the native Magyar magnates who were responsible for the functions that the monarch's court fulfilled elsewhere: the great noble families set up schools, established printing presses and libraries, founded scholarly societies and academies and patronised the various churches. In the rest of Europe governments or parishes had just begun to acknowledge a need to take care of the poor and to set up hospitals to tend to the wounded returning from wars and shelter the veterans who survived. In Hungary this had to be done by the aristocratic families who donated land and left legacies for the first hospitals and themselves cared for the sick on their estates.

The courts of the great landowning families depended on the concept of familiarity: a network and hierarchy of related aristocrats and gentry down to the poorest tenants and serfs, all owing a particular service to their lord. At the main Thurzó seat of Bytča, there were about fifty members of the close household resident in the castle. Young men of the middle nobility provided armed retainers and other officials and guards were stationed in the town. George Thurzó kept heavy armour and weaponry at the easily defended stronghold of Árva (Orava) where the family would repair in times of danger.[17]

Elisabeth Báthory's court at Čachtice was slightly smaller, with twenty to thirty people working in the manor house and castle and another thirty to forty tending to the fields and vineyards. The records of the estate show that the business of cultivation and husbandry was exceptionally well organised. Nobles sent their daughters to the courts of this most powerful of chatelaines from far away. It was a great honour for a girl to be given a position in her household, even that of a humble seamstress or chambermaid, and all her servants had to come recommended for a particular skill. Some witnesses testifying in the investigations into Elisabeth's alleged crimes, however, claimed that the Countess had to lure girls into her service, and one witness among the hundreds who were questioned said that the poor families around Čachtice hid their daughters when they heard that the Lady was approaching. In fact, Elisabeth Báthory was related by blood or marriage to nearly all the victims named in the testimonies, which makes it difficult for some modern commentators to imagine that she could wantonly slaughter them. Had the relatives been aware of such cruelty, they say, surely they would not have sent their daughters to be educated at her court. But social tensions in the Hungarian territories had been heightened by the male–female imbalance which the wars had created. Towns and villages were filled with unmarried or widowed women, with the result that a dowry and the chance to acquire a skill or trade were even more desperately sought.

It was the twenty or so wealthiest families who owned more than a quarter of the land. The hereditary governor (*comes*) of each county was a member of the senior aristocracy, but the county assemblies were administered by the lesser gentry, who were not usually refined, but rather rough squires addicted to hunting and tippling. Many of these 9,000 families, whose nobility consisted of a coat of arms and exemption from taxes, were impoverished and in debt: the charters conferring the lowest levels of nobility were referred to as 'dogskin

31

parchments', the lesser gentry as 'the mean puttee-wearers' or the 'lords of seven plum-trees'.

Countess Elisabeth Báthory owed allegiance to the crown of Hungary, and that crown was worn in Vienna by an Austrian. The Habsburg family had ruled Austria since 1278 and the Holy Roman Empire since 1438, a rich, ornate, cosmopolitan and complex edifice that was landlocked but diffuse, introverted and quite without any geographical reason for its existence. In 1576 Rudolf II succeeded Ferdinand as ruler of the Empire, having already assumed the crown of Hungary, which the Habsburgs had acquired as a hereditary right by marriage. Much as the Hungarian nobility disliked Rudolf personally and resented being ruled by a foreigner, their sense of realism and their veneration for the Holy Crown of Hungary itself prevented them for the most part from openly defying Vienna.

Rudolf was obsessive, introspective and morose at the best of times, and seems to have lapsed into deep melancholia for months on end. Until recently it has been usual to dismiss him as a weak ruler, a mythomaniac and a decadent, whose failing sanity eventually left him incapable of government. After rejections by Maria de Medici and the Spanish Infanta, the unfortunate Emperor did not marry, and, although he fathered children by his mistress, Barbara Strada, lurid rumours accused him of sodomy and paedophilia and ascribed his physical and mental peculiarities to the onset of tertiary syphilis. Rudolf may be seen more sympathetically as a failed mystic, who dreamed of reversing the Reformation and uniting Christian Europe under the divinely sanctioned control of his family. Protestantism was forbidden in Vienna after 1598 and he enraged the proud Hungarians by persecuting the Lutherans and Calvinists who made up a majority of their senior nobility. His own eccentric religious ideas led him to abandon all acts of worship and he was said to be terrified by the sight of the sacramental host, leading gossips to surmise that he had been the victim of an evil spell cast by his chamberlain, Makovsky. It was murmured that Rudolf himself practised alchemy and cabbalistic magic.

As a patron of science and the arts Rudolf excelled in inverse proportion to his failings as a politician and soldier. He detested the rituals of the Vienna court and the half-civilised pastimes of its inhabitants, and in 1582 he moved his seat to the ancient and beautiful Bohemian capital of Prague, which he determined to transform into a model of refinement that would outshine even the Renaissance centres of Italy. The mathematician Johannes Kepler and the astronomer Tycho Brahe were welcomed to the court of the now reclusive Emperor in Hradčany castle, as were the English magus, Dr Dee, and a host of artists, sculptors, jewellers and musicians.

Although Rudolf was, to put it charitably, an indifferent politician, he excelled as a patron, actively intervening in artistic projects, as when he directed the painter Roclant Savery to draw rare species for his still-lifes, which are some of the earliest produced in Europe. It was the bizarre constructs of the Milanese Archimboldo which are the most characteristic of Rudolf's tastes. Combining inanimate objects to produce portraits – a cook made of pots and pans, the Emperor as Vetumnus, god of the seasons, made of flowers and fruits. It is an aesthetic of novelty bordering on surrealism, but there is something airless and inconsequential about it.[18]

As the war against the Turks wore on, it became clear that the isolated Rudolf had become a liability to the house of Habsburg, and his brother the Archduke Matthias began to rally support for a palace coup. The actual events that toppled Rudolf were not the discreet decisions taken in family councils that Habsburg propaganda described, but rather a prolonged and undignified jockeying for power involving rival shows of military strength and threats of civil war. The result was a fortunately bloodless victory for Matthias, who, with George Thurzó's help, made peace with the Magyar nobles in 1606, took the crown of Hungary in 1608 and became emperor in 1611.

This, then, was the backdrop against which Elisabeth Báthory, blessed with a degree of privilege and wealth second only to the King, conducted her affairs and was eventually judged and condemned. The Empire was a wider reality to which the Hungarian aristocrats had access, and yet was one from which they could withdraw when they wished, to listen to their plaintive songs tinged with memories of the east, and reflect in the pauses between battles on the mystique of their Magyar heritage of pride and apartness.

All along the Váh valley as it winds north-east, the ruins of a string of feudal castles cling to the peaks on the river's edge. Not far north of Čachtice is the civic centre of Trenčín, then a free town and centre of trade, where a spectacular fortress begun by the Roman general Marcus

Aurelius still towers intact over the plague column, the hangman's house and the many churches in the streets below. Further along the riverside road – another hard day's ride for a traveller on horseback – lies George Thurzó's former fiefdom of Bytča, today a market town of 12,000 people. On a damp winter's day in the late 1990s, Bytča is a rather sullen place, its many featureless factories apparently deserted and the streets empty of all but a handful of expressionless passers-by. There is a market square of burghers' houses, once prosperous but now with shabby façades, and near by a crumbling synagogue, quite abandoned and ignored, on the edge of a small stream which links the moat of Bytča's castle to the river. The turreted castle too is grey and somewhat forlorn, but is undergoing a leisurely restoration to the splendid white-walled, red-roofed landmark, rising from the water-meadows and dwarfing the little settlement outside its walls, that is shown in the sixteenth-century woodcut panoramas.

The castle was built in the Renaissance style by the Milanese Giovanni Kilian for Count George Thurzó's father. In 1601 the famous wedding palace, decorated with frescoes of abundant fruits and fabulous animals, which still stands, was erected by George Thurzó just outside the castle proper, which at that time contained a school, a library and archive, a pharmacy and a prison. The Bytča estate was a centre of prosperity, enlightenment and entertainment for the aristocracy and their retainers, and was renowned for the lavish marriage feasts that the Thurzós regularly staged. For the peasants who lived in the surrounding countryside the court could be a source of largesse when the great families gathered there; at other times it was the fearful place from which unquestioned and absolute power was exercised.

On 27 December 1610 the young wife of the Count Palatine of Hungary sent a private message from Bytča to her husband, whom she had left behind two days' ride south of Čachtice in the capital, Bratislava. The note, which survives, from Elisabeth Czobor to her husband George Thurzó, is fragmentary and mysterious, in part because it was at the heart of a secret conspiracy, in part because the writer was an *ingénue* who had been taught the alphabet by her husband, but who knew nothing of written style and committed her unpunctuated thoughts to paper just as they occurred to her:

My dearest, beautiful spirit . . .
As you bade me, I have also sent my estate manager and the

old woman. They say that she [or 'he' – there is no gender in Hungarian] still says, but whether it is true or not only God knows. Those who do not obey the [first] commandment and act against it, then it is very likely that after this will do so easily [or 'after that would act contrary to the others, too'], and it is possible that those persons will bear false witness against their fellows. That one who is in the castle, they say that she says that with her hand she beat them, and if she feels herself to be involved and had she known for certain, would have been investigated thoroughly as your lordship ordered.

I am going to attend to these things as well as I am able. My beautiful beloved spirit and my lord.[19]

This insight into the unedited thoughts of one of those who was intimately involved in the Báthory case is unique. The impression that emerges from Lady Czobor's letter is of a rather garrulous, childlike woman (the terms of endearment are saccharine; the handwriting shows a mounting excitement as the note progresses) who is anxious to please her husband and to show herself as a clever adviser. Although she seems to be involved in the Palatine's secret plans, we cannot know whether she was really playing an important role or whether her husband is indulging her. We do know that George confided in his wife, which means that, whether she was interfering, gossiping or had performed a vital part in the preparations for Elisabeth Báthory's entrapment, her letter is a precious clue. If we could decode its text, we might know once and for all whether Countess Báthory was a monster or herself a victim, but the words are all ambiguous.

'I have sent . . . the old woman' – who is this that Lady Czobor has dispatched in the company of a senior servant, and where? A spy sent to infiltrate the Báthory court, an informant who will reveal the Countess's secrets, or a guide to lead the raiders to their victim? Next, 'whether it is true or not only God knows' – there seems still to be doubt in the minds of the accusers forty-eight hours before the soldiers moved in; 'it is possible that those persons will bear false witness' – will they lie to their judges about their own actions, or lie to implicate an innocent? 'That one who is in the castle' – can we be sure who is being referred to, the mistress or one of her trusted aides? 'She says that with her hand she beat them' – are the two 'shes' one and the same, or is the first the informer and the second the accused?

On 30 December George Thurzó replied to Elisabeth Czobor, who was awaiting his news:

My dear love . . . I have arrested Madam Nádasdy and they are taking her to the castle. Those who were torturing and killing the innocent ones, those wicked females, with a young lad who was the assistant in all these cruelties, I have sent to Bytča. And now with great care and security, they must be held in close captivity until God speeds me to the place and a court may be convened. The women may be held in the town, but the young boy placed in captivity in the castle. When our people went into the Csejthe manor, then they discovered a dead girl at that house and another one with wounds and dying from torture, and also there was a woman who had been tortured and was covered with wounds and another [or others] who was imprisoned who that damned woman was keeping for torture. I am waiting for that accursed woman to be taken up to the castle, and that they put her into her place. I have written in great haste on the Thirtieth day of December from Vág Újhely.
    Your love, who so much loves you
        Count George Thurzó[20]

'. . . that damned woman . . . that accursed woman . . .' – is there any doubt about which woman Thurzó is referring to? Lady Czobor's letter is intimate, cryptic and scarcely penetrable; his reads like a public declaration, which in a way it was. It contained his instructions and his authorisation for her to carry them out in his absence, and she would show it if necessary to his men in the town as a token of her authority.

When the visiting English gentleman and his companions looked over the scene of Elisabeth Báthory's arrest and incarceration in 1836, the letters that passed between Count Thurzó and his wife were lying still undiscovered among the unsorted papers of the archives in the depths of the Palatine's castle. Paget had only the terse narrative of the guidebooks and the legends as his inspiration:

With this tale fresh in our minds we ascended the long hill, gained the castle, and wandered over its deserted ruins. The shades of evening were just spreading over the valley, the bare grey walls stood up against the red sky, the solemn stillness of evening reigned over the scene, and as two ravens which had made their nest on the castle's highest towers came towards it, winging their heavy flight, and wheeling once round, each cawing a hoarse welcome to the other, alighted on their favourite turret, I could have fancied them the spirits of the two crones condemned to haunt the scene of their former crimes, while their infernal mistress was cursed by some more wretched doom.[21]

CHAPTER TWO

Ordeals and Confessions

and the false nurse shall be burnéd,
on the fire there close by.

'*Long Lankyn*', traditional English folk song

John Ficzkó's confession ~ techniques of torture ~ the evidence
of the accomplices ~ proclamations by the Bytča court ~
thirteen further testimonies ~ the sentencing and the punishment
~ a public burning

The authorities who had detained Countess Báthory knew who else
they were looking for. After being privately tortured and publicly
confronted with two of their supposed victims in Čachtice, four
members of her staff, three elderly women and one young man,
were taken under guard to the town of Bytča to be put on trial. The
four were examined again immediately after their arrival there and the
same set of eleven questions was put to each of them in turn. We should
pay especially close attention to the answers they gave since the accused,
although they may have had much to hide and good reasons to lie, had

38

been identified as the most intimate companions of their mistress and among the very few people in a position to describe the workings of the private inner court that operated wherever the Countess was in residence.

The trusted servants whom Thurzó's henchmen imprisoned and tortured were a former wetnurse, Ilona (Helena) Jó, whose surname (literally 'good') is a common one, but might also have referred to her vocation, Dorottya (Dorothy) Szentes, known familiarly as 'Dorkó', who oversaw the female servants, and Katalin (Katherine) Benecká or Beniczky, called 'Kata', a laundrywoman. Also accused was János (John) Újváry, known to everyone as 'Ficzkó', either a manservant or a humbler *Johannes Factotum* (a jack of all trades or odd-job man), who was the first to be brought before the court.

The evidence regarding Ficzkó, like the others, is given in the third person in the form 'he said . . ', but the third person pronoun 'he', 'she', 'it' is the same in Hungarian. This leads to great ambiguity in all the accounts given, because it is not always clear which of the protagonists is being referred to. Likewise the word *asszony*, denoting a married woman, so 'Mistress', 'woman' or 'lady', cannot always be ascribed accurately either to Elisabeth Báthory or to one of her female servants. Strange gaps and illogical links in the text may be due to the inarticulacy of the witness, compounded by editing or even wholesale reconstructing by the scribe. In inquisitorial procedures at that time, the quantity of evidence, so long as it went to support the charges laid, was more important than its quality, so inconsistencies were often not picked up and blatant untruths were sometimes allowed to pass unquestioned. It is implied in the original trial documents that there was at least one other version of the confessions, kept in another place, and the copies that survived in the Thurzó archive in Bytča, in the Erdő']dy archive in Galgóc and in the National Archives in Budapest differ in significant details.

Ficzkó's responses are set down here just as they appear in the records, with some comments inserted, but no attempt has been made to improve the style or impose this author's interpretation. (In the other testimonies which will be considered, some repetitions, irrelevancies and obvious errors have been removed for the sake of brevity.)

The preface of the 'protocol' or first draft summary of the servants' interrogation reads: 'This is the confessions of persons of low rank against Mistress Nádasdy, Elisabeth Báthory, on the Second of January in 1611 in the county town of Bytča. First János Újváry, otherwise known as Ficzkó, gave the following confession to the questions in order.'[1]

First question: How long has he lived with the lady and how did he come to her court?

Response: He has been living with the lady for sixteen years, if not longer. He was taken from Mrs Martin Csejthe, the wife of a student, by force.

Second question: From that time hence, how many girls and women had been killed? [Literally 'had he/she killed' – the reference is not clear.]

Response: He does not know of any woman or mistress, but of girls, since he has been living there, he knows of thirty-seven in number. Besides, when his Lord Palatine went to Pressburg, he [or 'she'] buried five in a pit, two in a small garden and one under a drain. The one is dead who was found and showed to him [the 'him' is ambiguous]. Two were taken to Lešetice [a small village now called Podolie] into the church by night and they were buried there. They were taken there from the castle because that is where they were killed. Mistress Dorkó killed them.

Third question: Who were they that she had killed and where were they from?

Response: He does not know whose daughters they were.

Fourth question: Which and what manner of women were summoned to the court and taken there?

Response: Six times he himself, this witness, with Mistress Dorkó went to look for girls, and the girls were promised that they were taken to be merchants or serving-women somewhere. This last dead girl was from a 'Horvát' [Croat] village somewhere over near Rednek, and she was taken from there. She [presumably Dorkó] was there with her, and then she had her killed [or 'caused her death' – the use of the Hungarian causative structure is likewise ambiguous throughout]. With Mistress Dorkó to look for girls were also Mrs János Bársony who lives close to Gyöngyös in a place called Teplánfalva, and besides this there was a Croatian woman living at Sárvár, Mrs Matej Ötvös, who lives opposite Mrs János Zalay. Mrs János Szabó also brought girls. She brought her own daughter and she [either Dorkó or Báthory] had her killed as well, of which she [presumably the mother] was aware, but despite that fact, she brought more and took more girls there. Mrs George Szabó also gave her own daughter to her at Čachtice and she had her killed, but more she did not take. Mrs Stephen Szabó also brought many; Mistress Helena also brought enough. Mistress Kata never brought girls, she just buried those who were killed by Mistress Dorkó.

Fifth question: With what kind of treatment and by which method did she have them killed?

Response: They tortured in the following way: they tied the arms of the girls with Viennese cord. The woman called Mistress Anna Darvulia who lives [sic] at Sárvár tied their hands behind them – like the colour of death, their hands were – and they were beaten until their body was opened up. Their palms and the soles of their feet they were beating for as long – five hundred blows – as they beat the other captive women. But they learned how to torture from this Mistress Darvulia first of all, and they were beating them until they died. Mistress Dorkó also cut with scissors the hands of the one who did not die at Čachtice.

Sixth question: Who assisted in the killing and torturing?

Response: Besides these three women, there is a woman at Čachtice called Mistress Helena who is also called 'the bald Mrs Kočiš' and she also tortured the girls. The woman, she herself pricked them with a needle if the lace was not tight. The old women took them into the torturing house . . . they burned them with an iron rod and she herself and all the old women burned them on the mouth, the nose and the lips. She put her fingers into the mouth, pulled it apart, and that is how she tortured. If they did not finish their needlework, then they were taken to be tortured. They took as many as ten a day. Like sheep they were taken there; sometimes four or five naked girls were just standing before him [the accused] and the young lads could also see that. And even in these cases they did their needlework or tied the lace. And again she punished Sittkey's daughter because she stole a pear. And she started to torture her and in the place called Piešt'ány with the old women they killed together those two who were suffering the pains of childbirth. She killed the Viennese girl Miss Modl at the place called Keresztúr.

Seventh question: Where did they bury the dead bodies; who hid the bodies . . . and how were they hidden?

Response: These old women hid and buried the girls here in Čachtice. He himself, the accused, helped to bury four of them: two in the place called Lešetice, one in the place called Keresztúr and also one in the place called Sárvár. The others were all buried in

Sárvár, accompanied by singing, and also in Keresztúr and Lešetice. When these old women killed one of the girls, the Mistress gave them presents. She herself tore the faces and other parts of the bodies of these girls and pricked them under their nails. And after that the tortured girl was taken into the frost-covered field and cold water was poured over her with the help of these old women. She herself also poured water over the girl. The girl froze and died. Here at Bytča when he was leaving, at the place called Predmier, one of the girls was put up to her throat in water and had water poured over her – the girl who escaped from her at Illava and who was found and then she died in Čachtice.

Eighth question: Did the woman herself torture them and what precisely did she do when she tortured them and had them killed? [Another version of this question runs: *What did she do then if she did not torture and did not have these unfortunate beings killed?* – this might lead us to think either that the transcribers were recording loosely, or that the wording of the questions was changed for the final versions.]

Response: When she herself did not torture, just left this work to the old women, she was in the laundry-house. She did not give the girls anything to eat for a week, and if someone secretly gave them food, that person would immediately be punished.

Ninth question: In Čachtice, in Sárvár, in Keresztúr, in Beckov and in other locations, in which places did she have these poor ones tortured and killed?

Response: In Beckov in the chamber. Inside the furnace-house she had the girls tortured. In Sárvár they were torturing in the inner part of the castle, where no one was allowed to go. In Keresztúr they were torturing in the privy. In Čachtice they were torturing inside in the furnace-house. When they were on a journey, at that time she herself tortured in the carriage. She was beating them and pinching and pricking the girls' mouths with a needle.

Tenth question: Of important personages, who was there, and who was aware of the deeds of the woman, and who saw the woman's actions?

Response: The steward Benedict Dezsö [more usually 'Deseő'] was aware of most things; he was more involved than the others, but he [presumably the accused] did not hear that this Benedict addressed the Mistress about these matters. It was also common knowledge among the servants, and the apprentices were also aware. There was also a person who was called 'Ironhead Steve' who had recently left the woman for Transdanubia: he was aware of everything – much better informed than this witness himself – and he had been playing freely with the woman [this tantalising comment could have a sexual sense, or mean that they literally played/gamed together, or that some power allowed him to toy with or behave over-familiarly with his mistress]. This man had carried more to be buried, but the witness does not know whither.

Eleventh question: For how long were they aware of the woman's terrible deeds and when did these date from?

Response: Even when the Master was alive she had been torturing girls, but in those days she did not kill them as she now did. The poor Master complained about this and he disapproved, but she did not care about the warning. But then after Mistress Anna Darvulia arrived, that one [presumably Darvulia] started to kill the girls, and after that the Mistress herself became more and more cruel and wicked. With the help of a tiny box with a little mirror set in it, she was beseeching. The wife of the *Majoros* [the tenant farmer] in Myjava prepared some water and at about four o'clock brought this water and had the woman bathed in a bread-pan. She poured the water out into the brook, and from the second mixture in the pan they wanted to bake a sort of bread which they wanted the King, my Lord Palatine and also Imre Megyery to eat and thus poison them. But these lords recognised this [enchantment] and moved against the woman, because as they ate from the first baking, they complained of their stomachs, and she then did not dare arrange the second baking.

What we know for sure about the real Ficzkó is little more than his name: he is mentioned in many of the accusations collected during Thurzó's inquiry, but the stories told by witnesses hostile to him were not all necessarily accurate. In the literature that grew up around the persona of the Blood Countess, Ficzkó features prominently; his precise age was not specified at the trial, although his youth was referred to in the judgement and in separate documents. George Thurzó and the pastor of Čachtice, Ponikenus, call him 'the young man'. This, coupled with his nickname, which can be translated as 'the Lad' or 'Boy', is significant as it helps to explain his transformation in fiction. Some writers, puzzled that an adult had kept this childish sobriquet, decided that it referred to his size or the fact that he was treated as a plaything. By the nineteenth century a French source was referring to him as 'Filsko [sic], nain de sa cour' ('her court dwarf'),[2] a hundred years later he is 'a kind of idiot hunchback gnome, very vicious, but at the same time docile'.[3] Just as Elisabeth herself seems to have provided a character for gothic romances, Ficzkó may be a precursor of a stock figure still to be seen in debased form in cartoons and video games, the evil and misshapen retainer.

There are several points in Ficzkó's confession which deserve attention. First and foremost, the way he frames his answers to the first four questions coupled with the ambiguity inbuilt in his native language mean that he may be accusing Dorkó rather than Elisabeth. Later, however, he does seem to be implicating the Countess herself.

There are some curious passages; for instance, Ficzkó says that as a very young boy and presumably an orphan he 'was taken by force' from 'the wife of a student' (deák, the Hungarian word, often also denoted an educated person or clerk). Although women were sometimes lured into service and homeless children were occasionally adopted by noblewomen, it was very rare for them to be abducted. Perhaps the comment is an error by the transcriber, or perhaps the accused is trying to emphasise his helplessness in the affair.

When Ficzkó reacts to the second question, he may be trying to impress the court with his truthfulness, or possibly it is a hint of bravado, or else simply the literal response of an unsophisticated person. Later, though, his testimony does seem questionable as he claims not to know any details of the girls who died, yet remembers the names and even addresses of the women who procured them.

Two other significant details are the mention – one of only two among the hundreds who testified – of a girl escaping from the clutches of the Countess, and the reference to magic. Ficzkó describes his mistress using her mirror to 'beseech' – to call up spirits, cast spells or ask for supernatural aid, and gives details of the ritual preparation of the deadly cake, although he does not explain how Elisabeth could have sent it to the intended victims or persuaded them to eat it.

Finally there is the strange matter of Istok (the diminutive form of István, Stephen), nicknamed 'Ironhead'. Here Ficzkó may simply be trying to shift some of his blame on to the other man's shoulders – may even have invented an *alter ego* in his desperation, but this is also the one and only possible reference to sexual impropriety in the thousands of words recorded against Elisabeth at that time. In other investigations of prominent women, as we shall see, allegations of promiscuity or infidelity were common. In the court records Elisabeth's 'Ironhead

Stephen' simply 'disappeared into Transdanubia', and strangely no one else even mentioned this memorable character.

While we are looking at the information provided to the court by Countess Báthory's assistants, we must keep in mind that their words had been transcribed shortly after they had undergone a second session of torture ordered by the Palatine, George Thurzó, and supervised by the examining magistrates.

Torturing those accused or suspected of crimes or their accomplices was an accepted part of judicial process in what the English historian Bindoff called 'an age of paid witnesses, faked testimony, of prosecuting counsel who were allowed to do almost anything they liked, and defendants who were allowed no counsel at all'.[4] It was institutionalised all across central Europe, and was unquestioned until the eighteenth century (and even then it was criticised as being an inefficient and counter-productive way of obtaining evidence, rather than as immoral or inhumane).

The methods of torture did not depend on sadism or arbitrary cruelty on the part of the torturers. Nevertheless it was well known that the quality of evidence produced in this way was likely to be inferior, and it was probably George Thurzó himself who struck out the words 'et tortura' in the draft of the report sent to the King about the executions of Elisabeth's accomplices, presumably to lend more credibility to their forced confessions.

The skill of eliciting such confessions entailed more than causing physical pain. By Elisabeth's day the inquisitorial process had undergone 200 years of refinement, culminating in handbooks for inquisitors which instructed them in exactly what should be asked, and what responses could be expected in a prescribed sequence of interrogation. In a telling precedent the Knights Templar – members of a hardened and supremely disciplined chivalrous order – had been forced in the fourteenth century to submit to interrogation. At first these warrior-monks proudly rejected all the accusations made against them, but once the torturer's expertise was brought to bear they confessed at length; in their delirium they scoured their imaginations for the most elaborate blasphemies and abominations to admit to. If paragons of knighthood were helpless before the rack, how much less resistant would a loutish young manservant and three elderly women have been?

The expert in charge of the torturing, usually the local executioner, would be a professional, rewarded for his services, typically by a fixed cash payment for each instrument applied.[5] Executioners lived well, but were local pariahs – the word executioner, *hóhér*, was a term of abuse (applied by her judges to Elisabeth Báthory and later by Lady Listhius to her despised husband) and even their touch was regarded as a cause of lifelong shame. The chief torturer would begin by displaying the instruments of torture to the subject, who would have been stripped naked and restrained: this in itself might prompt a first confession. The standard panoply included wooden wall- and floor-stocks, iron vices serving as finger-screws, iron collars spiked on the inside, the boot – a wooden or metal cylinder with studs on the inside that could be tightened by the driving in of wedges. There were also two-foot-long metal pincers and flails consisting of slender barbed chains attached to a wooden handle. Next, some of the array of torture devices would be placed on the victim's body. The mere touch of the thumbscrews or the iron boot would concentrate the subject's mind, but, if this was not enough, the various tools were put to work, starting with the agonies of crushed fingers and legs and proceeding if necessary through lighted matches under the finger- and toenails via the rack (either an upright bench or ladder on which the suspect was stretched with the aid of weights or a rectangular frame from which the subject was suspended) and the strappado to scourging, burning, branding, boiling and whatever local refinements were in vogue.[6]

In the twentieth century Hungary has a particular tradition of relishing the romantic barbarism of the exotic past in its popular fiction:

> But the real days of celebration were those when to cheer up the folk, to excite their fighting spirit, the *magister torturarum*, imported especially for the task, prepared and laid out his instruments of practice. This was the time for the hoisting up, the scorching with slow fire, the crushing of bones. This was a most effective method for quickening the lazy blood that was turning to whey in the veins. It was gaudy amusement, cruel amusement.[7]

After Ficzkó had replied to the interrogators' questions, it was the turn of the women – they are invariably described in the literary sources as 'crones', but we know nothing of their appearance or manner, only that they were all three elderly.

The next 'accomplice' to confess was the woman Helena Jó, widow of a certain Stephen Nagy. She informed the investigators that she had served the Lady for ten years (either the information was wrongly recorded or she was minimising her involvement – she must have been with Báthory for eighteen or nineteen years at least) and had acted as wetnurse to the Lady's two daughters and to her son Paul (she did not mention Andrew and Ursula, the other boy and girl born to Elisabeth, which suggests that they had died almost at birth). She knew that the crimes that her employer had committed had begun before she arrived, but during her service her mistress had killed many girls – perhaps more than fifty, but she could not be sure. She did not know whose children they were, but could remember some instances: a girl named Zichy murdered in Ecsed, George Jánosy's younger sister, a well-born girl from Pol'any, the two Sittkey women.

In answer to the fourth question Helena Jó supplied a list of those who had assisted in procuring girls, including three women from Sárvár, the wife of John Bársony, John Liptay's wife, and the wives of Stephen Szabó and Balthazar Horváth; she herself had accompanied Daniel Vas in the search for victims and had brought two girls, one of whom was dead and the other, 'the little Cseglei', was still alive. The latest victims from the Čachtice surrounds had been recruited to serve the Lady's daughter during her wedding celebrations. Helena explained that her mistress threatened some women who brought her serving-girls and rewarded others with gifts of clothing. For whatever reason, women continued to supply girls even though they knew that they were going to their deaths.

Helena Jó admitted assisting the Countess in torturing victims, but said she was forced to do so. She named Dorothy Szentes and Katherine Benecká as others who had tormented the maidservants, the former sometimes cutting the girls' swollen flesh with pincers (in another version they are scissors); Ficzkó would also slap the girls' faces whenever he was told to, but the cruellest was Anna Darvulia, who beat the girls when she had the strength to do so, but also forced them to stand in freezing water and poured more cold water over them. Darvulia had later become paralysed and, later still, blind, whereupon the other assistants had had to take over the tasks of punishment. The Countess had learned the techniques of torture from Darvulia, who was her intimate companion. Often the mistress herself would torture the girls unassisted, heating up keys and pressing them on to the girls' flesh, a technique which she repeated with coins if girls stole or concealed money they had found. Years before in the summer at Sárvár the Lady's husband had come upon a young girl bound and naked in the open air; she had been smeared with honey and left for a day and a night in the palace grounds to be bitten by ants, wasps, bees and flies. This girl who was a relation, she said (presumably of the Nádasdys), had fainted away in her agony. When that happened, said Jó, there was a method of revival that Lord Francis Nádasdy had taught his wife, which was to place coils of paper dipped in oil between the fingers or toes of the unconscious person and light them: the shock of the burning would jerk the victim back to their senses.

Helena told of the great volume of blood that was spilt around the Countess – so much that the Lady was forced frequently to change her saturated clothes and have the walls and floors of her rooms washed down. When the naked female servants were beaten by Dorkó in the Lady's presence (presumably *en masse* in their sleeping quarters), the blood around their beds was so thick that ashes or cinders had to be spread about to soak it up. At other times the Lady had used candles to burn the genitals of the maidens and needles (or knives) and even her own teeth to lacerate them. In a much quoted sequence, this witness gave evidence that when Elisabeth Báthory was in residence in her townhouse in the centre of Vienna, the cries of her victims were so loud and incessant that the monks living next door (the houses adjoined, probably on the corner of the Lobkowitz Square and Augustinerstrasse) used to throw their clay pots against her walls in protest.

When others were beating the girls, Helena stated, the Lady (or it might be 'the woman') would urge them on, shouting '*Üsd, üsd, jobban!*' ('Beat, beat, harder!')

Dorothy Szentes, known as Dorkó, the widow of Benedict Szöcs, was the third member of Elisabeth's entourage to be questioned. She said that Helena Jó had recruited her into the service of Countess Báthory and that she had been employed for only five years. She did not know when her mistress had begun to practise her cruel crimes; she was aware of about thirty-six maidens' deaths, but did not know the victims' names or their families or where their homes were located, only that they had been engaged as seamstresses and servants and had come from many different places. Szentes told her interrogators that she had

48

helped her mistress to torture girls because she had been ordered to do it. If she did not beat the girls, the Lady would do it herself, and would also pierce the girls' lips with needles, burn them with spoons and with irons on the soles of their feet and pinch their flesh with tongs. Once when the Lady was too sick to punish the girls, she was ordered to take them to her bedside, whereupon the Lady bit lumps of flesh from her victim's face or shoulders. On one occasion at Čachtice five girls died in the space of ten days as a result of torture. Szentes also implicated Katherine (Benecká), referring to her concealing corpses in Lesětice.

Szentes is said at times to 'declare as the others said' or 'agree with the previous witness', which might be a device by the scribes to avoid the tiresome transcribing of similar statements, or may demonstrate that the accused were giving evidence in each other's presence. Whatever the case, there was a consensus that local women had conspired with Elisabeth and her accomplices to supply the court with girls, that torture and murder had taken place over many years wherever the Countess was in residence, and that other members of the estate households, including the steward Benedict Deseő, the stablemaster Daniel Vas, the estate manager Jacob Szilvássy and others named as Balthasar Poky, Stephen Vágy (both of whom had testified at the earlier secret hearings in April 1610) and a certain Kozma had been aware of what was happening. All the confessions named the late Anna Darvulia, who had served Elisabeth and her husband at his court of Sárvár, as the instigator of the earliest and worst cruelties.

The last of the inner circle to be interrogated was Katherine Benecká or Beniczky, a woman whose name suggests a rank in the lesser gentry and whose husband, John Boda, and two daughters were still living at the time. She said that the wife of Bálint Varga, the mother of the present priest of Sárvár, had invited her to Elisabeth Báthory's court, where she had worked as a laundrywoman. She did not know how many young women had been killed, but thought that the number was around fifty. She herself had not recruited girls for the court, so she could not say where they had come from. She said that Dorothy Szentes had supplied the largest number of girls, including those who had died in the recent past. Helena Jó had also assisted the Countess on many occasions and joined her in her cruelty as she was an especially close confidante of the Lady, but Helena was no longer able to use her own hands in the beating (perhaps due to rheumatism or arthritis); nevertheless she was the most ruthless in supervising punishments. When Katherine Benecká had refused to help she had herself been beaten and had to stay in bed for a month to recover. Dorkó had deprived the girls imprisoned at Čachtice of food and drink and she and Elisabeth Báthory had tortured girls together, on one occasion killing five by beating them. The five corpses were stuffed under a bed and she (Benecká, or it may have been Dorkó or even the Lady) had continued to bring them food (another version has 'talk about them') as if they were still alive. The smell of decomposition had filled the manor-house so that everyone became aware of it. Then the Lady departed for Sárvár after ordering Katherine to scour the floor and conceal the bodies, but she had not been strong enough to move them and so, with the help of two women named Kate and Barbara, she dragged them to a grain pit, later burying them with Dorothy Szentes' help in an orchard (or, in another version, in a ditch). The Mistress had killed eight maidens within a short space of time and had tortured the daughter of Helena Herz or Harczy in Vienna. Benecká had also taken bodies to be buried in the graveyard at Lešetice.

Benecká also described how Anna Darvulia, originally the most adept at devising tortures, had been struck blind, after which the other women had learned to take her place. She also related how, when her mistress's daughter Anna, the wife of Count Zrínyi, was visiting Čachtice, the Countess cleared her servants out of the manor-house to make way for her, dispatching them all to the castle on the hill under Dorothy Szentes' supervision. Szentes kept the serving maids under lock and key without food or drink, doused them with cold water and made them stand stark naked overnight, deprived of sleep. She cursed and threatened anyone who thought of giving them food. When the Lady wanted to depart with her daughter to Piešt'any to take the waters, she sent Benecká to summon maidservants to accompany them, but Benecká found that the maids were in a pitiable state and not one of them was strong enough to travel. The Lady was furious with Dorkó, and the elderly Katherine had to accompany the group herself.

There are discrepancies in the surviving versions of the evidence, different documents ascribing the same statement to different witnesses. Variant versions of proper names and the confusion over pronouns and verb forms makes it difficult to decide exactly who is acting and who is being acted upon. Nevertheless it is possible to reconstruct a general summary of the testimonies of the four defendants which contains

The Čachtice portrait of Elisabeth Báthory (unknown date), stolen from the village museum in 1990

The Budapest portrait of Elisabeth Báthory, thought to date from the 17th century

Count Francis Nádasdy, the 'Black Bey', Elisabeth's husband (1555–1604)

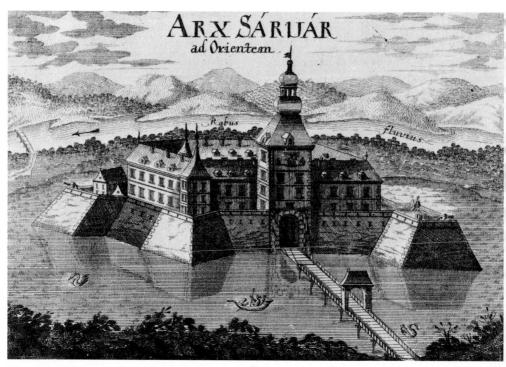

The castle of Sárvár in the 16th century

The castle of Varannó – the scene of Elisabeth's wedding to Francis Nádasdy in 1575

Count George Thurzó, Palatine of Hungary (1564–1616)

The obtaining of confessions: techniques of torture in the 16th century

The execution of traitors: a depiction from the early 17th century

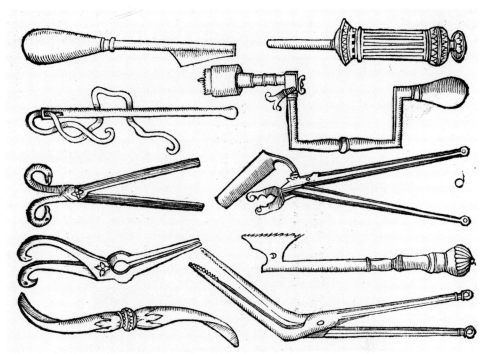

Medical instruments from the early modern era

A 16th-century witch is ceremonially burned

ANDREAS BATHOREVS

Cardinal Andrew
Báthory (d.1599)

The seal of the
Báthory family

themes and incidents echoed in the evidence given by others before
and after their indictment. All the accused agreed on the methods of
ill-treatment: beating, piercing, cutting, burning, biting and freezing
with water and snow. All said that girls had been buried, some with
and some without proper ceremony, in village cemeteries near the
Báthory estates, sometimes with the help of local priests.

The estimates of the number of victims vary but there is some
consistency: Ficzkó and Dorkó suggest thirty-six or seven, Helena
Jó and Benecká around fifty. Naturally, accomplices to mass-murder
are likely to minimise their involvement and knowledge, but if we
consider that these figures are very roughly accurate, but were actually
deaths from natural causes, the totals could be credible, given epidemics,
accidents and violence. A figure of five to ten deaths a year among a
female staff (in the Lady's larger estates across the country) of a couple
of hundred is not beyond possibility, but we will see these estimates
change dramatically as other witnesses are called.

The four accused were examined on New Year's Day, and the
court assembled on 2 January 1611. Unsurprisingly, given the venue,
the proceedings were conducted almost entirely by persons in the pay of,
or in some way dependent upon, George Thurzó. Theodore Syrmiensis,
a representative of the royal assizes at Bratislava (and a personal friend
of Thurzó), was presiding, with Eördögh from neighbouring Trenčín,
and Caspar Bájaky and Caspar Kardoss, who were both employed by
Thurzó at Bytča.[8]

The full court convened on Monday, 7 January, with a jury of
twenty including John David, sometimes known as Szent-Peter, and
Caspar Ordódy, the assistant justices of the nearby Thurzó seats of
Orava and Trenčín respectively, as well as the presiding dignitaries. The
prosecutor, Thurzó's secretary George Závodský, formally proclaimed
to the court that the Lord Palatine had acted to protect the goodly and
the innocent and to bring the Widow Nádasdy's inhuman crimes to
an end. He had gone, Závodský announced, with his retinue and in
the company of lords Nicholas Zrínyi and George Drugeth, and Paul
Nádasdy's guardian, the knight Imre Megyery, to Čachtice where he
had surprised Countess Báthory *in flagrante delicto* in the act of torturing
her victims. One girl was already dead and two others were dying.
The Palatine, in his anger at her bestial cruelty, there and then had
the Lady confined as 'a bloodthirsty female' and pronounced upon her
a sentence of life imprisonment in the castle of Čachtice. The woman's

accomplices had been tried there at the Bytča court and justice had been done. Závodský introduced the certified documents recording the accomplices' confessions into evidence and these were read out to the assembly. The four accused, who were deemed to have pleaded guilty by their confessions, repeated that they had been forced to do what they had done; they added nothing further.[9]

At this point thirteen other witnesses were heard. Nine of these were people of low rank brought from Čachtice, the other four had come from the Nádasdy estates south of the Danube in western Hungary, or at least had knowledge of events which had taken place in that region.

The first to testify, George Kubanović, said that he had seen the body of the last girl to have been murdered. She had lived at the manor-house and her body had been removed after the Lady's arrest. There had been signs of beating and burning on her body. (Kubanović did not name the girl but others did, calling her Doricza. The rumour was that she had angered the Countess by stealing a pear.) The next five witnesses, John Válko, Martin Janković, Martin Krsko, Andrew Uhrović and Ladislas Antalović, supported this evidence without adding anything significant. The seventh witness, Thomas Zima, said that he knew that two bodies had been buried in the cemetery in Čachtice and one in Lešetice. When the priest from Čachtice had criticised the Lady, bodies from Čachtice had been taken to Lešetice in secret.

John Chrpman supported the previous testimony and said that he had once asked a girl who had escaped from the Countess who her accomplices were. This girl had said that Báthory had acted alone, but was sometimes assisted by a woman who was disguised as a man.[10] Andrew Butora, the following witness, was recorded as giving similar evidence. The next to testify was a woman, identified only as Susannah, who said that Countess Báthory had been helped in her torturing by Helena, Dorothy and Anna, known as Darvulia (in some versions 'nicknamed Delbora'). John Ficzkó had also been involved, although Katherine was kindlier and had brought food to the maidens who were awaiting their cruel fate. Susannah said that several of her own friends had been killed by the Countess. She also informed the court that Jacob Szilvássy (the administrator of Léka and Keresztúr castles) had found a list of the Lady's victims in a casket (or chest) and that this list contained 650 names. The eleventh witness, Sarah Baranyai, agreed with Susannah and said that in the four years that she, Sarah, had been serving the Lady eighty people had died. She knew this from Bicsérdy, the castellan at Sárvár, but she had seen it also with her own eyes.

The penultimate witness was Helena, the widow of Stephen Kočiš (this may be the 'bald Mrs Kočiš' whom Ficzkó accused of joining in the torturing, but the name is a common one). She confirmed the stories of murder, but added that the Widow Nádasdy was also practising witchcraft and was adept at preparing poisons. She planned to kill the King and the Lord Palatine and Imre Megyery in this way. The last to be called, Anna, the widow of Stephen Gönczy, said that her own daughter aged ten years had been one of the victims and that she had not even been allowed to see her.

This part of the trial documentation also seems to be constructed from a number of different copies, signed by different notaries. Some phrases are entered illogically, out of place. It is also conceivable that some of the alleged crimes relate to Dorothy Szentes and not to Elisabeth Báthory. The witnesses once again employ the causative structure in Hungarian, which blurs the distinction between 'did' (oneself) and 'had done' (by someone else), even when less ambivalent forms could have been used. Some of the archaic vocabulary is also ambiguous: 'She used her teeth to tear the flesh of the girls' could also be rendered 'She used tongs to tear the flesh of the girls'.

The statement from 'Susannah' was one of the most sensational of the whole investigation. She estimated that 650 girls had been killed – by far the highest number mentioned in connection with Elisabeth – and said that the court official Szilvássy had seen the proof in the form of entries in Countess Báthory's journal. Those modern writers who have taken the depositions by witnesses at face value and who are convinced of Elisabeth's guilt quote this as the ultimate proof of the scale of the woman's serial sadism. The weavers of legend have included this strand, too; in their versions the notebook in its secret casket also contains, like a seducer's diary, comments on the girls' features and figures.

In a modern courtroom drama such a devastating allegation would be followed by gasps of incredulity and indignation, then an impatient shuffling while Szilvássy himself is called to the stand to corroborate or deny. The bare written records from 1611 are silent; the witness said no more and a full year elapsed before the name of Szilvássy was heard again.[11]

When the presentation of evidence was over, the court went on to pronounce its sentences immediately. The published judgement read as follows:

> The lady has committed a terrible crime against the female blood, and in this Dorothy, Helena and John Ficzkó were privy and purposeful accomplices and under interrogation the accusation proved to be well-founded and to determine more of the matter, Dorothy, Helena and Ficzkó were submitted to torture on the same occasion of the questioning. The accused persons then confirmed their previous statements and added even worse details of the terrible crimes committed by her ladyship, the widow Nádasdy. All the accused before the court, in the confessions that they made voluntarily and also under torture, and in other confessions, prove beyond doubt the guilt of the accused which surpasses the imagination in the many murders and slaughter and specific tortures and cruelty of all kinds and evil. And as these most serious crimes should be matched by the severest punishments, we have determined and we hereby decree that regarding firstly Helena and secondly Dorothy as those most implicated in the bloody crime, and as murderers, the sentence is that all the fingers of their hands which they steeped in Christian blood and which were the instruments of murder shall be torn out by the executioner with iron tongs, after which they shall be placed alive on the fire. As concerns John Ficzkó, his guilt and punishment is alleviated by his youth and his lesser participation in the crimes. He is therefore sentenced to lose his head; only his dead body will be placed on the fire with the two other condemned persons. And Katherine, as her two female companions stated that she had not participated in these affairs [sic], on only the basis of John Ficzkó's confession she cannot be condemned, therefore she shall be kept in close confinement until her guilt may be determined.[12]

In fact the truth was the reverse: Ficzkó had spoken in Benecká's defence, the two women had tried to implicate her.

> This sentence has been pronounced publicly before the accused and the punishment has immediately been carried out. As wider

proof and as an example for future times, this document is signed in our hand and affirmed by our seal, and we order that it be dispatched to his excellency the Palatine. Dated 7 January 1611.

There followed the signatures and seals of the twenty jurors.[13]

The punishments handed out to those found guilty were carefully graded and designed to match the crime. This was an age in which the idea of rehabilitation was unknown and punishing was carried out as a social ritual to deter and, just as importantly, to enact retribution, ensure public approval and to purify the whole community. As well as its pillory (instead of the wooden stocks, larger Hungarian communities favoured wrought-iron cages suspended above the marketplace) every village had its gibbet as a reminder to potential miscreants, and towns and castles kept their instruments of chastisement on public display. At Bytča there was a prison within the castle itself, where Ficzkó was kept, and a public jail for common criminals in the town, where the old women were held.[14] Public executions were held outside the town on meadowland by the river, overlooked by a line of hills. Here large crowds could assemble, and, if the wind blew from the right direction, the stench of the pyre could disperse along the valley. The condemned were usually brought out in carts early in the morning as bells tolled. They would be standing or sitting in an open cart, restrained by chains or a sort of scold's collar: a wooden yoke with a line of holes for the head and the two wrists held one before the other.

In death by burning it was thought that the forces of nature were annihilating the guilty, and not just the hand of man; it was one of the longest-drawn-out and most painful forms of capital punishment, usually reserved for witches or heretics. Hanging was considered to be the most shameful form of death and beheading the most noble in the prescribed range of capital punishment.

In Hungary, as in the rest of Europe, the moments before the act of execution could be a confused, sordid and shaming experience, or they could provide the chance for the condemned to enjoy, fleetingly, an audience before which he or she could repent, ask forgiveness and vouchsafe a few words for posterity. No account of the executions at Bytča has survived, so we do not know how Ficzkó and the women faced their deaths. In a comparable case in Engand, there would have been pamphlets printed and doggerel rhymes and songs composed, but Bytča was Thurzó's fiefdom, the few printing presses were all in the hands of the nobles and dissent was not tolerated, so any public response could only have been oral and transitory.

So died the human instruments of Elisabeth Báthory's cruelty, if the evidence and the verdict can be trusted. Apart from her, they were perhaps the only individuals who knew the truth about the deaths of so many innocents, and they could no longer be brought back to fill in the many gaps in their testimonies or alter their stories to exonerate the woman they served. Whether or not they deserved to die, the speed with which these lackeys had been condemned and the sentence carried out was unusual and irregular, but they were, with the exception of Benecká, who was spared, people of absolutely no consequence in society and therefore expendable.

The judgement pronounced on the three servants who had suffered the death penalty was proclaimed publicly in all the areas where Elisabeth's family had landholdings. Shame was a powerful weapon in the early modern period, and the potentates of the late Renaissance were experts in black propaganda: the 'facts' that had been revealed brought ignominy on Countess Báthory and by extension upon her late husband, but did so without smearing any other high-born individuals.

Of the ultimate fate of Katherine Benecká, the only one of the inner circle of servants to escape immediate execution, we know nothing at all. Arbitrary justice could work both ways; unexpectedly merciful treatment was almost as likely as disproportionate harshness, and Benecká, especially if she had relatives from the gentry to agitate on her behalf, may have walked free once a decent interval had passed (there were two men of the same family name recorded in documents of 1612 as living in the Bytča area and owing allegiance to the Thurzó family). Unluckier prisoners – war captives who could not be ransomed, minor miscreants without friends of substance, or victims of embarrassing miscarriages of justice – were generally left, literally, to rot.

There was one more gruesome entertainment for the citizens of Bytča that January. On the 24th of the month the stake was raised again in the meadow outside the town and the kindling and faggots piled around it. Without ceremony and without, it seems, any formal trial, the other named confidante of the Lady of Čachtice, the old woman Erzsi 'Majorosné' (the name translates as Beth 'the Farmer's

Wife'), the witch of Myjava, who had, it was said, helped the Countess to bake her magic cake with which to kill her enemies, was brought out and burned alive for sorcery. The farmer's wife was rushed to her death without being questioned, without being required to undergo the ordeal by water or the oath purgatory, which would have proved or disproved her guilt.

We might, as most historians of the last century did, accept the evidence presented here as being trustworthy, and take this as the whole of the story. But the trials of the servants at Bytča, the condemnation *in absentia* of their mistress and the burning of her witch was neither the beginning nor the end of the official investigation into the alleged massacre of virgins. Nor is it possible for us to judge Elisabeth Báthory finally for ourselves until we have considered her life and her age in more detail, and examined the remainder of the documents that have been left for us by her accusers and by the Lady herself.

CHAPTER THREE

The Pastor's Denunciation

Compassed about with so great a cloud of witnesses

Hebrews xii: 1

The secret interrogations of 1610 ~ hearings at Vág Újhely ~ the March testimonies ~ visions of purgatory ~ Pastor Ponikenus' denunciation ~ cannibal feasts ~ some rituals, portents and omens ~ vampires and other supernatural beings

All the indications are that Elisabeth Báthory was taken by surprise when the authorities arrested her, but the process which culminated in the raid at the end of December 1610 had been set in motion nearly a year before, almost as soon as George Thurzó, her neighbour turned adversary, had been confirmed in his post as Palatine of Hungary. Some historians have written that after hearing rumours of atrocities committed in his own city King Matthias had ordered the inquiry into Elisabeth's activities from Vienna; others, starting with the eighteenth-century Jesuit Father Túróczi, suggested that the parents of missing girls must have lobbied Count Thurzó until he was forced to take action.[1]

But there is absolutely no hard evidence for either of these theories.

Imagination, of course, also abhors a vacuum, so a more romantic rationale emerged. Paget introduced the tale to English readers:

At last, however, Elisabeth called into play against her two passions stronger even than vanity or cunning – love and revenge became interested in the discovery of the mystery. Among the victims of Csejta was a beautiful maiden who was beloved by and betrothed to a young man of the neighbourhood. In despair at the loss of his mistress, he followed her traces with such perseverance, that, in spite of the hitherto successful caution of the murderess, he penetrated the bloody secrets of the castle, and burning for revenge, flew to Pressburg [Bratislava], boldly accused Elisabeth Báthori of murder before the Palatine, in open court, and demanded judgement against her.[2]

It was normal to assemble a great volume of evidence before starting a trial against a high-ranking defendant, and the sequence of preliminary hearings, the actual trial and the post-trial deliberations would frequently take years. A lord or lady could expect to be formally summonsed to appear well before being taken into custody or having to present themselves before the court, and it was at that point that many defendants simply left the country and waited for the political climate to change, or petitioned for a pardon on the ground of their rank. In the matter of the rumoured crimes of Elisabeth Báthory the officials appointed to supervise the investigation made their first moves at the end of February 1610 when the Countess was staying at her usual winter residence at Sárvár.

The first letter of interrogation was issued on 5 March 1610. Andrew Keresztúry, a notary of the royal chamber, received this evidence recorded in Latin to be used later in a formal trial if needed. The thirty-four witnesses, all from the environs of Čachtice in Nitra county in Upper Hungary, were brought together in secret at the market town of Vág Újhely, the present-day Nové Mesto nad Váhom in Slovakia, only a few kilometres from Čachtice itself.[3]

The witnesses were mostly people of low birth: fourteen of them were the serfs of Daniel Pongrácz, the lord who shared the lands around the castle of Beckov with the Nádasdys, seven were the serfs of Peter Ráttkay and five were the serfs of Francis Mágóchy, lesser gentry owning adjoining estates.[4] These, then, are humble near-neighbours who would not have been allowed to enter Countess Báthory's properties without her invitation. They mainly refer to news that they had heard rather than to events that they had witnessed with their own eyes and are reticent in comparison with witnesses testifying later in the investigation – understandably so, given that the Lady they were being asked to accuse was still at large and was their most powerful neighbour.

Three of Daniel Pongrácz's tenants, George Predmerský, Nicholas Kochanovský and George Blanár, stated that Countess Elisabeth Báthory had killed two maidens and had taken them to the village of Kostol'any to be buried. George Gasparović, the fourth to be summoned, confirmed that there had been at least one mysterious death connected with Kostol'any, and many of the witnesses also referred to an incident which seems to have taken place there in 1592 in which a young girl was given an 'ice-bath' in a brook on Countess Báthory's orders, after which the girl died.

Another of Pongrácz's men, Nicholas Kuzchleba, testified that he had heard from a certain Potocký, who served Thurzó's fellow lord Count Stephen Illésházy, that the Lady had cruelly murdered two maidens from well-born families in Liptov by whipping them, then ducking them in the icy Váh river near the clifftop fortress of Strečno.

The eleventh witness, Nicholas Mezarić, a debt and tithe collector from the town of Nové Mesto declared that the Čachtice manor warden (he did not name the individual) had asked a John Sl'uka from Vrbové to obtain medicines from the pharmacy in Nagyszombat (today the town of Trnava). The pharmacist, Dr Márton, who called himself by the Latin name of Graimelius, had told Sl'uka that the drugs he had been asked for were sufficient to kill about a hundred people.

One Ladislas Šaary said that girls had been whipped until they bled, then lashed again with stinging nettles, before being submerged in icy water. The next-but-one witness John Moravčik also referred to the icy-water baths, which he had been told about by one of Báthory's servants named Mazalák; he further confessed that he heard from others who had been selling salt that when Stephen Báthory (Elisabeth Báthory's elder brother) died, the Widow Nádasdy, as she was travelling past his estates, buried two girls in Liptov. The next group to testify, John Mesar, John Pesthy, Nicholas Čisar, John Benco, John Krajčović and George Maidanek, agreed that before the wedding of his lordship George Drugeth of Homonna to Elisabeth's daughter, there had been two murders, and afterwards there was another mysterious funeral.

Stephen Mokor, the twenty-sixth witness, said he had heard many times that the widow in her court was cruel to the living virgins. The twenty-seventh witness, Michael Dubnický, confessed that he did not know or see anything personally, but he heard from many people that the widow, Mistress Nádasdy, her ladyship, did cruel things in her court to living maidens and girls. The next witness, Martin Komarek, endorsed the previous witnesses' stories. Some witnesses reported that they had seen maidens with their hands bound, others that girls in the Mistress's carriage appeared to have burns on their hands.

Several had heard that there had been a funeral without the prescribed tolling of the bells and without the due ceremonies, an assertion which was confirmed by Michael Fábry, the priest at Kostol'any, who was the last to give evidence at this hearing. He stated that two girls who had been murdered at Čachtice had been buried in Kostol'any without a priest so that no one should learn of their deaths.

There are several points worth noting in weighing up this first round of depositions, apart from the fact that the testimonies are cautious and based almost wholly on hearsay. Firstly, it is quite likely that the citizens of Nové Mesto itself would be hostile to the Nádasdy family, given that they feared the interference of this most powerful feudal clan in their relatively free trading activities (the town of Nové Mesto had been granted grazing rights, the right to sell its own wine and to hold a lucrative annual fair). Most of those heard, however, were tied servants of a rival feudal estate, that of the Squire of Beckov, Daniel Pongrácz, who was a descendant of the Hunt–Poznán dynasty which had ruled the region long before the arrival of the Nádasdys. Recent research has uncovered another intriguing connection between his family and the neighbouring Nádasdys which may point to a resentment deeper than the usual coveting of land. Daniel Pongrácz's wife was Anna Majláth, the daughter of the nobleman Gábor Majláth and Lady Anna Bánffy, and forty years earlier Francis Nádasdy's father, Count Thomas and his wife Lady Ursula Kanizsai, who were then without an heir, had considered adopting the boy Gábor Majláth and bequeathing him their vast inheritance. Before they could conclude this arrangement, Ursula became pregnant with a child, the long-hoped-for son, Francis, Elisabeth's husband, and the hopes of the Majláth family were dashed.[5]

The accusations made by all the witnesses, even if based on rumour, are fairly consistent – which does not itself say anything about their authenticity – and two main themes emerge strongly. The first is that bathing in icy water, for whatever reason, was practised by Elisabeth's entourage, and the second is that it was widely believed that girls who had died were being buried without ceremony and in secret. Not for the last time, the local priest was willing to give evidence against the Countess, but without explaining how it was possible that he knew so little about so much. The question of poison, which was strongly hinted at by Mezarić, was not developed by other witnesses, but the fact that drugs were being purchased by the Báthory court may be significant in another connection. The substance in question was not named, but Sl'uka later confirmed that it was antimony, indeed a poison, but widely used in very small doses by professional and amateur healers.

There is another strand within the evidence lodged against Elisabeth Báthory, one which first appears in the statement by Nicholas Kuzchleba. This witness refers to 'well-born' victims, and the theme of noble girls being abused is emphasised more and more as the confessions are collected. The wellbeing and the lives of commoners counted for very little in feudal Hungary and any serious attempt to indict the Countess would depend on proving that she had harmed persons of consequence. If, as some recent commentators suspect, the whole purpose of the investigation – at least at the beginning – was to outrage Elisabeth's fellow aristocrats and alienate them from her for political reasons, it was vital to show that she had scorned the inviolable status of the nobility.

The second stage of the investigation took place almost simultaneously, the mandate being issued on 25 March 1610. This set of hearings was organised under the supervision of Keresztúry's fellow notary, Moses Cziraky from the tabular court of Bratislava (the supreme legal assembly which was headed by the Palatine), and examined eighteen witnesses from the county of Vas, where the court of Sárvár was situated, and the surrounding districts of Györ, Sopron, Moson, Veszprém and Zala, all in the west of the kingdom.[6] The specifics – names and methods of torture, for instance – given in these statements show a consistency, but differ from those recorded in the north of the country. The language, too, is different: whereas the style of speech used by the serfs of Nitra county often seems like the repetition of a formula – one nervous peasant echoing his predecessor's words – these more privileged officials and courtiers provide 'colourful' detail and anecdotes.

The first witness, Benedict Bicsérdy, the warden of Sárvár castle, declared that 175 girls and women were taken out dead from the house of the Lady, but of the nature of their deaths he was ignorant, because he was not there unless summoned by the Lady. But he once saw that the wall was stained with blood; it must have been the blood of the torture victims, and he knew that she was beating her girls, so much so that when walking around the castle he heard the sound of the beatings, some of which went on for six hours at a time.

Gregory Paisjártó, the second witness, had not been to the house of the Lady. He could say nothing of what happened or of the attitudes of the people there, but he knew that girls were carried out in coffins, accompanied by singing. He could say nothing regarding the causes of their deaths. He was not permitted to enter the Lady's house.

The third witness, Benedict Zalay, was the estate bookkeeper, but said he had no business in the castle and that he knew nothing of the events there.

The fourth witness, Gregory Balázs, said that he had carried girls' bodies on the cart (another version has 'he knew that girls had been carried out in coffins on the cart') accompanied by priests singing, but he did not know what manner of death those girls had suffered.

The fifth witness was Ambrose Borbély, who was a 'doctor' (he was probably a humble barber–surgeon, but some versions describe him as a quack or body-snatcher), and said that when the Lady summoned him he would go, but otherwise he would not. When he was there, and saw some sick girls, he gave them some medicine because the Lady ordered it, and he saw the faces and mouths of the girls, but did not know if other parts of their bodies had been beaten or tortured.

The sixth witness said he, Michael Zvonarić, was the priest of the place, and confessed that when he was in the Lady's house nothing could be seen, because they were very careful and they had enough staff to ensure that it was cleaned. There was a guard on the door and none could enter without permission. And there inside she had a secret place, and he heard from others that she tortured the girls, but he himself saw nothing. He had been told that on one occasion the Lady had had three girls laid in one coffin and buried together in that way, so he had gone to the Lady and reproached her, asking why she had three maidens buried in one casket. She had replied to him that there were only two bodies in the coffin, and that she had ordered it to be done so that suspicions would not be raised that they had died one shortly after the other. Zvonarić said that he asked her not to do such things because her household was suffering as a consequence.

The seventh witness was a squire named Adam Szelesthey from the village of Dienesfalva. He stated that he had heard that the two daughters of Gábor Sittkey were killed cruelly by torture, as were the daughters of Stephen Szoltay. He also heard from a coachman called Peter that when he (or 'she', it is not clear) was travelling from Ecsed, she was torturing the daughter of a noble for a long time. When the girl died they just buried her by the road. The same Peter said that when they returned at the time of the coronation ceremony (of King Matthias in 1608) there was an exhausted girl who had suffered torture, having been stabbed and burned with hot irons; it was in this state that they brought her from Pressburg (Bratislava). She died after a few days in Keresztúr.

The next to testify was Francis Török, a knight and magistrate, who swore that Countess Báthory had done nothing before his eyes as she had before others, but he knew that when she was travelling to Ecsed after the death of Stephen Báthory, her brother, in 1605, she had been carrying with her the corpses of three girls who had died after torture. The Countess ordered the bodies to be buried at Branisko, beyond Siroka (near the Polish border). A girl of noble birth had been brought to Ecsed and had later been killed at Keresztúr: when Elisabeth Báthory had come to Füzér the girl's relatives had asked after her and the Countess told them that she had died of the plague. On her first journey to Ecsed, he said, she had cruelly tortured a maiden in Varannó. The witness went out hunting hares and when he returned, the footmen told him, 'Sir Francis, the girl you saw being tortured was strangled in the Turkish way.' (This was a harem technique of discreetly dispatching domestic victims in private with a silk scarf.)

Here occurs for the first time in the testimonies the oft-repeated story of the young woman from Bratislava who was employed by Elisabeth Báthory at the castle of Varannó. The Countess, who was short of serving maids, ordered this woman to dress as a maiden to wait at table. (There was a tradition that only virgin girls should attend the table at marriage feasts.) When she refused, saying she was a married woman with an infant son, named Francis, her mistress became furious and gave her a log and forced her to suckle it as if it were a child, and then she tortured the girl to death using many kinds of torment. (This story was repeated by two other witnesses at this hearing, but the woman concerned was not named.) Before Lord Homonnay's wedding to her daughter, Török added, the Lady had two dead girls in her chambers and she caused them to be buried at night. A witness had seen the marks of torture and of burning on their bodies.

Török said that he had heard that the Lady had inserted a hot iron bar into the girls' vaginas. Her household servants had declared that she had already murdered 200 victims and he himself knew that the daughters of Sittkey had died not of the plague, but of torture. He knew too of the means employed: the Lady had had the maidens' hands tied so tightly that they turned blue and blood spurted from their fingers. 'God alone', he said in conclusion, 'could account for all her brutalities.'

Sir Balthazar Poky, who spoke next, was also a castle warden at Sárvár. He stated that the total number of victims involved was more than 200, who he heard had probably died of different forms of torture.

Stephen Vágy, an official at her court, then asserted that the Lady had a kind of grey cake which she had been given by sorcerers. In the centre of this cake was a wafer through which the Lady peered while she recited words against the Lord Palatine, the judge (Cziraky was named in some versions) and the head of the county. When she looked through this wafer she looked at a picture of the person she was thinking of and repeated the following formula: 'I am looking at you through a wafer, and as I cannot see you there, do me no harm.' This would sometimes continue for an hour.

The twelfth person to be questioned was Stephen Szabó (a common name, then and now): he volunteered almost nothing. It may be of significance that Elisabeth Báthory's confidants later named the wife of a Stephen Szabó of Sárvár as one of many women who procured girls and brought them to the court.

The sixteenth witness, Andrew Lakatjártó, said that he had been told that a woman named Anna and nicknamed 'Delbora', had tortured maidens, and that the Countess had had her kill Matthew Fekete's younger sister and others.

The nineteenth witness, Francis Bornemissza, a nobleman, related that Stephen Magyari, the former priest at Sárvár, had told the people of the village that they should remain (behind in the church after the service) for he had something important to say. He said that he was bound to warn her ladyship because a girl who was buried the day before had died as a result of cruelty. The girl who predeceased that girl had also died from cruel treatment, and the lady should desist because God would be offended, and the priest would be damned if he failed to admonish her. That is why he suggested that the body should be exhumed and the signs upon it examined to determine how she had died. And then her ladyship said, 'You will see, priest Stephen, that I will make you regret this. I have relatives who will not tolerate your behaviour: you are creating a shameful situation for me and exposing me to public disapproval, and I will write of this to my husband.' Then the priest answered, 'Well, if your ladyship has powerful relations, so have I, and mine is the Lord; like it or not I will have the corpses exhumed and you can see what you have done.' Then the Lady went into the castle and wrote an aggrieved letter to her husband to the knowledge of the witness (her husband was in Vienna at the time).

The final witness in this part of the proceedings was Paul Bödy, described as a student (usually meaning an educated person with scholarly or clerical duties) and assistant castle warden at Sárvár. He claimed often to have seen the bodies of girls taken through the gates of the castle to be buried with the accompaniment of singing. He himself did not witness their deaths because he did not go into the Lady's quarters. He heard that they had died of torture. On one occasion when John Mogyoróssy, the captain-in-chief of Sárvár, and Gregory Jánossy were together, the priest Stephen Magyari was with them and they were speaking as follows: 'Beware that, as well as punishing her, God will also punish us. We had better leave this place, and you sir, Stephen, as a man of God, it is your duty to reproach her, and if she does not cease, then you must declare it from the pulpit!' Magyari did just this and his master (Count Francis Nádasdy) was furious, but the priest eventually pacified him.

During this round of depositions the number of Elisabeth's supposed victims is estimated for the first time and rises from 175 (the figure given by Francis Nádasdy's faithful servant, Benedict Bicsérdy) to 'more than two hundred'. The tormenting and killing, they say, was not confined to the secret places inside the Lady's properties, but went on behind the curtains of her carriages in transit between one estate and another. There is a first mention of sorcery by Stephen Vágy, who describes a ceremony of sympathetic magic that was typical of the era. Obtaining magic cakes from witches was something that many noblewomen were commonly supposed to do and the principle of framing your enemy or victim in a transparent surface was widespread – the Elizabethan magus Dr John Dee had a 'scrying-glass' for just such a purpose. This same Stephen Vágy was named by Elisabeth's servant Dorothy Szentes ('Dorkó') during her trial at Bytča as one of those who knew all about their mistress's secret activities.

Several of the witnesses stress the high social status of the girls who were mistreated, including the daughters of the Sittkey family, who were related by marriage to the Nádasdys. Other victims came from what the Slovaks call the Zemani, the lowest rank of the gentry.

Several also refer to the sermon preached against the Nádasdys at Sárvár in 1602. The letter that Elisabeth was said to have sent to her absent husband complaining about the local priest's interference has been preserved, but it does not specify the reason for the complaint.[7]

When witnesses describe burials 'accompanied by singing', this refers to the custom of hiring students or trainee priests to chant prayers and sing hymns over the bodies of paupers and plague victims. Here it implies unorthodox funeral arrangements, but of course it argues against these burials being carried out in total secrecy.

The story of the German servant-girl who was publicly humiliated by being forced to suckle a log is one which recurs throughout the testimonies and must refer to an authentic incident, although it is not clear when it happened – the dates given differ by almost a decade. It is fairly easy to rationalise what looks at first sight to be a grotesque and arbitrary ritual, lending weight to the idea that many of Elisabeth's supposed cruelties were in fact instances of imaginative punishments meted out for real misdemeanours. It makes sense to assume that Miss Modl's insolence was connected with the mood of defiance among the Germans living within the Kingdom at the end of the Bocskai rebellion when they took advantage of the Imperial anger at the Hungarians' disloyalty to express their own ingrained resentments. It was at this time that Elisabeth was humiliated by the Germans of Bratislava, who refused to let her cross the Danube on their ferries; she would have been doubly enraged at the thought of a wave of disobedience spreading through her households, and an effective means of stopping this was to parade the bare-breasted maidservant through her estates as a lesson to the other domestics. The log was a refinement that Elisabeth probably borrowed from a widespread form of punishment, the so-called 'stone of shame', suspended from the neck of a wrongdoer who would be displayed in a village square to expiate the crime of slander or disrespect to one's betters.

In passing we can also note that one aspect of this testimony rebuts the idea that the age was so brutalised that the death of an individual was quickly forgotten. That may have been tragically true in the case of the unbaptised babies of the poor, who up until the end of the nineteenth century were buried in unmarked graves around crude crosses at the roadside. But here the death of a girl in a brook at Kostol'any was clearly recalled from eighteen years before – if it was true.

There is perhaps a parallel between the witnesses' evidence and the visions of disorder which preoccupied the European mind and can be seen in such masterworks as Brueghel's *Fall of the Rebel Angels* and *Dulle Griet* ('Mad Meg') and in the cruder, more lurid depictions on the walls of churches right across the troubled eastern regions of Hungary. The early modern imagination was informed – or inflamed – not only by sermons dwelling on sin and retribution, but by the sensationalist content of pamphlets and broadsheets which circulated among the just-literate and the educated alike, and which were read to those who could not decipher them. One popular theme was visions of purgatory or hell. Those of George, the son of Krizsan, from 1353 were still recounted in Báthory's time:

> then George saw . . . souls who were hanged aloft with burning ropes, but when he saw better those ropes, he realised that they were rather snakes, which could bite and burn the souls, too. And each soul was hanged by eyes, ears, lips or tongue, or other parts of their bodies wherewith they had sinned . . . He saw male and female souls, who were pierced with heated iron pikes in their stomachs, but the spikes went through their vulvas or penises. Female souls were pierced through their wombs as well. The devils put heated iron tools on the penises of the male souls . . .[8]

This second phase of the inquiry made mention in passing of some sort of feud between the aristocratic couple who presided over the Sárvár estates (and were also hereditary administrators of the whole of Vas county) and the Lutheran priests who officiated there. As well as these hints of a religious aspect to the campaign against the Countess, there is one other document, a letter, in existence which is central to the Báthory mystery and which sheds unique light on the volatile relations between factions from the church, the noble families' courts and the local communities of Royal Hungary, as well as hinting at the secret agendas that were operating at a more rarefied level. The document is a rich mixture of the minutiae of life in the village and the imaginative landscape of the Lutheran mind. It was sent on New Year's Day, 1611, by the Vicar of Čachtice, the Slovak pastor Jan Abrahamides Ponický, who had latinised his family name according to humanist custom as Ponikenus, to his superior, Elias Láni or Lányi, and was found attached to the investigation papers in the Thurzó family archives, but there is no indication that it was ever formally introduced in evidence, or officially certified as a case document. Láni was the Lutheran Superintendent in the area and Thurzó's own minister. The letter was certainly passed on to Thurzó by him, which was probably Ponikenus' intention when he wrote. The handwriting, which is clear and workmanlike, is probably Ponikenus' own, and the text begins in competent Latin with the conventional lengthy expressions of respect and piety, then . . .

On the first Sunday of Advent past, during the evening service when I was explaining the lesson, a person named Andrew Priderović – a living instrument of the Devil – dared to contradict me publicly – did I say 'me'? – dared to oppose the pure Holy Spirit itself, saying aloud to a student standing next to him: 'Does this priest preach the truth? I do not understand!' The student answered him holding the New Testament before him: 'Behold! See the text itself.' He left the church spouting all kinds of evil words. On the following day a certain nobleman, who was betrothed [or 'at a betrothal ceremony'], for no reason greeted me thus – pardon me for using these words – 'You are a rascal, a bastard, I will drag you out of this parish by the scruff of your neck like a dog.' I protested and left, and in accordance with the decision of the Synod in Žilina reported the case to the superior authorities, who promised me protection.[9]

This glimpse of the tensions in the local congregations and the bullying behaviour of nobles may be an example of provocation by rival Calvinists, or else is part of a personal feud between Elisabeth and her agents and her Lutheran enemies. (It was Count Thurzó who had personally convoked the Žilina synod to establish Lutheran privileges and agree procedures for the new faith.) Ponikenus then exults:

> But behold, beyond all expectations – my good Lord! – what has happened! It is at once miraculous and evil. Our Jezebel (my meaning is Elisabeth Báthory) has had just punishment for her misdeeds. She was incarcerated. She was put into a stone-walled prison for ever. What should I add to that? (I believed that it was my official duty to invite some of my fellow-priests to console her with prayers and to protect her from temptation [presumably the temptation to take her own life].)
>
> No sooner had we saluted her and expressed our pity at her case but she said straightaway: 'You two pastors, you are the reason for my imprisonment.'
>
> Reverend Zacharias, the pastor from Lešetice, offered excuses in Hungarian which she accepted and she became calmer saying to us, 'You are not the reason, but the parson of Čachtice certainly is. For he fulminated against me in each of his sermons.'[10]

The power of sermons must not be underestimated; these were the means of disseminating news, opinions or propaganda, but also gave the opportunity for clerics to mesmerise, entertain and terrify their parishioners with their eloquence. Comparisons with the power of the modern mass media are not necessarily facile or overstated. Among the non-Magyar populations of the Kingdom of Hungary, the local priests and their rhetoric had another vital function: they began to legitimise the people's language. Before the Reformation the Slav dialects of Upper Hungary had been ignored or forbidden, but with their use in church they began to be written down, then standardised and codified. We can imagine the situation in Čachtice where the Lutheran priests trod a wary path between defending the serfs whose language they conversed in, appeasing Lady Nádasdy their local patron, and sometimes acting as spies for their ultimate master, the Palatine.

> Reverend Zacharias answered: 'Do not believe that, Madam!' The woman said, 'I can even prove that with witnesses!' I said, 'I was preaching the Gospel and, Madam, whenever your conscience felt itself pricked, it was not because of me, for I never mentioned you by name.' The prisoner answered: 'You, you must die first, then Sir

Megyery. You two are the reason for my grievous imprisonment. Do you not think that it will provoke turmoil? East of the Tisza an uprising will start and soon they will be here. Even the Duke of Transylvania will take revenge for the injustice done me.'[11]

The writer is tactful enough to substitute the title 'Duke' (*dux*) for the 'Prince' (*princeps*) by which Elisabeth's nephew was honoured in Transylvania: this very issue of titles had enraged Thurzó in his negotiations with Gábor Báthory. The Tisza was the river which separated the politically unstable counties of eastern Hungary from the mainly loyal Habsburg dominions of the west. After this devastating suggestion of treason – a capital crime – on the part of the Lady, Ponikenus hints at the existence of co-conspirators before turning abruptly to a more sinister:

I discovered what she said in Hungarian from my interpreters only at home. But she never mentioned who she was going to entrust with the task of requesting the army. Nor did she name the person whose idea it was. I believe she trusted in the service of those whom she asked for help when she was captured. Much has recently been brought to light; what must be taken into account most especially and above all, is what happened this year [sic], before the twenty-ninth of December, 1610. Before she was caught she had lost a superstitious prayer which had been given her by the tenant-farmer's wife [Erzsi Majorosné] from Myjava. When she missed it she sent her steward to the woman and asked him to write it down immediately as he heard it from her and to bring it to her. The woman, who was an adept in witchcraft, did not want to say it at once, but timed it for midnight. Then she went out, and looking at the stars and the motion of the clouds prayed with the following words, asking the steward to record them:
   'God help! God help! You little cloud! God help little cloud! God grant, God grant health to Elisabeth Báthory. Send, send me little cloud, ninety cats, I command you, who are the lord of the cats. Command them and gather them wherever they are, whether beyond the mountains, or beyond the waters or the sea, gather those ninety cats and send them away to bite King Matthias' heart, to bite my lord Palatine's heart, and let them eat

the heart of the red Megyery, and Moses Cziráky's heart, too, so that Elisabeth Báthory may come to no harm! Holy Trinity do these things!'

According to confessions, this and others similar have been written down and kept by the steward. See, Reverend Sir, how the Devil makes his subjects blind and by what means he leads them astray. Before the steward returned with the bewitching words (she commanded him under penalty of beheading to write down accurately the words of the tenant-farmer's wife and bring them to her) the Lady had already been led to the castle.[12]

Cloud-conjuring formulae seem to have been particularly common, perhaps because at certain times it was easy to predict changes in the weather and then claim credit for them. Elisabeth's incantation is also notable for mixing Christian sentiment with pagan superstition in the manner of Caribbean voodoo or *santeria*.[13]

Ponikenus continues: 'A man whose name was Torkos, and who used to live a mile from Sárvár, gave this advice to her: Choose one black hen, beat it with a white stick, keep its blood and use it against your enemies in this way; if you touch with the blood your enemies or their clothes, they will not harm you . . .'[14] He underlines the pernicious prevalence of witchcraft, a Protestant obsession which led his church's rivals, the Calvinists, to mount wholesale pogroms among the country's peasantry later in the sixteenth century:

You can judge my Reverend Lord what a sinful soul is within this paragon of evil! But she still places her hopes in the county court, and is still blaming the Lutheran priests for her disaster, just as the local people are saying that the Lutheran priests have caused this scandal.

Yesterday we had much difficulty with her. Reverend Zacharias asked her: 'Do you believe in Christ who was born and died and rose for you and won the remission of your sins?'

'Even Peter the Smith [the personification of the simplest rustic] knows that!' she said. Reverend Zacharias wanted to give her a prayerbook, but she refused to take it: 'I do not need it.' Then I asked her: 'I wished to know, who was it who said to you that I was the cause of your trouble?' 'I am not obliged to answer to your question. Now you are furious with me, soon you will have twofold cause to be angry.' But I said, 'I am not angry, but I should like to be fair, and make it clear that I am not the cause of your imprisonment.' Then she said again: 'I was the patron – like a mother – to your priests, from the smallest to the highest one, I have never done anything against them, neither the slightest nor the highest, I have done nothing even against you yourself.' I asked her to remember me always with good feelings, because I pray always to God for her prosperity and to grant mercy to her for her sins. She answered: 'Praying to God for the prosperity of others is always praiseworthy behaviour.'

We can picture Elisabeth's furious sarcasm in the face of the pastor's pious condescension and nervous bumpkin manners. Then Ponikenus pauses, fearful that his message might be intercepted: 'We were discussing in this way, but the subject is more fit to speak of in words and not to be written in a letter. But I was writing this because I want the three old women and the young Ficzkó to be questioned, who were carried from her to Bytča, I want them to confess their sins, how much they enjoyed the killing, and what else they have done . . .' Here is the ostensible reason for the letter: to ensure that the truly guilty individuals will be brought to book.

We heard from those maids who are still living that they were forced to eat their own flesh, which was fried on an open fire. The flesh of other maids was chopped and mashed, as with mushrooms in the preparation of a meal, and was cooked and served to young men who knew not what they were eating. Oh Thyestean banquet! Oh what brutality! I think there were no greater executioners under the sun than they were. But I must hold my feelings, I can write no more of it for the pain of my soul is so great.

Cannibal feasts were a staple of the horror-folklore of the time, and were probably based on historical fact. As well as the roasting of the rebel Dózsa on an iron throne, anyone living in Hungary at that time would probably have heard of the Tatar Khan's treatment of envoys from Hungary that was reported by Edward Barton, the English ambassador to Constantinople in 1593:

73

This Prince of the Tartars is sayd lately to have taken sixe Hungarish spyes, whom calling before him, he commanded presently three of them to be rosted in the presence of their fellowes, and calling his captaines about him caused them all to eat part of the said rosted spyes . . . and cutting off the noses and ears of the other three spyes, had them returne and report what they had seene . . .[14]

The Vicar of Čachtice's thoughts turned to his own vulnerability:

However I have too many enemies, therefore I have to ask your protection my Reverend Lord, pray for me to our Lord and please ask his Lordship [Thurzó] to take me under his protection, because I am afraid that Lord Homonnay or the son of the lady or her daughters will attack me. Although I am sure that Elisabeth Báthory was already killing maidens ten years ago, because in the time of my predecessor, Andrew Berthoni, maids were buried in the church at night, which is well known by the inhabitants of Čachtice. Even Stephen Magyari, who died eight years ago, warned the lady in his speech publicly, and this is also well known in her court among the servants who are still living. I have spoken the truth.

Rejoice in our Lord

Čachtice, the first day of January 1611.

Jan Ponikenus, priest and senior

At the end of his letter Ponikenus has not managed to unburden himself of all that he has to express. Before the message is sent, he takes up his pen again:

P.S.

The paper was not able to hold all that I wished to let you know, although I do not wish to abuse your patience, but you must be aware of the following: in the last days of December, when I returned from the castle and sent home my priestly brothers from Lešete and Vrbové, I was thinking upon my sermon. Then I took supper, after it I prayed with my servants, and then I went back to my study. Shortly my wife came to me and we were discussing these horrible matters. Suddenly I heard cats mewing on the upper floor, I can explain it clearly in my own language ... [here Ponikenus switches to Slovak][15] ... so that voice was not a normal miaow, I went after the voice and ordered my servant, 'Jano, if you see any cat, just beat it!' But we found no cat. My servant said: 'There are mice in the storeroom.' I checked the said place, but there was no cat in there. But when I was descending the staircase, straightaway six cats and dogs were biting my legs. 'Get you to hell!' I shouted and they disappeared so soon that my servant did not see them. See, my Reverend, this was a game of the Devil.

The presence that had terrified him was presumably that of the ninety cats and their canine allies. It is not clear whether Ponikenus could see them, or merely felt their teeth, but the Protestant clergy firmly believed that evil was tangible – Luther himself saw the Devil sitting on a wall and mocking him.

On Christmas Eve Majorosné was bathing the lady using several herbs, and as I heard, they wanted to bake bread using that water. They wanted to bake that bread for their enemies.

So the devil was caught in his own trap. You will hear other things from others, but pray God with me to help us against our enemies. God be with us!

The said Majorosné, as I have heard, has withered.

Ponikenus himself says that the purpose of this hasty communication is to 'investigate well those servants taken to Bytča': singling them out and taking for granted their guilt, as he does here, must have helped to seal their fate, as well as making Erzsi Majorosné's death inevitable. (His closing words, the reference to that woman's 'withering', are obscure, but suggest some form of divine retribution: 'wasting away' was a common description applied all over Europe to the victims both of sorcery and of God's punishment of it.) But his letter concentrates rather on the sins of their mistress and indicts her for mass-murder, sorcery and high treason – three separate capital charges. It is no wonder that Ponikenus appeals to the Palatine for protection.

The wealth of incidental detail is fascinating, but no guarantee of veracity: it has been shown that the barbarities the priest ascribes to Elisabeth have their parallels in contemporary folklore, and the novelty – so far-fetched to the post-Enlightenment way of thinking

– of shape-shifting was a magic technique that most of his parishioners and many of his fellow-clergymen would have believed in.

It has been suggested that Ponikenus' letter was actually composed in three separate stages, an idea supported by changes in the handwriting and by the fact that he gives two different consecutive accounts of his visit to the imprisoned Countess, and that the accusations he makes against Elisabeth increase both in gravity and in sensationalism as the letter progresses. It may be that the priest began to compose the letter spontaneously, fearful of the repercussions of his feud with the most powerful noblewoman of the locality. When he heard that Countess Báthory had been arrested, he paused before restarting the letter in a distinctly different style and with a shift in focus. According to this interpretation, the penultimate part of the letter may even have been dictated directly to Ponikenus by Thurzó or one of his agents, expressly so that it could be introduced in evidence if needed. In his postscript Ponikenus launches into the realms of the supernatural with his story of being attacked by phantom cats; this outburst of superstitious paranoia was not likely, in the formal setting of the court, to help the credibility of the case against Elisabeth, and was never referred to again, even when Ponikenus gave evidence orally later the same year.[16]

The world that Countess Báthory and her parish priests inhabited was one in which people of all classes sought desperately to make sense of the bewildering series of torments that fate was subjecting them to, and also to exercise a little more control over their lives than their static society (with the hugger-mugger intimacy of village life and the cramping proximities of the servants' quarters) normally allowed. The many examples of magic help to illuminate the mind of the age and of those who aided the Blood Countess and those who condemned her.

Until the oppressions of the Counter-Reformation took hold, and the tensions in society heightened to intolerable levels, superstition was quite respectable and not by any means limited to the poor. At the end of the seventeenth century Count Francis Esterházy, the military commander of Csesznek and head of the county of Fejér, compiled a small handbook of magic cures. His recipe against toothache prescribes the reciting of an incantation on the first Friday after the new moon. (The words must be said standing at the door and looking at the moon, just as Majorosné did when reciting her new spell for Elisabeth.) Esterházy adds the standard 'probatum est' (it has been tried and proven).[17] Like Esterházy and like Elisabeth, George Thurzó, the Count Palatine, also made use of formulaic cures which combined piety and superstition. In a letter he says he is upset to hear of his daughter's illness and tells his wife that he has written a plea for a cure on a piece of paper to be attached to the girl's neck 'when the fever is upon her again', while saying three 'Our Fathers'.[18]

People of all social stations were constantly on the lookout for portents in nature that would mirror and confirm the chaos that regularly overwhelmed their human realities. This habit, and the forms that these portents typically took, were not exclusive to Hungary, but life for Hungarians must have seemed particularly precarious, with attacks by marauding Hajdúks, unpaid foreign mercenaries and local brigands a daily possibility, the ever-present likelihood of war and the threat of the Turks finally overwhelming the nation always in the back of the mind. Battles in the sky, when the clouds parted, the sky turning red and phantom armies clashing with fireballs and thunder, were regularly seen and entered in the 'miracle books' that each town compiled.

If portents did not actually occur, they were imagined into existence. It was commonly believed that Elisabeth's uncle, Prince Sigmund Báthory, had been born with bloody hands, signifying his warlike nature, and that when he was being bathed by his nurse in a basin, he turned into a fish and slithered out of her grasp, neatly anticipating the fact that he moved his seat of power many times during his political career.

Another kind of folk superstition common to all cultures was a fear of the dead, most keenly felt when it was believed that the deceased retained a physical appetite and the means to satisfy it. If Countess Báthory is known at all in the anglophone countries, it is usually in the context of vampire literature, a fact that is not surprising in that the vampire myth has been especially identified with her native lands – but the connection does not stand up to scrutiny any more than the tenuous links with the Romanian Dracula. In Elisabeth's lifetime, between 1560 and 1614, the vampire craze in central and eastern Europe had not yet begun, but stories of ghostly revenants were common. In 1600 in the north of Hungary there was a local epidemic in which at least 2,500 died. Once the epidemic had subsided, strange phenomena disturbed the people of the region. Schoolchildren and their tutors fled when a phantom hunt was heard in a schoolhouse, reappearing the following night even after guards ('including educated persons') had been posted. More disturbingly the dead victims of the epidemic started to reappear in their villages, causing doors to creak and slam, moving furniture, moaning and touching their surviving loved ones with cold hands.[19]

One particular returnee from the dead was Gasparek of Lublo, who reappeared in his village looking just as he had before his funeral. This ghost indecently assaulted the maidens working in the fields and tried to lie with his widow in her bed at night. He continued to torment and annoy his neighbours until his body was exhumed and burned, after which he was never seen again, but his name served as a nickname for the foolish or mischievous until the 1980s. Peter Plogojowitz, the Serbian vampire whose exploits triggered the eighteenth century's fascination with the blood-drinking undead was part of the same widespread tradition, in which those who managed to live through epidemics were then plagued by the reappearance of their loved ones.[20] Modern rationalism explains this as shock, grief and guilt at surviving an inexplicable bereavement preventing the living from coming to terms with what had happened to their community – something too awful for the therapeutic effects of prayer to efface. The exhaustion, lassitude or even prostration that followed these traumas were similar to the effects of bloodletting, and was put down to the vampiric activities of ghosts or zombies.

Long before the now familiar regalia of fangs, batwings and silver crucifixes had accreted to the vampire, there was a rich body of folk-legend surrounding a slightly different creature. The common attribute is blood-drinking, but the original vampire was a malevolent soul – a witch, a suicide or simply someone tainted by evil or ill luck – who would escape from the grave to prey upon humans and their animals. The word itself has been known in English only since 1732, but is much older in the regions of its origins. Cognates, including the Serbian *vampir* and *úpir* in Czech and Russian, are found in all the Slavonic languages and seem to be based on the root *pi*, to drink.

Hungary's vampire-craze, which coincided with lesser epidemics in Bohemia, Moravia and Silesia, lasted from the end of the seventeenth century through a further eighty-odd years. Probably initiated by rumours from Istria and the Balkans coinciding with waves of hysteria among the common people, who were suffering intolerable social stresses, it was fuelled by the inquisitions launched by the Calvinists and Catholics and by the attentions of officials of the Austrian Empire and German-speaking scholars, prompted by genuine concern but also by suspicion of heresy, immorality and subversion among their Slav and Magyar subjects.

Distinguished writers such as the sceptic Calmet in his *Treatise on the Vampires of Hungary*', Karl Ferdinand von Schertz in his *Magia Posthuma* and Guiseppe Davanzati in *Dissertazione sopra i vampiri* analysed the phenomenon, as did the Imperial bureaucrats and bailiffs who were sent to investigate the outbreaks of vampirism *in situ*. The published works became bestsellers and the names of the most notorious undead – Jure Grando of Carniola, Peter Plogojowitz of Kisilova, Arnold Paole of Medvegia, as well as the aforementioned Gasparek of Lublo – became familiar throughout the continent. (Although it is significant that Father Túróczi's tales of Countess Báthory's blood-bathing coincided with the first vampire reports and an upsurge in witch-trials elsewhere, Nitra county where Čachtice is situated actually recorded fewer persecutions of witches than most other parts of Hungary.)

Local people would often report the sound of chewing coming from the coffins of their deceased neighbours: when graves were opened, the corpses of suspected vampires were often found to be perfectly preserved even months after their deaths. Blood – or what appeared to be blood – might be seen around the mouth and on the fingernails, and the flesh might be rosy and firm. Once again there are explanations. Where local conditions or intense cold do not actually preserve a body, the effects of decomposition can mimic preservation. The actions of bacteria can reinflate the body, liquefy the blood and cause reddish secretions to seep from the orifices. Surface skin can peel to reveal healthy-looking pigments beneath or there may be 'rubefaction' from internal chemical changes which can even heat up the corpse to a lifelike temperature. When exhumations revealed a lustrous, well-fed cadaver, the standard procedure was to cut off the head, drive a stake through the heart and then burn the remains, scattering the ashes as widely as possible.

By 1848 the Carpathians had been made the setting for the many vampire romances produced in Paris. The archetype of the undead *femme fatale* which was embodied in Elisabeth Báthory had also begun to filter into the literature of the west. Although the best-known eighteenth-century revenants of central Europe and the most famous fictional blood-drinker have been male, it is notable that in a recent survey of the most important vampires recorded in folklore, prose and poetry between 1687 and 1913 the list of forty-three (which includes Elisabeth Báthory) contains twenty-three women and three supernatural creatures of unknown gender, and another six female 'semi-vampires' are mentioned in the accompanying text.[21]

A spectral being which can be found in Hungary is the 'beautiful lady', an ambivalent witch/fairy who rarely appears alone, but dances and sings with her companions on lawns and in meadows. The beautiful ladies will entice their victims, then dance them to death. They also live in whirlwinds and steal the milk from the cow's udder, but they are said to be invisible at high noon and from midnight to dawn, unlike the Slovak fairies – the souls of girls who died while preparing for their weddings, or in childbirth – who, like the Romanian *Pripolniza*, can only be seen at those times, especially on St George's day, 23 April, when the earth opens and they dance forth from its crevices and caverns. In central Slovakia the noonday fairies are ugly crones, while further east the *Rusalka*, or water spirit, also known to the southern Slavs, is more prevalent; she lives in wells, in channels, in rain and dew, and can be recognised by the water dripping from her left eye. These were among the denizens of the faery world in which Elisabeth's make-believe persona also found a place.

If old Hungary was a land often visited by the supernatural, its neighbour to the east was a veritable magic cauldron. The nineteenth-century gentlewoman Emily de Laszowska Gérard wrote of Transylvania: 'It would almost seem as though the whole species of demons, pixies, witches and hobgoblins, driven from the rest of Europe by the hand of science, had taken refuge within this mountain rampart, well aware that here they would find secure lurking-places, whence they might defy their pursuers yet awhile . . .'[22]

Old Romanian legends, probably influenced by rumours from the time of the Crusades, recount that the stability of castles and churches was guaranteed by walling up a live victim, preferably a female virgin, in their foundations. Emily Gérard noted that in Transylvania the practice had been replaced by the custom of stealing the shadow of a passer-by and sealing that into the building instead – not such an innocuous alternative, as the unwitting donor would sicken and die within days.

The connections between the world of magic and virgins and castle foundations, and the links between the real Countess and her counterparts in myth, do not end here. And more elements – the female provinces of herbalism and curing, and the associated concepts of witchcraft, the persecution of women, and myths of femininity and blood, as well as the pastimes of the privileged, both innocent and not so innocent – must be considered before we can displace ourselves into the vanished landscape of the early modern mind.

CHAPTER FOUR

The Black Bey and the Heiress

On to the dead gois all Estatis
Princis, Prelatis, and Potestastis
Baith rich and pur of all degree
Timor mortis conturbat me.

William Dunbar, *Lament for the Makers*

The origins of the Báthorys ~ Elisabeth's childhood ~ criteria of marriageability ~ Francis Nádasdy, the golden youth ~ a young lady's wealth ~ betrothal ceremonies ~ Sárvár castle and court ~ a secret affaire ~ Hungarian weddings ~ potions and charms ~ life on the frontier ~ the Mighty Black Bey ~ the priesthood and 'an evil woman'

The Báthory family was an illustrious one, distinguished even among the supremely proud older aristocracy of the Hungarian Kingdom. Their personalities fascinated their contemporaries, and if references to them sometimes make them seem almost more than mortal, this no doubt was how some of the family saw themselves. They had in common a conviction of their inalienable rights and privileges as the

82

foremost among an all-powerful noble caste; they were headstrong and self-willed. In Hungary today it has become an unquestioned truism that the family were all, in the word most often employed, 'touched', alternately by greatness or by madness and degeneracy.

Like many Hungarian noble families of the early modern era, the Báthorys claimed mythical origins for themselves; they included Bathus, the King of the Roman province of Pannonia, Alaric the Goth and Vencellinus among their ancestors, as well as the warrior Vid Báthory, who was perhaps real but whose importance is that, Siegfried- or Beowulf-like, he was said to have slain a dragon with a mace in the Ecsed marshes, providing the family with their coat of arms: three dragon's teeth surrounded by a dragon biting its own tail. The real origin of the crest is obscure (conjecture that the teeth are wolves' and reflect the family's disposition was a conceit of nineteenth- and twentieth-century werewolf enthusiasts), but is much more likely to be a version of the symbols of the Order of St George, a knightly honour bestowed on some of the greatest warrior families – among them Vlad, Count Dracula – at the end of the fourteenth century.

The Somlyói branch of the family was the princely line, with their seat a small palace in the village of the same name, now in Romania. During Elisabeth's lifetime four magnates from this dynasty, Christopher, Sigmund, Andrew and Gábor, ruled the Principality of Transylvania, and Stephen became King of Poland. Through marriage, the family was related to the Austrian Habsburg and the Polish Jagiełłon royal lines. The lesser Ecsed branch of the Báthory family had owned their castle, incongruously set in the middle of an expanse of marshland at the place now known as Nagyecsed, near the modern Romanian border, since 1317.

The blood of Elisabeth Báthory was compounded of a long interbreeding between a few noble clans, her own family reuniting the two branches of the Báthorys; her mother Anna, the sister of King Stephen of Poland, was from the Somlyóis, her father George, the ruler of several counties (and her mother's third husband), was from the Ecsedys. Countess Anna was a devout Calvinist and a strong character, revered especially by her son. No scandals were ever associated with Count George Báthory, who resigned his official posts in the service of the Habsburgs to marry his 'Transylvanian' cousin. But, apart from this, nothing is known of their private lives. Elisabeth was christened with one of the small stock of family names that occurred at least once in every previous generation on her mother's side; the first names of boys were likewise reused again and again, confusing historians and even more so the literary embellishers of history. Elisabeth's elder brother, who inherited the Ecsed estates and ruled the surrounding counties, was one of many Stephens, and she had two younger sisters, Klára and Sofia, who have disappeared from history without leaving any traces – not even the usual rumours of madness and wantonness. All that is known is that they survived long enough each to marry a respected middle-ranking nobleman and to die childless.

Elisabeth had been formed first at Ecsed, a Renaissance court of great splendour in a complex of palaces and fortifications amid meres and quicksands, later at her husband's equally eminent family seat of Sárvár, also a centre of humanist culture. All the aristocratic courts, particularly those of whoever was the current Lord Palatine, vied to promote learning and literature. Among those who had no intrinsic interest in the cultivation of the mind and spirit it was nonetheless a question of prestige to pose as a patron.

The story that is being told here will return again and again, as it is bound to, to the barbarism and desperation which permeated European society in Elisabeth Báthory's lifetime. But the young Countess spent her childhood and the first couple of years of her married life in a brief period of tranquillity for Hungary: not an idyll, but at least a respite from the troubles. Sickness, local disputes and lawlessness did not disappear, but between the Drina Treaty of 1566 and her future husband, Count Francis Nádasdy's first recorded battle in 1578, the Turkish occupiers and their free Hungarian neighbours learned to coexist and began to trade with one another. Even Transylvania was at peace after 1574.

In 1571 Elisabeth Báthory, at the age of eleven, was promised in marriage. A betrothal at such an early age was commonplace, marriages were not love-matches but dynastic unions for the upper classes of Hungary, contracted principally to ensure that family wealth was concentrated and increased. The first offer of marriage might come from either the girl's family or the boy's, and although it was sometimes spontaneous (the Polish Count Dembinsky abruptly offered his stepdaughter to the Hungarian John Kemény while the latter was visiting on a diplomatic mission),[1] any attempts to sidestep the strict etiquette of supervised courtship were severely punished.

The criteria that senior family members considered before making or accepting an offer of marriage were set out in a letter from Count

George Thurzó, Elisabeth Báthory's later enemy, to his younger cousin Stanislas in 1598. George has been asked to put his views in writing, as well as in an oral message, and says he is flattered to be consulted. He first congratulates Stanislas on his arrangements for his daughter's wedding to Lord Sigmund Forgách, a young man, he says, who is virtuous and of good family (not surprisingly; George's stepfather and mentor was a Forgách).

He then comes to the more testing question of Stanislas' own marriage, which he has been pondering at length: 'You could gain much or lose everything, and then better to die than to live,' he comments, before considering in turn the ladies who have been offered as partners. He counsels against the daughter of the Pole Lubomirski, saying that Polish morals are quite different from Hungarian morals, and that in any case the Poles dislike both the Hungarian people and their sovereign. Becoming a member of the Polish nation would bring the King's displeasure – and everyone who has taken this path before has regretted it. He clinches this part of his argument by reminding Stanislas that he would have to pay the woman an impossibly high dowry of more than 40,000 florins. As for the daughter of the Austrian Prince of Teschen, this would bring great honour, but the woman 'does not look nice and is old and sickly'. George had also been offered her as a bride when he was a widower; he refused her then and so he cannot possibly recommend her now.

He finally comes to the daughter of Squire Listhius, and here he is cautious, saying he has not seen her and cannot comment on her family as Stanislas knows them better. He urges Stanislas to listen to his own heart, but also to listen out for more information about her health and morals: 'If you choose, choose not only with your eyes, but with your ears as well. Our family obliges you so to do.'[2]

George's ambivalence about the fifteen-year-old Lady Listhius was not resolved when he went with Count Stephen Illésházy to inspect her personally on Stanislas' behalf. 'She is no Dido [Queen of Carthage and Aeneas' lover in Virgil's *Aeneid*],' he wrote to his own wife, 'but if Stanislas likes her so much that he cannot live without her, what can I do against it? I am quite unsure how the matter should proceed.' Stanislas did marry Anna-Rosina Listhius and we will meet her name again in much more sinister circumstances.

Elisabeth Báthory's husband-to-be was the fifteen-year-old Francis

Nádasdy, scion of a fabulously rich family, and probably the most eligible bachelor in Hungary at that time. The marriage was arranged not least so that the Drágffy inheritances of which each child possessed a part could be united.

The golden youth Francis was the cherished only child of the Palatine, Thomas Nádasdy, the highest official of Royal Hungary after the foreign King, and his wife, Lady Ursula. The Nádasdys traced their lineage back to a quite spurious English ancestor: they had only recently been elevated to the senior aristocracy and Lord Thomas, born in 1498, had enormously increased the family's wealth by marrying in 1535 the teenage heiress (she was fourteen and he thirty-seven) Ursula Kanizsai, whose family seat was in the south-west on the borders of present-day Croatia and Slovenia. Thomas had inherited an array of feudal privileges, to which he added a cultivated mind formed in his student days in Bologna and Graz. He was respected and admired by his serfs, and the Habsburgs entrusted him with diplomatic missions and military commands and rewarded him richly in return. Although Nádasdy's loyalties wavered – he defended the capital Buda against the Turks for the Empire, but after the débâcle of Mohács he supported the Magyar Zápolya's claim against the Austrian Archduke Ferdinand – by mid-century he was one of the most powerful magnates in the Kingdom and back in favour with the Habsburgs, whose cause he re-espoused, not least so that he and Ursula could be allowed to keep their vast tracts of land along the western borders. He was created ban (governor) of the province of Croatia and later elected to the highest office of Count Palatine of Hungary. Thomas was also a loving and affectionate husband who helped his young bride to learn to read and write.

The baby Francis was doted upon, especially as he was born when his parents had almost given up hope of an heir. The couple had, very unusually for that time, a relationship based on real and mutual tenderness, as their letters to one another show, but for many years Ursula could not conceive. Her husband was almost always away from home attending to affairs of state on behalf of his master, the King, or supervising the Nádasdy–Kanizsai inheritance, which included vast estates spread across western and northern Hungary, and the south Transylvanian castle of Fogaras, which had belonged to the historical Dracula.

Several techniques of contraception were used at the time, but there seems no reason why the couple should not have sought an early birth: the many other cases of temporary infertility among the nobility, including that of Elisabeth herself, may have been due to unbalanced diet or ill-health, or, as later writers suggested, to the depleted gene pool within which the great families intermarried. Whatever the reason, in January 1555, just as the Palatine and his lady, now thirty-four years old, were about to adopt a male child, Ursula discovered to her surprise that she was pregnant.

The fabulously wealthy Nádasdy family were able not only to employ their own private doctor, but to buy the services of one of the very best, Caspar Szegedi Körös, known as Praximus, who supervised Countess Kanizsai all through her pregnancy. As was customary, the family also called in a traditional healer, a German midwife, to assist at the delivery, and without her the lady and her child who was born on 7 October might not have survived. His valet, Antal Sárkány reassured the father, 'the baby is now in fine fettle, he resembles you, his nose is quite big; he certainly will not be cursed with a snub-nose . . .'[3]

It seems that Lord Thomas did not see his son in the flesh until some time in the following year: Sárkány wrote to tell him of the christening, which took place on 21 October. In the new year Sárkány reported: 'The little lord is in good health, he is nicely plump and sucks his mother's milk most greedily: nor does he often allow his mother rest, even at night. But it would be a blessing if your lordship could return home for Easter.'

Although he indulged his son, Thomas also subjected him to the strict regime of discipline and piety that was the norm, writing to his wife on one occasion that she should have a servant administer a spanking to their son every three days without fail.[4]

In the legends which have been woven around his wife Elisabeth, Francis has usually been depicted as a dashingly thoughtless man of action or as a heavy-set dullard, but this is not how friends of the family viewed him during his early years. Francis could write in his Hungarian mother tongue at the age of five, and Lord Francis Batthyány wrote to his father complimenting the boy on his handwriting. 'I know for sure that neither of you, his parents, could write when you were his age,' he adds. 'I strongly recommend that you send him to the court and chancellery of His Majesty [the Emperor in Vienna], and after two or three years he will prove to be a great man there.'[5] Plans were indeed made to have Francis educated at the royal court, but they were interrupted by the death of Thomas Nádasdy, who succumbed to the plague in Egervár in June 1562 at the advanced (for that time) age of sixty-four. Lady Ursula, now solely responsible for her son's upbringing, decided that he should first be taught by Stephen Bythe, the schoolmaster at Sárvár. In 1567 she dispatched Francis to Vienna to continue his education under the protection of the Austrian Archduke Ernest and the tutelage of two Hungarians, Francis Sennyey and Christopher Lörinczfalvy. In common with many boys of his class, Francis was attached to the household of a fellow-countryman, in this case George Bocskai, Secretary of the Hungarian Chancellery, rather than being lodged in his own family's house in the city. The twelve-year-old lived and studied with Bocskai's son Stephen, later to become Prince of Transylvania, and the two of them attended the Imperial Court, where they were obliged to serve for three years before becoming members of the King of Hungary's official entourage. Francis had free access to the private apartments of the Emperor's own children and would visit them each morning between nine and ten o'clock and again after four in the afternoon.

At the age of twelve Francis Nádasdy could compose his letters in Latin; at thirteen he was hunting with the Habsburg children, and in the same year he appeared in a theatrical entertainment at the court in the role of a goddess. He also took part in the most important ceremonial events of the court and, when he was seventeen years old, the chronicler Eunonius Urbanus singled him out as the most promising of the young Hungarian nobles in Vienna at that time and predicted a glittering future for him.

By that time Francis had been engaged for two years to Elisabeth, eldest daughter of the Ecsed branch of the Báthory family. As long ago as 1557 Lord Francis Török, the commander of the nearby fortress of Pápa, had approached the Nádasdys of Sárvár and proposed his daughter as a bride for their two-year-old son. For whatever reason this offer was declined, and it is likely that other matches were suggested for the eminently eligible heir, but by 1562 Thomas Nádasdy and George Báthory had discussed the betrothal of their children, and in February 1570 the widowed Ursula Kanizsai concluded a formal agreement with Lord George and Lady Anna Báthory that they would reserve the hand of their daughter Elisabeth for her suitor Francis Nádasdy. The records show that the notary Michael Szássay certified the arrangement whereby the ten-year-old girl's parents promised to give the fifteen-year-old

Francis first option on their daughter until All Saints' Day, or longer if war or illness intervened. At that stage no dates for the engagement ceremony or marriage were set.

As for the bride, a document dated New Year's Eve 1572 confirms Elisabeth as Lord Francis Nádasdy's bride-to-be and lists her personal possessions from just one of the estates that already belonged to her as follows: 31,000 florins in cash; two gilded silver basins; six large silver platters; six gold and six silver plates; twenty-four gilded silver spoons; twelve silver forks; four gold necklaces; five gold necklaces for maidservants; two gilded silver bowls; two large silver sconces; two gilded silver cocks; one golden carpet set with jewels which had belonged to King Mátyás Corvinus I; thirteen tapestries; six new carpets; one gold pendant set with rubies and sapphires; one gold medallion set with four crystals and one amethyst; six silver belts with attached small golden chains for maidservants; two large rings set with sapphires; several other pieces of jewellery; a portrait of an ancestor, Bartholomew Drágffy, in a gilded frame; and many items of clothing, including a gold-trimmed fur coat with silver hem. It is known that at a later date Elisabeth also possessed the sword of her uncle King Stephen Báthory, a great gilded silver cup decorated with a gold cross, twenty-six diamonds, thirty-eight rubies, nine sapphires, two hundred and sixty-six pearls and a cup decorated with views of the castle of Fülek.[6]

Elisabeth and Francis waited four years to marry. This was quite normal, given the age of the couple and the need to uphold the dignity of the families. In the intervening months or years the future bride would be 'finished' – instructed in her household duties and the social skills and arts appropriate to her new position, and this would often take place in the household of her mother-in-law, as was the case with Elisabeth.

The young Elisabeth was sent from Ecsed to Sárvár, the main Nádasdy family seat in western Hungary, where she was placed in the care of Lady Ursula Kanizsai. By all accounts, Elisabeth had already been well tutored in her parents' court and could read and write Hungarian, Greek, Latin and German as well as any man. This was still an exception in an age when some male aristocrats remained semi-literate all their lives, and most women, including Lady Kanizsai, could not read and write their own language at the time of their marriage. The stories say that Elisabeth was sent to the court of the martinet Ursula to be instructed in the wifely arts, and they describe in detail how a mutual hatred grew up between the two women which helped to feed the bitterness and cruelty that Elisabeth later showed to other, weaker women. We know nothing of the young heiress's temperament and the later legends that she hated the strict regime of her mother-in-law are groundless; there was certainly no lengthy feud, as Lady Ursula died in 1571 when Elisabeth was only eleven years old, two years before the engagement party and four years before the marriage took place. There is no proof that Elisabeth ever even saw her mother-in-law face to face. We can be fairly sure that Elisabeth was not physically abnormal or in poor health at the time of her betrothal: as the Thurzó correspondence shows, prospective brides were carefully inspected or vetted by third parties, and Francis Nádasdy could have had his pick of the Kingdom's female suitors.

Sárvár (the name – 'mud castle' – commemorates an earlier fortress on the same site) in the third quarter of the sixteenth century was an ideal place for the cultivation of learning and the civilised virtues. Today the castle lies on the edge of an elegant market town amid meadows and flat countryside luxuriant in summer with reeds, marsh marigolds, willow and deep yellow-topped weeds.

The streets of Sárvár are hot and dusty in summer, and the pungent smell of horses wafts from the riding stables by the castle's outer wall and hangs on the air just as it has done for more than 300 years. The sight of the intact Sárvár castle comes as a surprise; it is not rough-hewn, severe, austere, as the sixteenth-century woodcuts showed it, but spacious, airy. The Renaissance style which replaced the earlier gothic and became common after the Battle of Mohács was imported from Italy, as were the architects and some masons; the standard form was a quadrangle with turrets at each corner or a star shape. The castle roofs were a striking red, according to contemporary Austrian admirers; the main gate is said to have been designed by Palladio himself; and the outer fortified wall was added by Francis Nádasdy in 1588 following a Turkish raid; his son Paul completed the work in 1615 and celebrated the fact in a plaque proclaiming him as his father's legitimate heir.

In Elisabeth's day the castle stood surrounded by a moat as wide as a river. The town, which then consisted of little more than the castle and its garrison buildings, was an island in the waterlands created by the Rába and Gyöngyös rivers, which join there. In the still heat of the long summers, clouds of insects would torment the men and horses in the stable blocks and liveries; during the hard winters the waterways and meres round about would freeze over for weeks at a time.

The Sárvár court was a magnet for Protestant humanist scholars during the years that – Thomas Nádasdy and Lady Ursula presided over the household. The succession of priests who served the family included Matthew Dévay Bíró, known as the Hungarian Luther, János Sylvester, the first translator of the New Testament into the Hungarian language, and the religious propagandist Stephen Magyari, who became embroiled in Elisabeth's controversies. To disseminate religious tracts and books one of the very few printing presses in the Kingdom was set up by the order of Thomas, who played host to visiting intellectuals from the Netherlands, the German Principalities and Italy.

During the period of their engagement the young couple probably saw little of each other; Francis spent time completing his academic education in Vienna and being trained in military discipline and the techniques of warfare at the garrisons along the Austro-Hungarian border. There would have been a hundred innocent diversions with which Elisabeth could counteract her own boredom, but the tedium which might have afflicted the delicate, intense adolescent heiress has been compensated for by a fictional love affair recounted by her Austrian biographer, von Elsberg.

The story goes that across the Danube, in the walled town of Trnava where the family of the future groom owned a small mansion, the girl Elisabeth gave herself to Ladislas Bende, a man of fine physique and heroic bearing (the standard attributes then as now). In von Elsberg's cosmopolitan prose, 'virginitatem suam geraubt und sie dadurch *in perpetuam infamiam* gebraucht' ('he robbed her of her virginity and thereby consigned her to perpetual shame').[7] Elisabeth conceived immediately and an illegitimate child was born, to be spirited away into Transylvania and never heard of again (until, that is, she reappears in Nižňanský's later Slovak novel). The family hushed up the scandal as best they could, and propriety dictated that the marriage went ahead despite the bride's secret transgression.

The property in Trnava existed and there was indeed a László or Ladislas Bende, although his relations with Elisabeth, if any, are unclear. The story of the love child, embroidered around snippets of real history, is a standard ingredient of melodrama and romance and helps to create the persona of a headstrong and passionately amoral teenager. It was useful, too, to explain why the Countess might have been shunned in her adult life (which was not in fact the case), and why she did not reward her new husband with their own child for many years.

The wedding between Lady Elisabeth Báthory and Lord Francis Nádasdy took place at the small turreted palace of Varanno, now Vranov, known as an island of gaiety in the backward eastern part of the Kingdom, on 8 May 1575: the bride was then fifteen years old and the groom nineteen. A nineteen-page announcement was printed in Vienna[8] and the Habsburg Emperor Maximilian himself was invited, but as was usual the Austrian grandees stayed on their side of the border and sent representatives bearing lavish gifts of golden goblets, wine and jewelled ornaments. There were probably around 4,500 guests, not counting the commoners from the surrounding countryside who would be allowed to join in the celebrations with open-air pig- and ox-roasts and wine and bread. Those celebrating inside the castle would be ministered to by fifteen or so wedding stewards and ushers, catered for by around twenty master-chefs and their assistants and serenaded by gypsy bands and Polish or Italian ensembles, as well as Hungarian musicians.

Guests would compete in the finery they and their servants could display at such an occasion; in 1559 Lady Anna Thurzó had to extort two pounds' weight of gold from her estate manager to pay for her attendance at the nuptials of Lord Christopher Országh, then the owner of the castle of Čachtice. A typical aristocratic wedding might cost more than the whole estate of a member of the minor gentry: in 1603 George Thurzó spent over one thousand florins on supplies from Vienna for the feasting at the wedding of his daughter Susannah, which Countess Báthory attended. The shopping list comprised 200 pounds of pepper, 50 pounds of ginger, 25 pounds of cloves, 4 pounds of nutmegs, 4 pounds of saffron, 1,000 lemons, 500 oranges, 253 pounds of honey. Other ingredients for the standard three days of feasting could be requisitioned from the surrounding demesnes. Thurzó demanded 36 oxen, 118 calves, 103 sheep, 58 lambs, 119 pigs, 33 deer, 185 rabbits, 526 hens, 381 capons, 785 chickens, 420 geese, 130 small birds (probably starlings and sparrows), 5,333 eggs, 70 *galóca* fish, 1,600 trout, 240 small fish, crayfish 'without number', 200 *menyhal* fish, 238 cubic feet of oats and 35 wagons of hay.[9]

The groom, his friends, familiars and guests would traditionally travel together in procession to the place of the nuptials where the bride-to-be was waiting. Certain rites had to be observed at each stage of the proceedings: two members of the groom's entourage would ride ahead to pay their respects to the bride's family on the groom's behalf and, before returning, the two messengers (whose title translates as 'heralds of happiness') would take wine and dance three times with their hosts. The bride's wedding steward would then send a group of prize horses and a ring to the approaching party, and young men from both retinues would pause at a suitable site *en route* to race against one another for the ring. Given the Hungarians' cult of horsemanship, the races were in earnest and the winning of the ring an important public honour.

Only when the races were over did the groom's party continue on their way. When all the guests had assembled, the groom would send an envoy on horseback to deliver gifts to the bride and her family and to any representatives of the King, neighbouring rulers and the church who had agreed to attend. The humbler female guests would receive rich clothing, the men fine weapons, while the betrothed couple would exchange jewelled ornaments, sumptuous tapestries, carpets and robes which would take pride of place in their family treasury. For the young Elisabeth her husband's wedding gift included the manor of Čachtice with its seventeen neighbouring hamlets, a holding that Ursula Kanizsai had acquired in April 1569.

As the company moved to the appointed venue, a castle hall, a temporary pavilion or a specially constructed 'wedding house' annexe, there were cannon and musket salutes and serenading by musicians. Before the ceremony proper there was one final formality, a lighthearted test of the groom's sincerity. The best man stepped forward to hail the bride's family and called forth the bride herself, but instead the bridesmaids would emerge one by one to confront the young man and he would have to identify his wife-to-be from among them. Once the real bride had been chosen, the marriage ceremony itself could be enacted according to the religion of the couple.[10]

Post-wedding feasts in sixteenth-century Hungary were much as they are today, with toasts to the couple's future health and happiness between the many courses of the banquet, followed by dances – to Hungarian, Polish and Italian music, but all unrestrained and exuberantly Magyar in execution. Visitors from the west, used to a sedate, courtly ambience, were fascinated by the frenetic play of primary colours, the fierce brio of the social rituals, all set to urgent, haunting music.

During the succession of wedding balls, the bride was obliged to partner every one of the guests, even the bishops and cardinals who had attended and who would not touch her hand but held the other end of a ribbon or kerchief as they wheeled about. The dancing would continue long into the evening and at the end of the first day of carousing the young couple would be escorted to their chamber by young nobles carrying flaming torches to light their way. It was usual for marriage festivities to last at least three days, allowing ample time between the many changes of costume, the elaborate and gargantuan meals and the dances and games, for the younger guests to take stock of the personal charms and social prospects of their fellows, while the older lords and ladies withdrew into secret corners to gossip and conspire.

It has been calculated that sterility and infertility among the Hungarian ruling class, along with a low life-expectancy and the effects of intermarriage and syphilis, meant that every second generation there was a strong risk of a family being left without a male heir of an age to inherit. For more than ten years after their marriage, no children were born to the Nádasdy couple, and in this masculine society it would be the woman who was assumed to be deficient, even if the tension between notions of pious celibacy and the pressing need to procreate, not to mention simple fear of sex and venereal disease, could play havoc with a man's potency. The cures on offer for women's infertility were legion, but almost completely ineffectual. From her fellow-aristocrats and her relations Elisabeth would have borrowed or bought the *grimoires* translated from the French and on sale in Venice, or acquired the Persian and Turkish recipes carried by word-of-mouth through Transylvania. If it was fecundity she desired, then there were simple procedures – watch a cat as it licks its genitals, sprinkle a tortoise with cold water – or more costly ones, such as buying a holy relic or the appropriate magic stone. Emeralds and aquamarines, sharing as they do the colour green, would strengthen the bonds of marriage and guard the owner against infidelity by a spouse or the temptations of a would-be seducer.[11]

Perhaps an aphrodisiac was in order, to stimulate a husband who was a lion on the battlefield but a mouse in the bedchamber (or had he already spent his energies with the camp-followers and well-born lady admirers who had managed to have themselves smuggled to the front?). The simplest of the remedies available meant slipping fireflies into his food, or spicing his meals with red grass and mistletoe. If it was the wife whose ardour was feeble, the answer was to mix the powdered heart of a dove, the liver of a sparrow, the womb of a swallow and a hare's kidney with drops of the husband's blood. This concoction was to be used with caution as only three thimblefuls could, it was said, madden a woman with desire. There was another source of potions and enchantments near at hand, and nineteenth-century writers, trying to explain how a virtual princess had taken the lowliest peasant women into her confidence, decided that it was during her years of barrenness that Elisabeth had fallen under the influence of the local witches who promised to cure her.

Elisabeth's contemporary, the gifted amateur healer Lady Éva Poppelová, was contemptuous of orthodox medicine as practised by men and strongly recommended that women's ailments, infertility included, were better treated by traditional folk remedies. She went further and warned, probably not without justification, that male surgeons could do more damage than good to a woman's body.[12] Perhaps Elisabeth stumbled on a charm or a medicine that worked (it may even have been the clumsy attentions of the gynaecologists of Vienna which had caused Elisabeth's inability to conceive in the first place, and the herbal baths and infusions of the wise-women which restored it), for in 1585 she gave birth to a daughter, Anna, followed by Ursula and Andrew, both of whom died in infancy, another daughter, Kate, and a surviving son and heir, Paul, who was born in 1598.

The military frontier between the Hungarian and Turkish lands, a second home for Francis Nádasdy, his peers and the men at his command, was made up of a chain of fortresses stretching about a thousand kilometres from the Dalmatian coast to the borders of Transylvania.

The frontier lands bred a frontier mentality with its own values and customs, shared by both sides in the endless war. Criminals and runaway serfs could get shelter there, among the military outposts where the *robot* was not enforced and where allegiance was limited to one's own captain and comrades; booty from raids and ransoms might occasionally enrich the poorly paid, hard-bitten soldiers, but for much of the time it was harsh, unremitting discipline that kept them in check.

Francis Nádasdy excelled at his military duties and mastered the strategies of war as well as inspiring the men who served under him, who were also awed by his sheer physical strength. For the whole of his adult life, war against the Turk was his vocation and for nineteen years his wife hardly saw him in domestic surroundings at all. (Sárvár itself, well to the west and the north of the war zones, had been raided by the Turks in 1532 and again in 1588, but Elisabeth was well guarded and the walls had been strengthened to withstand a siege.) With no hope of real political and cultural progress or social stability in Hungary, the energies of the men were of necessity devoted to war. The romantic uncertainty of 'life on the marches' provided a setting for a cult of heroic chivalry that became the only *raison d'être*.

Francis Nádasdy was first appointed Master of the King's Horse and then named Captain of the Field Army of Upper Hungary – the equivalent of a modern general. With his co-commanders Pálffy, Zrínyi and Batthyány, all four of them drawn from the country's noble elite, Nádasdy led his troops in a series of brilliant campaigns against the Ottomans under Amurad III, who honoured their enemy by nicknaming him the 'Black Bey of Hungary'. He played a leading part in the battles of Bajcsa and Sissek and the siege of Pápa in 1600, after which he was joined in his soldiering by a fellow-Lutheran aristocrat and patriot whose seat was in Upper Hungary, Lord George Thurzó. For his own side, Francis the 'War Thunderer' was and still is a national hero: his strength was said to be more than that of a mere human and the admiring folktales that were told have him dancing at victory celebrations with the corpses of Turks, tossing them in the air and catching them and playing bowls with their severed heads. The official iconography can be seen in the Sárvár castle frescoes which show the glowering bearded champion besieging castles and transfixing dozens of Ottoman foes on the end of his lance.

Francis had covered himself in glory in the service of Hungary and the Empire: his fame as a soldier spread all across Europe and he was honoured and rewarded in Vienna, although he quarrelled with the Habsburgs over ransoms for Turkish prisoners which he thought they had denied him and over the return of the funds which he had loaned to the Imperial Treasury. He was at the same time a man of strong principles and when the Catholic Austrian King conspired to flout Hungarian law and have the Protestant Count Illésházy dispossessed and beheaded, Nádasdy dared to declare his support for Illésházy, in opposition to his comrade-in-arms, the Habsburgs' catspaw, Thurzó, who had helped to orchestrate the plot. Lord Francis had earlier taken a risky and courageous stand against Elisabeth's own family when he protested at Prince Sigmund Báthory's judicial murdering of the Hungarian lords during the purge of the pro-Turkish party in Transylvania in 1594.[13]

Francis was also a staunch patron of the Lutherans, occupying the Catholic churches on his lands by force and handing them over to worshippers of his own faith. Elisabeth had been brought up in a devoutly Calvinist household whose religious principles had inspired her brother Stephen but seem not to have been infused into the personalities of her nephew and niece, Gábor and Anna, who were raised there. Elisabeth's deeper thoughts on her faith are lost to us, but in common with most of their peers the couple's religious beliefs were probably held sincerely and not just factors of social tradition, although piety did not seem anywhere in Europe to enforce kindness or pacifism. The earnest discourse of the Reformation, with its emphasis on humility, redemption and an all-pervading awareness of retribution, can be seen not only in the many published homilies and editing works that were circulating, but in every recorded conversation, every letter and every essay.

The extreme puritanism seen in some western societies was never embraced by the Magyars, nevertheless in the sixteenth century the nobility had welcomed the Reformation, not least because it restricted the power of the Catholic king. Although the church of Rome remained the official faith, it was practised widely only in Croatia. Reformers preached to the people in their own languages and readily took on a role as the champions of the oppressed against the feudal landlords. Disputes between the noble landowning families and the priesthood were commonplace. When the aristocrats and their followers had first converted, the Protestant pastors took full advantage of their status to criticise the excesses of their rulers and to intercede zealously on behalf of the oppressed peasants, but soon the real status quo became clear again; the senior nobility had a monopoly of power in Hungary, and not even the new church would be allowed to interfere with that. The Calvinists and Lutherans excoriated one another, and for a while the Catholic influence was blotted out altogether. The priests continued to agitate, but more circumspectly, speaking out only when they were sure of the patronage of a strong local grandee.

In the early 1600s the Catholic Counter-Reformation, backed by Vienna, began to gain ground in Hungary and by the second decade of the new century the number of recusants among the aristocratic families and their serfs was growing in earnest, encouraged above all by the efforts of the noble Protestant turned ardent Catholic propagandist, Cardinal Peter Pázmány. One of Pázmány's most energetic opponents in the theological battles of the time was Lord Francis Nádasdy's family priest, the Lutheran Stephen Magyari, who published an important tract, *On the Present Troubles Afflicting the Two Nations* (the two being Hungary and Transylvania), which provoked Pázmány to produce his even more influential *Response*. In the meantime, in the smaller world of Sárvár, Magyari was negotiating the dilemma that faced all of the favoured ecclesiasts in his position: he had been sheltered and sponsored by a noble family, but in theory at least he was also answerable to his parishioners who, whether they were themselves of the gentry, or servants, or just humble soldiers or peasants, were living at the mercy of his patron's whims. From the archives, we know that those whims included the seizing of grazing land, the forcible rededication of churches, and the collecting of punitive taxes. Perhaps there were also other, more sinister reasons for the resentment that was communicated to the priest, reasons that concerned one of the other protégées of the family.

It is known that by the turn of the seventeenth century Elisabeth Báthory had added to her personal entourage the teenage boy, Ficzkó, and, from around 1595, a widow named Anna and known as 'Delbora' or 'Darvulia'. Darvulia is a mystery that has perplexed all those writers on the case who have paused to consider her. In 1610 and 1611 she was posthumously accused both by the senior servants who had known her and by other witnesses of being the most evil of Elisabeth's confidantes, indeed of being the Lady's guide and inspiration in her torturing. Even Darvulia's name, which was a nickname transcribed in several different forms, is mysterious; it is not Hungarian, nor does it seem to be Slovak, unless, as has been suggested, it is a corruption of the words *dar* (give or gift) and *bol* (sickness or pain), which can be found in Croatian and Serbian, too, the implication being that she had the gift of curing sickness. Unfortunately, Slovak linguists cannot find a precedent for this ingenious etymology.

According to the evidence, while Anna Darvulia was in charge of the domestic arrangements at the castle in 1602 the pastor Michael Zvonarić wrote to Gregory Pythiraeus (or Piterius), the preacher in Keresztúr near the Austrian border, to inform him that Stephen Magyari, the Sárvár deacon and the family's personal priest, had been discussing certain matters with him upon which he desired Pythiraeus' advice. In particular the two of them, with fellow-ecclesiasts, had decided that a decision must be made 'regarding the admonition of his excellency [Lord Francis Nádasdy] and his wife for their acts of cruelty, and there is a woman about whom everyone knows who the Lady uses as her assistant in that place'. The letter is extant and is preserved in the Lutheran archives in Budapest. It is a key document in the armoury of those who believe in Elisabeth's guilt, as it is the only confirmed example of an accusation which predates the final investigation. Even then Elisabeth's defenders have pointed out that the letter may be a reaction to Anna Darvulia's cruelty, and that Elisabeth and Francis are guilty only of harbouring her. These apologists point to the suggestion in the letter that the cruel woman be deprived of the eucharist and, if she refuses to repent, be excommunicated, as an indication that this was actually a doctrinal feud between Lutherans and Calvinists, in which, they think, Elisabeth sided with her servant and co-religionist against the cabal of local priests.

Magyari did indeed denounce the couple from the pulpit for what he termed the 'tyrannical cruelty practised in their court by an evil woman'. (The quotation is again from Zvonarić, and there is no ambiguity about the word *kegyetlen* – 'cruelty'.) Witnesses, such as Bornemissza and Bödy, who recalled the incident years later said that Elisabeth was reprimanded in the absence of her husband and that she complained in a letter to Lord Francis that she deeply resented the behaviour of the preacher (this document has also survived, but the text is ambiguous).[14] Magyari nevertheless continued to serve the family for another eight years, asking pardon from Lord Nádasdy and later delivering the eulogy at his funeral in which there was no mention of the matter. Zvonarić took over the parish on Stephen Magyari's death, but strangely when he was called upon to testify against Elisabeth in 1610 he insisted that he had himself reproached her in the meantime, but did not mention Magyari's denunciation, although it was still being talked about by the people living around Sárvár eight years after the events.[15]

CHAPTER FIVE

At the Court of Lady Nádasdy

O, that it were possible
We might but hold some two days' conference
With the dead!

John Webster, *The Duchess of Malfi*

Two letters from Lady Nádasdy ~ customs and duties ~ the Hungarian table ~ pastimes for noble ladies ~ the death and burial of Count Francis Nádasdy ~ the widow's correspondence and some purchases ~ love and lust ~ health, healing and wise women ~ pictures of the past

Standing in the cool, quiet halls of Sárvár castle, in the museum ambience that fills them today, it is almost impossible to re-create in the mind the noises and smells and the subtler sensations that invested the place in the days when the Nádasdys held court there. We do not know if the household, only a day's hard ride from the war front, was a fraught, manic environment of bustle and suppressed hysteria, or a haven of ordered calm, an asylum for the warrior-lord and his senior aides when they returned from the fighting.

Like all other Hungarian ladies of her age, Elizabeth Báthory was forced to adapt to the almost constant absence of her husband during the years of skirmishes and military manoeuvres, which were followed by the fifteen years of continuous war against the Turks. Between 1591 and 1604, during her years of motherhood and maturity, Elisabeth would have seen her lord and his retinue for only brief moments, if at all, in the campaigning season from February to late November, and would have attended him dutifully once he had put his official tasks aside for the Christmas period. It was customary for the great ladies to send to Vienna for special delicacies, then turn their head cooks out of the kitchens at the return of their menfolk and prepare an extravagant meal with their own hands. Even while at war, the men were not incommunicado, and Francis could still decide important family matters and transmit his judgements in local disputes. But Elisabeth's responsibilities were hugely enlarged when he was away. There were retainers left on the estates to take care of the collection of tithes, the buying and selling of produce, harvesting and husbandry, and staff to carry out administration in the houses and farms. But the Lady was now the authority to whom they all reported, and it was she who was entrusted with the patronage of the local church, the education of scholars, the direction of repairs and the hiring and dismissing of officials and artisans.

The fact that Countess Báthory coped so well with her extra burden is another proof that she was not the weak-minded degenerate that some history and some fiction has suggested. Francis and Elisabeth's marriage was outwardly exemplary and, if the private reality was otherwise, the option of divorce was available to a Protestant couple. There is absolutely no evidence to support the literary accounts of her infidelity and his whoring during the many months they spent apart.

If there was no verifiable scandal attached to the marriage, nor were there any external signs of anything more than dutiful commitment. Elisabeth sent news of the childrens' health in May 1596: 'I can write to your lordship of Anna and Orsik [the pet name for their daughter Ursula, named after Elisabeth's mother-in-law] that they are in good health. But Kate is in misery with her mouth because that rot has appeared, and the rot is even in the bone of her jaw. The barber–surgeon went in with his iron up to the middle of her tooth, and says that she will be fortunate if she does not lose some teeth. Of myself, I can say that I am better than formerly.'[1] In July the same year she writes: 'Anna, thank God, is in good health. Ursula's eyes are quite painful, but as for Kate, again she has a rot [it was probably trench mouth or gingivitis, which was endemic] in her mouth. I am well, thank God, only my eyes pain me.'[2]

Writers have taken these scraps of domesticity and from them deduced that Elisabeth was a neglectful mother, that the family were afflicted with inherited defects and that Elisabeth was suffering from epilepsy, but they are surely no more or less than the banalities that would fill a letter to an absent father in our own time. If news of health is given prominence, it is because a desperation to cling to one's own life and protect one's dependants was uppermost in everybody's thoughts in an age when some women had lost ten children by the time they were thirty years old.

Letters were of two types: those written privately, in the certain knowledge that they would not be intercepted, and those written on the assumption that they might be examined by enemies. The latter were particularly important in Transylvania, where one's neighbour might well belong to the rival political faction. Sensitive diplomatic correspondence was written in numerical code, while other important messages were conveyed orally by servants in the wake of a note naming the person and indicating their time of arrival. Many of Elisabeth's letters were in her own hand and were articulate, forceful, contrasting with the clumsy conversational style of Thurzó's wife Elisabeth Czobor.

Elisabeth Báthory had been taught to read Greek and Latin by her tutors at Ecsed, understood classical models of structure, in short wrote as well as any man, but without the long-windedness, pomposities or poetic flights to which men were prone. There were no spontaneous intimacies in Elisabeth's letters, only the prescribed and respectful forms of address – 'your loving wife', 'your servant'. The letters from Elisabeth's father-in-law, Thomas Nádasdy, to his young wife Ursula contain jesting allusions to their age differences – he calls himself 'your old grey vulture' – and are full of phrases such as 'the arrival of your letter caused me to rejoice', whereas Elisabeth's to Francis are businesslike and dry (though this, not her parents-in-law's playful intimacy, was the norm in those days). 'I commend my service to your mercy. They have brought some letters to me which I include in my letter to you. May the Good Lord keep you in good health . . .' is typical of the conventional style she employs.[3]

Apart from her articulacy, there were other signs that Francis

Nádasdy's wife was not a passive partner in the relationship. Also in 1596 she upbraided her husband, saying, 'I understand from your lordship's writing that you were almost sent to Transylvania, and everyone wonders at this since you can enjoy no good from Transylvania and the soil from which you take all good things is this soil. We are at a loss to understand this news which I heard first from a friend who wrote of it to me and I have suffered bitterly of this . . .'[4] From the correspondence of fellow-nobles we learn that Elisabeth accompanied Francis when he was required to attend the Diet in Bratislava. Francis's comrade at arms, George Thurzó, reported to his own wife, the unsophisticated Lady Czobor, that he envied the other lords 'who have their loving wives with them in Pozsony, like Mistress Nádasdy'. At this time Thurzó, the man who would later seek to destroy her, seems to have had a special admiration for Elisabeth Báthory, and may have seen her as a model for his gauche partner to emulate. 'When Mistress Nádasdy journeys to Ecsed by way of Bytča, send, my dear heart, to her and ask her to visit you that you might have an opportunity to know her better, if you do not already . . .'[5]

Only the humble local squires were able to live, except for their hunting expeditions and displays of horsemanship, a lazy, sedentary life among their vineyards and orchards. The senior lords were preoccupied with their duties, which involved attendance at court, dealing with the affairs of local government, inspecting their own estates and either making war or preparing for it. In most noble families in post-Reformation Hungary the strict education they had been given by their tutors and parents had instilled in the boys a sense of public responsibility: the fifteen-year-old Lord John Révay wrote to his parents in a mixture of pride and some distress that his mind was preoccupied with public matters both day and night.[6]

For the elite class, Hungary was very much part of Europe: aristocratic boys studied in Wittenberg, the Low Countries, Vienna, Padua or France; future politicians were sent to be formed in Vienna. In their everyday habits Turkish and Balkan manners did have some effect on the Hungarians, but in terms of conscious behaviour the orientation was towards Germany and the Netherlands, and to a slightly lesser extent Italy, whence came artistic, decorative and literary influences, as well as, some said, a familiarity with the more recondite arts of the bedchamber.

The paragon Lord Francis Nádasdy was, apart from his high-sounding official titles – Comes of the County, Master of the King's Horse, some-time Captain-General of the Danubian Army – a living embodiment of a cult of heroic savagery and a way of life that found its fulfilment in bloodletting and blood-sports. It was the nineteenth-century Austrian writer von Elsberg, an Imperial patriot and a man who knew the soldier's life well, who linked Francis' triumphs on the battlefields with Elisabeth's campaigns conducted in the privacy of her own houses. Von Elsberg speculated that the brutalities of war must have infiltrated the home life of the family and even affected the womenfolk from the early days (the only real evidence, gleaned from the investigations and trial, that he and others cite is that Francis showed his wife the technique, presumably learned while at war, for reviving an unconscious person by lighting paper between their fingers and toes).[7] This is not wholly convincing, but the family members did live surrounded by active soldiers and pensioned-off veterans and could not have separated the two worlds entirely.

In the courts of the Nádasdys and Thurzós the household would begin to stir just before dawn when the lord and lady would rise and wash their hands and faces in a basin brought into their chamber, before dressing or being dressed. A small breakfast would then be served, consisting mainly of an invigorating drink: men favoured bitter-sweet wine or brandy, women might take cinnamon-water or a concoction of honey, figs and raisins dipped in brandy and set alight. They ate bacon or health-giving titbits of ginger and lemon or other fruits.[8]

The tasks of the morning had to be completed by ten o'clock when the cup-bearer would set the table for a lunch that might last for two hours. Dinner was usually taken at six or seven o'clock in the evening in summer, sometimes earlier in winter, and all but the watchmen would retire not long after night had fallen.

The diet of the privileged was heavy and included far too much meat. When the senior aristocrats travelled across the country, one or more kitchen wagons would accompany them, hung with whole carcasses of venison, game and sides of beef and pork; in a noble household an average meal for the senior members would consist of eight courses, and the more abstemious men would drink around a third of a litre of wine with each one. Over-indulgence was one of the main causes of illness: gout, of which George Thurzó is thought to have died, was prevalent, and digestive disorders and poisoning from eating tainted food were a commonplace. The rich suffered from a lack of ascorbic acid and vitamins whereas the poor, who mainly subsisted on grain and vegetables, lacked protein. Water was not potable, and had to be drunk boiled with herbs, so Hungarians of all classes constantly drank the wines which were produced all over the Kingdom: cloudy brown beer, brewed by the Saxons in Žilina and elsewhere, was an occasional alternative for those living in the north and east.

The great families were unrestrained in their feasting, not only on special occasions but every day that the lord or lady was in residence. A Friday diet of fish was the rule, but dishes of grouse and veal were slipped in among as many as twenty different preparations of the freshwater fish (great and small sturgeon, pike, loach and catfish were the favourites, and the prehistoric *fogas*, the pike-perch which is found only in Lake Balaton, was also prized), which were cheap and plentiful.

While the humbler maidservants practised the skills of sewing as they repaired and adapted clothing and linen, the noblewomen of all ages would pass a great deal of their time in needlecraft: sewing, knitting, crochet and embroidery. Women competed to excel in these crafts as well as spinning and weaving, using models and methods from Italy, Spain, Poland and the Low Countries and Turkey as well as Hungary itself.

Women of the aristocracy passed their time also in hunting, nearly always in the company of their menfolk. Riding was also a popular recreation, and so, more surprisingly, was fishing. The ladies would organise outings to fish without the company of the men of the household and would combine the excursion with elaborate picnics. When bad weather or delicate health did not permit the genteel outdoor pursuits, women would read (edifying literature was recommended by husbands and priests, and more entertaining works were exchanged privately between ladies) and indulge in letter-writing, which in the sixteenth century began for the first time to be a literary art or hobby for the most cultivated families as well as the main means of communication.

Unfortunately, very few of these personal letters have survived; most private notes were not thought important enough to preserve in family archives, and many of those which were collected were lost in the upheavals that racked Hungary over the next 300 years. (One result of this is that when a noble line died out or fell from grace, its collected papers might be destroyed or scattered: there is no 'Báthory archive', as there is for the Thurzó, Nádasdy, Zrínyi or Drugeth families.)

105

This means that there are two areas of the lives of these inhabitants of the past, the women in particular, that have been frustratingly closed to us, areas which bear directly upon the crucial mysteries of Elisabeth Báthory's story. The first concerns the mundane minutiae of everyday life: the interplay of social relations within the household, the pattern of duties and tasks and the quarrels and reconciliations and petty transgressions that attended them together with the transient thoughts and feelings of the players in the domestic drama of the castle or the manor-house or the village. There was no need to objectify these things, no outsider to describe them to; everyone from the Great Lady to the serf was living inside this reality and was utterly familiar with it. To try to reconstruct it we must fall back upon wedding lists, menus, payrolls and contracts, together with the few oblique references to the trivialities of life that we find in more important communications such as official notices of births and deaths.

In March 1601 while Count Nádasdy was staying at the capital, Pozsony (Bratislava), he was afflicted with an illness that caused him intense pain in his lower limbs and left him unable to stand. He recovered enough after a few weeks to resume his round of public duties, and the sickness was not mentioned again in his letters, but in late 1603 he was seriously ill again and this time he prepared his family for the possibility of his death. On 3 January 1604, a letter was carried from Francis to Lord George Thurzó, informing him that 'God hath visited me with sickness', and formally entrusting the wellbeing of the heirs and the widow to Thurzó's protection and benevolence should he not survive.[9] Nádasdy was too ill to sign the letter himself and died in his bedchamber in Sárvár castle on the day after it was sent. This observation of a common aristocratic convention may have been a sincere reflection of a close friendship between the two that had endured from the times in which they had made war on the Turks together, or more probably was a tactical move to ensure that Thurzó, already one of the greatest powers in the land after the King, would be shamed if he tried to harm the family's honour or their fortunes in any way.

The instructions for Francis Nádasdy's funeral, written by an anonymous senior member of the Sárvár household, have survived, although the names of the notables who were able to attend have not.[10] The funeral procession ceremony and burial were nonetheless as impressive as the embattled nation could manage: the lord's body in its coffin was displayed on a decorated catafalque hung with black cloth and lit by four giant candelabra, there were public readings from the New Testament throughout the night before the funeral and the singing of hymns began at seven in the morning.

There was a first sermon when the body was brought out of the castle and then, at the end of the proceedings, the eulogy was delivered from a specially constructed mobile pulpit by the same Stephen Magyari who had denounced the Count and his lady for cruelty two years earlier. This was not a time for truth-telling or provocations, but for an inspiring peroration, and he praised his dead patron fulsomely. Where once the Lutheran priest had chastised Francis for oppressing his serfs, he now reminded his congregation how Nádasdy had given food and clothing to the needy and had paid for poor scholars to pursue their studies. The late lord had taken food and drink always in moderation and had never indulged himself to excess. The more exalted he had become, the priest said, the more modestly he had behaved, for pride was no part of his being.[11] The body of Francis Nádasdy was then placed in a covered carriage and taken to the graveyard to be interred. Despite conflicting suggestions, its whereabouts today is unknown.

The great ladies of feudal Hungary, more emancipated perhaps, but essentially living like the wives of mediaeval crusaders, had not only to bear the burdens left to them by their absent husbands but to prepare themselves for bereavement which might come at any time. Elisabeth Báthory was more than equal to those responsibilities while Francis lived and also continued to exercise her husband's legal rights and maintain his sponsoring of students after his death, as well as pursuing his debtors, who included the Imperial Treasury itself. On Francis Nádasdy's death she immediately took over the responsibility for the running of the estates, as attested by the letters confirming the annual taxes levied on her villages which she signed during 1604. When these letters and others are examined, what is notable, if we compare Elisabeth's correspondence to that of her peers, is how terse they are, often to the point of curt aggression.

On 12 May 1588 Elisabeth had written in her telegrammatic style, but also in what were for her the very warmest terms to a certain Mrs Ponticzka:

After my greeting, Mistress Ponticzka our good sister, I wish to say to you that you should send to me immediately that book which is about pains in the back, and write to me of Ghéczi, how is he, and write to me also of how you find yourself, are you at peace or not.

Her Ladyship Elisabeth Báthory in her own hand[12]

On 5 November 1589 a more typical letter was sent from the twenty-nine-year-old Countess to one of the family retainers, a minor noble named Imre Vasváry:

Egregio Domine Nobis salutem . . . We have received your letter together with the food. Especial thanks for the bustard [a large game bird], we will keep it to await my husband, but you should know, Sir, that these provisions should have been sent to us during the last week. Therefore for next Saturday send to us all that you are accustomed to send, and even the provisions for the week to come, or you will see our anger, for we will expect guests and my husband, too, will return home. For tomorrow evening send fishes and crayfishes. You excuse yourself that you have distributed food amongst the poor, but we set you in your office for the government of our estates, that we might have everything that we require in our kitchen.

May God bless you.[13]

To modern eyes there is an ironic contrast between the required salutation and blessing and the message itself. Perhaps Vasváry deserved her anger, but this same tone of haughty impatience is also seen in her letters to her steward Benedict Deseő, whom she several times chastised, and in most of Elisabeth's surviving correspondence; it is echoed in the few reports of her conversations as they were remembered by (admittedly hostile) witnesses.

Elisabeth's pride and independence manifested themselves in other ways. She appears to have ignored the convention that a widow should retire and mourn for one year after her spouse's death, attending a function in Vienna only four weeks after Francis' passing and continuing to buy the finest clothing for herself and her ladies-in-waiting as shown on her bills from September 1604, 'to a total sum of 2,942 forints and 11 denar'. The bill was signed by the purchaser and by George Péchy the merchant, who probably brought the goods from Vienna. The sum of money involved was enormous – the annual salary of a senior steward of noble blood or one of the few doctors of good reputation was around 150 silver florins – and this was only one of many similar bills paid, always on time and in full, that same month.

The correspondence shows that Elisabeth also bartered valuables, mainly jewels, with merchants such as the German Péchy, and that on occasions she borrowed the cash that was in short supply from her stewards for brief periods, but far more often it was the Lady who advanced money or quantities of grain or other produce which her servants could then trade on their own account. The names of the servants who were indebted to her include the Sárvár bookkeeper Zalay, the squire Zamobothny and Benedict Deseő and Benedict Bicsérdy, all of whom later came forward to speak against her. There were also transactions with other aristocrats of more senior rank, including Count Paul Zichy, who wrote to Elisabeth in February 1607 acknowledging the receipt of a lease of land. Zichy's letter, although brief, is almost ingratiatingly respectful in its tone.[14]

Elisabeth was the authority to whom local lawsuits and other personal disputes were brought, and a great deal of her time was taken up with ensuring that the outbreaks of petty lawlessness, and the vendettas and misunderstandings which occurred on her lands were resolved. The names of the officers who assisted her in this are again familiar from the documents of the later investigations: an undertaking sworn by a constable, Mihály Tulok, to let drop a three-year quarrel with the bookkeeper Benedict Zalay, for instance, is countersigned by the castle warden Benedict Bicsérdy and the local dignitary Adam Szelesthey. Bicsérdy's behaviour later is cast in a new light by the record of a gift that Elisabeth and her nine-year-old son (who was required to add his signature to the deed) bestowed on him and his family in April 1607:

> We, Lady Elisabeth Báthory . . . declare to all who should be aware thereof, that those ownerless allotments in the village of Hegyfalu to the value of one hundred florins are hereby granted to Benedict Bicsérdy by me in recognition of his true and devoted service in his office and to my husband in the late Wars . . . We give these lands to him, and to Orsik Mesterházy, his wife, and to his children, namely John Bicsérdy, Francis Bicsérdy, and to his daughters Anna, Kate, Orsik and Elisabeth for their lifetimes, on condition that they serve us with the same devotion. If otherwise we or our successors

should wish to take back possession of these allotments, in such case we shall pay one hundred florins to Benedict Bicsérdy or to his successors.[15]

The irony of Bicsérdy's subsequent betrayal lies not so much in his ingratitude for this not inconsiderable reward, as in the fact that he and his wife had obviously named their younger children after his master and mistress and their own daughters.

The other vital part of sixteenth- and seventeenth-century lives that is missing from the archive documents is, not surprisingly, the whole panoply of the sins of the flesh that we know the inhabitants of that world must have indulged in. Later romantic literature and sensationalist religious tracts are full of hushed-up pregnancies, incestuous *affaires*, adulteries and poisonings, but if they were confessed or were gossiped about, as they certainly were, this was in the marketplace or at the wedding feast and was only very rarely entrusted to ink and parchment. Of the lesser excesses little was written: a few pious instructions to family members to drink and eat in moderation hardly does justice to a society in which it is thought that most of the squirearchy and the more affluent peasantry were habitually wine-drunk from dawn to dusk and gluttony was endemic at all levels. Crime itself was not restricted to the poor and desperate, but the privileged were able to beat, extort and seize their weaker neighbours' property with impunity and without coming to public notice, not least because it was they who controlled the local administration of justice.

The Hungarians were suspected by their German neighbours of indulging in peculiar Venetian or Turkish sexual practices, and there were signs that libertinage and the erotic refinements of the harem had taken hold in Transylvania even before the antics of Prince Gábor Báthory became the stuff of gossip throughout the region. But in Hungary itself George Thurzó, for instance, was much affected by Protestant ideology, and like all his family strictly avoided any mention of sexual practices in his letters and private papers. Hungarians were seen and saw themselves as hotter-blooded and less physically inhibited than other races, and Calvinism and Lutheranism in Hungary never involved the same degree of self-mortification that they did in colder climates. Nevertheless, for all but the most sophisticated, the discourses of love and lust did not even allow for concepts such as sex between women or sexually motivated sadism. In the Magyar and Slav lands, these were not so much taboos as unexplored and unacknowledged areas until early in the twentieth century.

Male homosexuality was practised, but how prevalent it was is not known: one of the few references to it comes in a visitor's uncorroborated aside: 'There is a great number of gentry in this kingdom, but being untravelled abroad, they are far less mannerly at home, being luxurious and ill-taught, and damnably given to that masculine misery the whole southern world is defiled with.'[16]

The concept of family honour was taken very seriously and, although men at war may have indulged themselves sexually with partners of both sexes, open infidelity or violence to a wife would breach the Renaissance codes and invoke the dangerous wrath of another family. Thurzó did write teasingly to his wife Elisabeth that he was looking for beautiful women in Bratislava, but could find none as beautiful as her and would cease to look henceforth.[17]

The other, illicit side of love is illustrated by the many stories that are still recounted with relish about the sixteenth-century noble poet Bálint Balassi. This half-mad philanderer had an amorous technique that was considered robust if not actually scandalous in his day; today it would be characterised simply as rape. Balassi habitually assaulted women and only afterwards became infatuated with them and dedicated his verses to them. It is said that while riding in the countryside he found himself behind a miller's young wife seated on her horse and accompanied by two servants. Even though her face was turned away from him, the sight of the woman so inflamed him that he knocked her from her horse and straddled her then and there as she lay on the ground. The young lady's honour was saved by her servants who, after a moment's hesitation, beat the distracted poet unconscious.

Of women's sexual needs and how they satisfied them nothing was written and nothing is known for certain. The nature of Elisabeth Báthory's private desires will always be a mystery, but, whatever they were, once her husband was gone the absolute power she wielded within the closed world of her court meant that anything she wanted was, providing some discretion was observed, in theory within her reach.

Such women's duties as overseeing the servants, attending to the herb gardens and cultivating and trading in honey, milk and eggs were taken for granted and went almost unmentioned in correspondence or chronicles (although Lady Révay declared proudly in a letter of 1560 that she had refused to give credit, even for three florins' worth of butter), but historians have discovered another important part of the aristocratic lady's routine, one which reinforced the power of life and death that she held over her serfs and minions. This was the healing of the sick and the dispensing of advice on health and hygiene, in particular to other women, inside and in the surroundings of the court. Although high-born ladies could choose whether or not they would undertake this curing (many but not all aristocratic women were practising healers), there was a desperate need for such a service in a country – or rather a long arc of territory stretching from Croatia to Wallachia – in which nine out of ten people lived in rural isolation, far from the few qualified doctors, who were needed in any case to tend to the war-wounded on the ever-shifting front-lines.

When the late-mediaeval epidemics were ravaging western Europe, the baths there were closed down because it was thought that water was the conduit for disease. In contrast, the spas of Hungary remained open and the wealthy took the waters to ease their maladies and enjoyed their visits there as an important social ritual. Before the seventeenth century sheets, nightclothes and clean underwear were rare, even among the rich, but in the inventories of castles there are always washbasins, tubs and ornamental baths and these were given as wedding presents. Hungarians knew to wash their hands before eating, although in his memoirs, which were written during his imprisonment by the Habsburgs, Lord Nicholas Bethlen says that water touched his skin only once or twice a year. So in spite of the army of 'balneators' who operated in Hungary and despite the great ladies' attendance at the many spas, cleanliness was by no means universal. Bathing in hot or cold water or herbal mixtures, dieting, the drinking of herbal infusions and purging were very common practices, usually applied according to astrological indications.

After the death of Lady Ursula Kanizsai, the Nádasdys did not have a male doctor or barber–surgeon resident in their court, so the women may have undertaken minor surgery, bloodletting and the prescribing of ointments and medicines. In towns and cities poisons and strong medicines were not to be administered without the permission of a doctor, but once again Elisabeth and her court ignored the strictures binding ordinary citizens.

There were respected and respectable doctors whom the wealthy were able to consult, but they were few and usually resided in cities or at a major court. Typical of these exalted physicians was the Hungarian Praximus, who had cared for the infant Francis Nádasdy. The rest of the very small number of trained medical practitioners were all male and were organised in a hierarchy which ran from physicians with degrees from foreign universities down through apothecaries, barbers (who doubled as dentists and were regulated by their own guilds), chirurgeons (who were qualified to set bones, administer simple potions and carry out crude surgery) and bath attendants, but the most numerous members of the health system were the lay healers, herbalists and shamans who were almost all women. These untrained local practitioners, who learned their craft from their parents or by unofficial apprenticeships, were given many different names which reflected their overlapping functions in the community: there was the healing woman (*orvosló asszony*), the woman doctor (*orvos asszony*), the wise woman (*tudós asszony*), the learned woman (*tudományos asszony*), the herb-woman (*füves asszony*), the seer (*néző*), the bed-maker (*agyvető*), the smearer (*kenő*) and the midwife (*bába*), whose profession was further subdivided according to her social status and where she practised.[18]

These women might be illiterate crones living in shacks in forest clearings, but they might as easily be the wives or widows of peasants, tradesmen, county officials or noble lords. They often claimed to have supernatural sensitivity and the gift of a healing touch, and their treatments consisted of secret potions and rituals as well as folk medicine and common sense. But in the late sixteenth and early seventeenth centuries even the humblest traditional healers were generally tolerated by their neighbours as well as by the priesthood – even the zealot Cardinal Pázmány commended the use of natural remedies – and by the gentry, who made full use of their services. (It is important to remember that what now look like 'alternative' methods were then as much part of orthodoxy as the early 'scientific' approaches.) The attention of a qualified male doctor even for a short time was beyond what most patients could afford, but, even when the physician had ministered, many wealthy clients asked their local healer for extra help, particularly where women's afflictions or fertility or childbirth were concerned, as these were both symbolically and practically the province of women. The women of the local aristocratic family, even if they were not themselves practising healers or sorceresses, would act as patrons for the poorer women who had inherited or learned

113

the skills of magic and to whom, in the idiom of the time, 'the herbs and flowers talked'.

Although uneducated women could claim extraordinary powers and draw upon folk wisdom dating back to pre-Christian times, they relied on an oral tradition of spells and incantations and could not decipher the language of the *grimoires*, herbariums and medical handbooks that were imported by the cosmopolitan rich, nor could they afford to supplement their native flowers and plants with the drugs that had become available at pharmacies in the larger towns. The noble lady with her bath-houses, laundries, clean linen and capacious medicine chest was well placed to operate an unofficial health service if she so wished, and some of Elisabeth Báthory's contemporaries were well known for their personal healing expertise, among them Lady Anna-Rosina Listhius, whose family contained many alchemists and whose later fate echoed that of Elisabeth herself, and Lady Potencia Dersffy, who lent her book of cures to Elisabeth's father-in-law. Those aristocratic women who were herbal experts included Thurzó's wife Elisabeth Czobor – a renowned healer in later life – and Éva Poppelova Lobkowitz of the Batthyány family.

Dispensing health care from the courts would bring Elisabeth and her inner circle in contact with other women in the most intimate surroundings, in which all occult wisdom and all power to inflict or assuage suffering was invested in them. The mock-surgical techniques that she and her female assistants resorted to in the absence of better-qualified male surgeons were indistinguishable from torture, and anyone carrying them out would need to become hardened to others' suffering.

In central Europe a popular medical handbook of 1586, the *Ars Medica* (written by György Lencsés, a member of the entourage of Prince Christopher Báthory's wife, Lady Elisabeth Bocskai), recommends that patients be bound tightly in chains to help expel poisons from the body, after which they should be bathed or steamed. Applying plasters – 'emplastures' or poultices – was a very popular process, as was 'cupping', whereby small ceramic or glass cups were heated and fixed to broken skin: the suction effect would draw off blood or pus.[19] (These practices involved using hot candlewax to fix the plasters or cups in position, a fact that possibly explains the reports of Elisabeth holding candles to the naked bodies of her maidservants.)

Leeching was also widely used and, for boils, open sores or lacerations, cauterising with a hot iron was the standard treatment. Purging, to rid the body of unhealthy excesses of the humours and purify the blood, was universally approved of, but the most popular technique in the healer's repertoire by far, and the one prescribed for the widest array of quite different physical and behavioural symptoms, was venesection or phlebotomy: bleeding. The more these methods caused pain, the more efficacious they were, claimed the healers; and the more drastically invasive they were (they might have added but did not), the more the patient's desire for a dramatic cure was satisfied.

Just as happened in England, the local wise woman, especially if she was reclusive, harsh and strange (whether those qualities were part of a carefully cultivated mystique or whether they were forced upon her), was a useful target when panic seized the village. Sometimes a cure would go wrong and a child would die, or an ailing patient declared themselves bewitched, sometimes a rival healer would lay charges of witchcraft to usurp a lucrative practice. Although in this early period there was a good chance that any woman accused of witchcraft would be acquitted, it was nevertheless one of the easiest ways to have an enemy arrested.

The use of magic cosmetics, which Elisabeth was accused of posthumously, was also part of the spectrum of herbalism and healing. The Hungarian scholar Ferenc Schram, in his exhaustive account of the witchcraft trials taking place in Hungary between 1529 and 1768, tells the story of women villagers fighting over possession of a magic cosmetic. Desire for the substance caused a wave of hysteria which died down only after the local wise woman had been condemned to death and her ointment had been carried off by her enemies.[20]

If we can apprehend the way of life and thinking of Elisabeth Báthory and her contemporaries, perhaps we can perceive the logic in their actions and they will cease to be unreachably alien. For most people in that era society was static and inert, Enlightenment concepts of improvement, progress and the power of understanding were unknown. During the endless conflicts, time sometimes seemed to have been reversed: the waterways became choked with weeds and silt, the fertile plain became dusty desert, fields were overgrown and dry land turned to marsh. Hungarians started to measure time then, and became extremely conscious of its running out, of a sense that the sins of the present were jeopardising the future; children were

115

at the centre of this consciousness. The national psyche was very insecure after the religious schisms and the change of faith, the threat from the Turks, the political pressure from Austria. Continuity and futurity became important – matters of desperate concern, not the leisured consideration of the stability of the spheres with telescopes and astrolabes as practised by Emperor Rudolf or the wise men of the west. All over Europe there was a sense of what was termed by Rembrandt 'lamenting the future', as shown allegorically in paintings like Brueghel's *Massacre of the Innocents*.

The complexities of emotional attachments are not easy to deconstruct even today, and those of that strange transitional society even less so, but it appears that true intimacy and deep affection among the ruling caste of Hungary was restricted to the family, in particular to the relationships between brothers and sisters, and with favoured sons or daughters. Two of Elisabeth's children, Ursula – 'Orsik' – and Andrew, died in infancy, and almost as little is known about the early years of the surviving Nádasdy children as is known of their mother's life in her childhood home at Ecsed. The first recorded landmarks in the girls' lives were the splendid dynastic marriages that Elisabeth arranged for them with partners from the few ancient families of comparable status. As was customary, the education and wellbeing of Elisabeth's son Paul, who was only twelve years old when his mother was arrested, was shared between his mother and a male, Imre Megyery, who was appointed as the boy's tutor and guardian.

Anna, the eldest child, married Count Nicholas Zrínyi, the grandson of another Nicholas, the hero of Szigetvár, whose son George had been a companion of Francis Nádasdy on the battlefields; the second daughter, Kate, married Count George Drugeth of Homonna (now Humenné in eastern Slovakia), whose family blood had been intermingling with the Báthorys' for generations (Elisabeth's mother's second husband had been Count Antal Drugeth and her brother Stephen married another Drugeth, Lady Fruszina). It is said that the Drugeth family had come to Hungary from Naples to serve the Angevin King, Charles Robert, who ruled Hungary from 1310. The dynastic connections had a strategic basis, too; Drugeth's stronghold of Homonna, which dominated the north-east routes into Poland, and Zrínyi's estates in the south-west meant that the combined families controlled a string of vast landholdings across the whole remaining arc of Royal Hungary.

There has been nothing from which we could resurrect Elisabeth's conversations with her children, no authentic record of their voices. During this author's research just one fragment came to light in the form of a letter that Elisabeth's elder daughter, the twenty-year-old Lady Anna Nádasdy, wrote to her mother on 22 December 1605 to describe her reception at the home of her new husband, Count Zrínyi, at his castle of Csáktornya (now Čakovec in Croatia). The letter is polite and dutiful, with a hint of spontaneity relegated to the postscript (often the most revealing part in letters of this period):

> Thanks be to God, I travelled hither without trouble and my health is good. My lord husband came to meet me two miles before our home, we are in good spirits and health. He has only a slight pain in his hand, for he fell from his horse. But it is nothing grave, his hand will soon be well. As concerns his servants, they are all obedient to me, they do as I command them. Do not worry for us, all is well with us, even his servants respect me greatly. God keep you happy.
>   Your poor servant and sister
>   Anna Nádasdy
>
> P.S. I have sent to you and to my beloved brother a basket of figs, I would have sent others, too, but this is all that we have received from the seaside.[21]

Anna and Kate Nádasdy may have simply obeyed their mother, or perhaps they married for love, but their husbands also wanted to share in the inheritances which their wives brought with them, and would expect to do so before they were too old for it to matter. Their mother-in-law's skill and tenacity in running the estates was an obstacle that could not be tolerated indefinitely, and Imre Megyery, the protector of the principal male heir, knew that his charge would have to compromise with these ambitious young men sooner or later if open conflict between the families was to be avoided.

Some writers have speculated that, even before the death of Francis Nádasdy, Elisabeth was abandoned by her relatives for some shameful transgression, excluded from the family council and so forced to consort with common servants, falling prey to their superstitions and like them resorting to black magic when flight was impossible. The few demonstrable facts tell a different story. Letters unearthed by this author prove that, far from being excluded from her family's social and political dealings, Elisabeth played an important and independent role in the international intrigues carried on by the male Báthorys in Hungary and Transylvania.

An example was the private note sent from Cardinal Andrew Báthory to Elisabeth in 1587, prefaced: 'may this letter be given into the hands of my most beloved sister . . .':

> I wish all the best to my beloved sister. I had to travel to Rome, I informed them of the sad news of the death of King Stephen [Báthory of Poland and Transylvania]. I pray that the man who has presented my letter to you remain unknown to the others in your court, for his mission requires secrecy and it would not be good if others knew him. Please ask your husband to forgive me, we shall certainly meet one another on the next occasion. A certain Venetian gentleman has accompanied my man, he is a great friend to our family, therefore I pray you to take care of him. I hope he will be given all that he needs in your court.[22]

After Francis was gone, some also speculated that his loss combined with Elisabeth's menopause, aggravated by the lurking family taint, tipped her into madness from which she never recovered. Once again there is no evidence for this: no change of tone in the letters she wrote, no abrupt withdrawal from public life. If she was insane, it was a carefully concealed insanity which went unremarked by her fellow aristocrats.

Although no one spoke up publicly on her behalf when she was arrested, she had not been friendless. She may have enjoyed the dubious attentions of Ironhead Stephen and the loyalty of her crones, but far from being a social pariah, a famous madwoman, Countess Báthory was also, in the words of one recent commentator, 'much respected and loved by other aristocratic ladies: many corresponded with her and more visited her'.[23] She seems to have been especially close to Lady Margaret Choron, the wife of Lord Christopher Nádasdy, her father-in-law's younger brother, with whom she exchanged frequent letters around the turn of the century and she also corresponded with Lord Bathóry who advised her on political matters after her husband's death.[29] If witnesses at the interrogation sessions are to be believed, she boasted of the calibre and number of her advisers and supporters: whoever they were, they failed her when she had most need of them.

★   ★   ★

The letters and the bills and contracts and the statements lodged in official records are not enough in themselves to bring the people of the past fully into existence: to a modern 'western' eye, the surviving portraits of the protagonists look like quaint caricatures, even grotesque, but we must remember that the Hungarian aesthetic of the time was constrained in two ways. Firstly, the artists available to the far-flung courts of the Hungarian and Transylvanian aristocrats were usually itinerants, mainly Italians or their local imitators, working quickly on one-off commissions for which they sometimes simply substituted heads on to a standard set of shoulders or on to the template body of a rider on horseback. In a time of almost permanent warfare the true likenesses of men, at least, were subordinated to the need to show their power, ferocity and heroism: piercing eyes, bristling moustaches and thick, curling beards were *de rigueur*. Cardinal Andrew Báthory appears in his portraits first as an intense and nervously alert presence, then, with raised eyebrows and half-smile, as a severed head on display. Prince Sigmund is shown at the age of twenty-six with the large eyes, long nose and sensual lips common to many images of the Báthorys, then at a later date as a blustering tyrant with bulging eyes and a curlicued topknot. Francis Nádasdy is pictured, full-length, as a stooping, kaftanned bear of a man, with the uncomfortable look of a warrior impatient to return to the fray (his father's fears regarding a snub nose had been quite groundless). From several portraits the bushy-bearded Palatine, George Thurzó, glares fixedly at the artist with a sort of savage imperiousness from beneath luxuriant black eyebrows, while his arch-enemy, Gábor Báthory, the great seducer, is painted as a jaunty clown. The results are in all cases quite different both from the delicate-featured dandies in their colourful finery who appear in Elizabethan English portraiture and from the more austere and haughty elegance of Habsburg likenesses.

The first reference to the existence of a portrait of Elisabeth Báthory comes in R. A. von Elsberg's 1894 work, *Die Blutgräfin*, in which he includes a poor black-and-white copy of a picture which he had seen in the gallery of the aristocratic Zay family. The image is of a dark-eyed young woman with dark hair drawn under a cap, and wearing a starched lace collar above a bodice and apron. The person depicted in the somewhat bland portrait seems a pert rather than sinister figure, but von Elsberg sees more in it than that:

She is Elisabeth Báthory, but is she at the same time the tigress? She is a lady of high rank with a cultivated mind, but her great eyes let us see deeper within to her devilish passion. Her finely chiselled nose, her wilful and obstinate lips show her siren-like personality, her wild heart . . . long white hands and in contrast to her white skin, her black hair: these are the features which perfectly define her difficult nature.[24]

The costume worn by the girl in the von Elsberg picture and her pose are almost identical to those in the two portraits which survived into the twentieth century, one of which can still be viewed. His picture and the portrait kept until recently in Čachtice are probably one and the same, although it is possible that there still exists a third version, hanging forgotten in a private gallery in one of the great houses of middle Europe.

The only portrait of Countess Báthory which can still be seen, although it is not on public display, is kept in storage in the National Museum in Budapest. The shades of red, red-brown and gold on this full-length canvas are rich, and the overall condition is excellent, partly because the painting was restored in 1974 when 75 per cent of the surface, excluding the face, hands and apron, were overpainted and some detail, particularly around the subject's right hand, was lost. Still, the whole work is convincing as an early modern family portrait and, although no masterpiece, it meets the criteria of official portraiture; it expresses a dignified formality at a distance which gives way to a different sense of intimacy when seen from close up.

The woman in the painting stands stiffly and stares gravely out at the world, but when the viewer gazes into her face, a more sensitive and enigmatic expression, an awareness in the eyes and the hint of a smile, is revealed. (For the historian Katalin Péter, the Budapest portrait is genuine but reveals a sullen, 'ugly moth', a stupid woman, oppressed physically and socially by her huge vulgarian husband. Another Hungarian, the art historian István Kelényi, disagrees: 'I like her, I think she is pretty in that painting.') She has the large brown eyes, the high forehead, long nose and prominent ears common to her fellow-Báthorys, but these are to some extent stylistic conventions of the period. Other conventional features are more significant. The artist uses the late Renaissance language of symbolism in the detail surrounding the figure. Elisabeth holds in her right hand an almost invisible key, a sign that she was accomplished in domestic organisation, a perfect mistress of her household. On her little finger is a ring, signifying in those days generosity (and not the coquettishness which it later came to mean), and she is wearing pearls, which stand for nobility of character as well as great material wealth. On the table upon which Elisabeth's hand rests there is a little ornamental clock, at that period a rare and precious object which also symbolised life and continuity. The clock is standing on a small box, which can denote a knowledge of medicine and healing, or may just imply the possession of secrets, which Elisabeth's own box, described by witnesses and by her son, certainly contained.

Of the known portraits, this is the most likely to be authentic, but there are problems in proving beyond doubt that it is a likeness taken from the living lady. The painting bears the date 1594, but this does not mean that it was produced at that time (dates inscribed on canvases could also refer to famous events, battles or the birthdates of children); the costume that Elisabeth is wearing is almost identical to one shown in a portrait of Christina Nyáry, the wife of Palatine Esterházy, dated 1625, leading some to suspect that it was reconstructed using that better-known painting as a model. (The Dutch expert Dr J. van Wadum saw the Báthory portrait when it was on loan to The Hague and pronounced it genuine, dating it to the period 1594 to 1620 and pointing out the Italian rather than Austrian style, which would accord with the close family links with Venice and Padua.) More importantly, the portrait of Elisabeth seems to be the work of the same artist who produced portraits of her son Paul Nádasdy and his wife Judith Révay around the year 1633 and it seems probable to this writer that all three pictures, together with the matching portrait of Francis Nádasdy, were commissioned then, either by Paul to fill the portrait cabinet of one of the Nádasdy properties, or by his widow to commemorate Paul's death the same year.[25] This would mean that the work was not taken from life, though it may well be a copy from a lost original painted while Elisabeth was still alive.

One of the first consequences of the opening up of eastern-central Europe after the demise of communism was a field-day for art thieves, who took advantage of the naivety of curators and the almost total lack of security devices and quietly looted museums and churches all over the region, often stealing to order on behalf of collectors from wealthier neighbouring countries. In Čachtice in 1990 someone broke into the little museum in the manor-house and made off with several early oil paintings of local dignitaries, including what is thought by some to be an authentic image of Elisabeth Báthory created in her own lifetime, but which is dismissed by others as a fake. The technique of that painting, which was ascribed to one Valentino, was also mediocre but by no means abysmal: examination of photographs shows that it bore the date 1593, or possibly 1598, but this rendering appears to be the likeness of a young girl and not a woman in her thirties, as Elisabeth was in that decade. At some point – certainly not during Elisabeth's lifetime – the caption in Latin, *Hyena Chejtensis* ('the Hyena of Csejthe'), has been added, and lower down on the canvas and almost invisible is a second date, 1869. The canvas had been crudely cut down but was originally full-length, and the costume details seem to have been overpainted at some point perhaps to conform to late-seventeenth-century fashions. The young Countess which this portrait gives us has a haunting, tantalising expression into which many other qualities can be read, from bruised innocence to cool cunning, and it has been widely reproduced as being the definitive incarnation of the real Elisabeth.

Unfortunately, although it fascinates, there are good reasons to think that the Čachtice portrait is a reconstruction produced in the nineteenth century, either to coincide with an upsurge of local interest in the case in Slovakia (two books that might have been inspired by the painting appeared in 1870)[26] or again as a commission for the collection of a noble family, perhaps the Zays. Apart from the inconsistencies implied in the two dates inscribed on it, there is one glaring anachronism in the picture: the artist has given Elisabeth a pointed nineteenth-century rather than straight baroque bodice; and the cuffs and collar she is wearing seem to be a crude imitation of those on the Budapest portrait.

As always with Elisabeth Báthory, the fascination felt for her by later ages has tended to obscure rather than reveal the truth.

CHAPTER SIX

The Palatine and His Enemies

There is little friendship in the world,
and least of all between equals . . .

Francis Bacon, *Essays*, 'Of Followers and Friends'

Count George Thurzó ~ the Hungarian lords and the Empire ~ the trial of Illésházy and the Bocskai insurrection ~ plots and counterplots ~ gruesome folktales ~ the Báthory–Thurzó correspondence ~ a widow's defiance ~ Elisabeth's domains

In the National Museum of Arts and Crafts in Budapest is a fabulous, nameless object. If the thing has any practical use it is not obvious, but as an ornament, a gift for someone already possessed of wealth and power in abundance, it is exquisitely impressive. It is a model about eighteen or twenty inches high of a hilltop or a steep mound cast in gold; at its foot tiny figures sculpted in silver are depicted toiling in a mine, worker-mannikins, bent double under their burdens of rubble, run up and down its flanks on glistening steel ladders, its upper reaches are set around with gems and minerals, and the whole miniature edifice is crowned by the figure of a Renaissance knight,

123

kneeling in homage before a silver–grey block of ore. It is not known who fashioned this celebration of industry nor whom it was intended for: the kneeling knight is clearly an allegorical figure, but could as well have been a representation of Elisabeth Báthory's nemesis, Count George Thurzó.

Lord George Thurzó of Bethlenfalva, Count of Árva, was one of the richest and most powerful grandees in Hungary by virtue of his birth, but he was acutely conscious that by comparison with the Báthorys or the Nádasdy and Zrínyi families he was to some extent a parvenu who still had to prove himself, socially and politically. He was the principal heir to hereditary rights – the governorship and regional judgeship of the counties of Orava and Spiš; patronage of the Lutheran church in Trenčín, Tematin, Hlohovec, Bojnice, Hricov, Lietava and Bytča in what is now Slovakia – as well as to enormous incomes from investment in mining, metallurgy and trade. The Thurzós were recent additions to the ranks of the nobility, originating, they said, from the village of Bethlenfalva, then in Upper Hungary. Their name is not a Magyar one and the usual fanciful origins were proposed, including an unlikely theory that they had come from the Norse port of Thurso in the far north of Scotland. What was known for sure was that they had made their fortunes at the end of the fifteenth century from development of copper- and ironworks and silver mines in their own region as well as in Poland, Bohemia and Baia Mare (in present-day Romania), where they leased gold mines with the German Fugger family of Augsburg, the famous moneylenders – or infamous usurers – who with Genoese financiers bankrolled the Spanish and French in their imperial adventures and exercised more real power in Europe than most royal houses. Together the Hungarian and German entrepreneurs founded the Thurzó–Fugger Company, one of middle Europe's first and largest transnational concerns.

The family member who confirmed the Thurzós' rise to pre-eminence was Count Francis Thurzó, George's illustrious father, who had been educated in Italy and became Catholic Bishop and Governor of Nitra county (by inheritance; he had not been ordained), head of Orava county and Prefect of the Royal Chamber. Like many of the Magyar lords he later converted to the Lutheran faith. When George Thurzó was only seven years old his father died and his mother, Lady Katherine Zrínyi, remarried to Count Imre Forgách, who was not a politician but a distinguished humanist intellectual who wrote treatises on history and the nature of marriage. The couple's relationship was warm, and it seems that the young George and his stepfather were quickly on good terms with one another. Imre Forgách was the centre of a very important humanist circle in northern Hungary, whose members corresponded with major Reformation figures in western Europe. George Thurzó inherited his stepfather's library on his death and collected for himself the works of Erasmus and books on Protestant theology as well as the writings of such luminaries as Castiglione (on courtly etiquette), Lipsius ('on Constancy') and Macchiavelli.

Thurzó's relationship with his second wife, Lady Elisabeth Czobor, was unusually good and exceptional for the age in the expressions of intimacy the couple exchanged. Their marriage produced many daughters, of whom six survived, and one son, and on one occasion when his wife was visiting her mother and Lord George was alone with the children, he wrote to her of the affection he felt towards his little daughter, that he was kissing her and playing with her – something very rare in itself at that time and hardly ever mentioned in correspondence.[1] There were two girls from the first marriage, and the first child from the new marriage, Barbara, was always her father's favourite. George asked after her constantly in his letters and after Imre, his only son and heir.

George began his political and military career at the time of the Fifteen-Year War against the Turks, first acting as a political adviser to Rudolf II, the absentee King of Hungary, later becoming commander of the Cisdanubian armies and of the Fort of Nové Zámky, then known as Érsekújvar. While he was engaged on diplomatic and court business in Vienna, he developed some sort of admiration for the Habsburg Archduke Matthias and remained loyal to him when Rudolf was replaced first as king and then as emperor. Elisabeth Báthory's husband, Francis Nádasdy, and Thurzó fought together in the wars against the Turks and together rode their horses into the courtyards of the Stára Radnica – the Old Town Hall in Bratislava – to attend the sittings of the Hungarian Diet. Their estates were close to one another in Upper Hungary and the families exchanged invitations to their children's weddings. There was a later cooling of the relationship between the Thurzós and the Nádasdys, as evidenced by letters, but no clear indication of whether political or personal differences triggered the change.

George Thurzó was a cultivated man who spoke Latin, Greek and

German, could communicate in Slovak and Croatian and wrote poetry in Greek. He was popular with his Slav tenants, not only because he supported the spread of their Lutheran religion, but because he allowed both the estate managers and the scholars and clerks who worked for him to communicate in their own Slovak language:

The Count Palatine of Hungary was elected by the whole of the Diet – the parliament made up of an upper house comprising the senior aristocrats and a lower containing representatives of the cities and towns and the lesser nobles – from a choice of four candidates put forward by the King, of which two had to be Catholic, one Lutheran and one Calvinist. The Palatine was not only the representative of the King in Hungary, but the mediator between him and the native aristocracy – and indeed the defender of that aristocracy all at the same time. During those years of the early seventeenth century Thurzó, elected Palatine in 1609, could rely on the tacit support of the Hungarian nobility for virtually anything he did, given that he was their only champion against the growing absolutism of the Habsburgs, against pressure from the Catholic Counter-Reformation and against the establishment all over Europe of a state apparatus that would eventually sideline the traditional ruling elites. Thurzó saw his political mission as modernising and strengthening the mediaeval office of the Palatine as the one guarantee of stability in the fragile remains of a kingdom. In this he was successful, and he is remembered today in Hungary as a master tactician and a shrewd statesman, if not for being one of the country's truly charismatic leaders.

In private Thurzó, like many of his fellow-lords, nursed more grandiose dynastic dreams. He had probably coveted the throne of Transylvania himself, but lacked the glamour of illustrious ancestors or a name that resounded throughout half a continent. Nonetheless, once he had attained the office of palatine it was not unreasonable to suppose that he might achieve his other ambitions, if not for himself then for Imre, his only son. Count George Thurzó died still in office in 1616 at the age of fifty-one and, in spite of the predictable rumours of poisoning, the cause of his death was probably gout.

The arrest of Elisabeth Báthory was not the first manoeuvre executed by George Thurzó during the dead time of midwinter, when social and political life was in temporary suspense. On Christmas Day 1600, Thurzó had tricked the twenty-three-year-old lord, Michael Telekesi, into leaving his forest hiding place and travelling to Thurzó's seat at Bytča in the hope of an amnesty. The young noble had ambushed and robbed a convoy transporting gifts to the Habsburg Emperor, Rudolf II, who deemed the crime high treason and ordered the Hungarian aristocrats to respond. When George Thurzó, eager to ingratiate himself with his master, agreed to besiege Telekesi's stronghold at Lednice, not one of his fellow-lords would accompany him or provide troops – all of them were suddenly indisposed. Thurzó, with his own 150 horsemen and 400 footsoldiers, took the castle anyway and chased Telekesi into Poland, whence he returned in secret, hoping to negotiate. Once he had surrendered at Bytča, Telekesi was summarily imprisoned, then taken by Thurzó to Bratislava, tried by the compliant tabular court and quickly beheaded. Thurzó's actions were judged unnecessarily cruel and his part in the affair was widely resented in Hungary: Telekesi was nobly born, young and as popular as Rudolf was unpopular; he had fought heroically against the Turks; and he was the last male of his line, all of which should have won him clemency.[2]

There were plenty of other instances showing Thurzó, the loving husband and father, to be utterly ruthless where his material interests were concerned. In 1605, at the time of the Bocskai rebellion, someone looted the Thurzó family crypt in Bytča, later abandoning some of the stolen objects near the Thurzó country estates. George suspected his neighbour Jan Kubinyi and his wife Magdalena Esterházy and without warning seized and burned Bodina, a Kubinyi village, and executed several family servants without trial. The robbery had in fact been carried out by marauding Hajdúks with the probable help of Thurzó's own servants, but no apology or compensation was ever offered to the less powerful victims of Thurzó's anger.[3] The young and intensely ambitious Lord Nicholas Esterházy, among others, is unlikely to have forgotten this incident, which was only one of many in which Thurzó harassed the Kubinyis, and when the new generation of aristocrats came into their own and Esterházy became palatine, retribution rich in irony was visited on George's own heirs. The Platthy family also owned land adjoining Lord George's estates and Thurzó took eleven of their villages by force, daring the weaker Platthys to resist. This one-sided feud simmered for twenty-seven years, during which time Thurzó turned his attention to persecuting Lady Kate Pálffy, the widow of his predecessor as Palatine, Stephen Illésházy, and many lesser members of the squirearchy.

Even at the peak of its power, which had not yet arrived, finesse was not a quality associated with the Vienna court, and in their determination to keep Hungary allied to the Empire, to rule it in what Henry VII of England described as 'the French manner' – by absolutist decree – the Habsburgs often employed heavy-handed tactics. One of these was to organise show trials to discredit the more troublesome, or simply more powerful, members of the native aristocracy who were associated with Transylvanian politics. The easiest charge to trump up was high treason (the crime was ill-defined and there was no shortage of pro-Vienna Hungarian officials who would help in the concoction of a case), the penalties for which were death and, most attractively, the forfeiture of property. In this way the Habsburgs hoped to cow the rest of the aristocracy, to rid themselves permanently of troublemakers and to redistribute the estates of those accused among their own German- or Czech-speaking nobles. Religious motives were also mixed up in this policy: it was the Protestant lords whom the Catholic Habsburgs moved against, and the dispossessions were also designed to weaken the Calvinist and Lutheran hold on the Magyars and hasten the spread of the Counter-Reformation. The problem was that, for all its fierce frontier ways and outbreaks of local lawlessness, Hungary had a long tradition of observation of the law – and high expectations of the crown – at a national level. Rightminded lords, among them Elisabeth Báthory's husband Francis Nádasdy, were outraged by the Austrians' blatant injustices, particularly during the most famous of these trials in 1602, in which the new Palatine himself, Count Stephen Illésházy, stood accused.

In Illésházy's case, once King Rudolf had ordered a trial from Vienna, the proceedings were carried out according to Hungarian law and the defendant was acquitted by the Hungarian High Court of all the charges against him. At this point the King simply overruled the judgement and forced through the death sentence and the confiscation of lands, tithes and treasures. Before the sentence could be carried out, Illésházy followed the convention of escaping to the sanctuary of Poland, thence to Transylvania, where he intrigued against his enemies until 1606, when he was pardoned and allowed to return. The war-hero Francis Nádasdy openly opposed Vienna, and by implication its agent Thurzó, during the Illésházy trial and it may be significant that ugly and damaging rumours of cruelty by the Nádasdy-Báthory family at Sárvár began to circulate at just this time.

During the Fifteen-Year War, the Hungarians had seen for themselves that their western allies were cynical, rapacious and, worst, incapable of once and for all expelling the Turk. The aggressive policies of the Counter-Reformation served to inflame feelings even further and many became convinced that not only the infidel, but the 'Germans' were the enemy. As the noble poet Peter Bornemissza lamented at the end of the sixteenth century:

> The haughty Germans persecute me;
> The infidel Turks surround me:
> Shall I again enjoy, and when,
> A residence in old Buda town?[4]

After all the blood spilt in the fight against Islam, a serious collaboration with the Ottomans was out of the question, but the welling indignation and the resurgence of national pride were coming to a head. The existence of a free Protestant state, embodying Magyar traditions and dealing with both Vienna and Constantinople on equal terms, became an irresistible prospect; indeed, that state had already come painfully into being twenty years before but was still not recognised by all parties as an independent entity. That nation was not Hungary but Transylvania, which once again became the stage on which Hungary's conflicts were played out. The Imperial troops had occupied and despoiled Transylvania and the eastern Hungarian counties during the Fifteen-Year War, and, once the fighting had died down, Archduke Matthias and his clerical advisers decided to use the armies' presence there forcibly to restore the region, which had enjoyed religious toleration since 1580, to Catholicism. In protest against the seizure and reconsecration of their church by the agents of Vienna, the Lutheran Saxon burghers of Košice (Kassa) refused to speak their own German mother tongue and conversed in Hungarian: they were among the great majority who rushed to support the figurehead of a new nationalism, the man who raised the flag against the Roman Empire and inspired the 1605 declaration, Count Stephen Bocskai.

Bocskai had been brought up with Francis Nádasdy in Vienna as a Habsburg protégé, the two men had been lodged together as boys, and Bocskai's family had served the Báthorys, to whom they were related by marriage. When they reached adulthood the two men functioned in tandem for a time as the Empire's strongmen

129

inside Hungary, Nádasdy in the west and Bocskai in the east. The ruthlessly determined Bocskai, a member of the newer nobility who had himself been counsellor to Prince Sigmund Báthory (and the real power behind the throne) became the ruler of Transylvania and was made a gift of an 'alternative' crown of Hungary by the Turks. He agreed to accept the crown only in its capacity as a fabulous object, knowing that its symbolic power was meaningless unless he could first bring the Principality under his military control and then end the war between the Habsburgs and the Turks. To strengthen his hand within Transylvania and to prevent interference from Hungary, Bocskai, whose power-base was in Kassa, fomented a revolt against the crown in the north-eastern Hungarian territories and moved to annex the Seven Counties with the help of a fighting force, the Hajdúks, which, to paraphrase Wellington, frightened their commanders as much as they terrified their enemies.

The Hajdúks, who in later centuries became a sort of police force within Hungary, were originally Balkan shepherds and cattle-drovers who had formed a military order whose members fought as mercenaries against the Turks during the Fifteen-Year War. They lived outside the feudal system of servitude and were joined by Hungarian peasants and refugees who had renounced serfdom. These homeless warriors were notorious for their fanatical savagery and their bisexuality; they fought on foot and wore a uniform of sheepskins or furs and caps in which three crows' feathers were stuck. During the winter of 1604–5 Bocskai's Hajdúks – characterised by one historian as 'miserable, landless, lawless, godless creatures of an inhuman epoch'[5] – matched the brutal excesses of the Empire's troops and fought a guerrilla campaign with no quarter given to military foes or civilians who happened to get in their way. Bocskai knew what he had unleashed, but kept his part of the bargain with the Hajdúks, to whom he gave land where they could settle with their animals and camp-followers and begin to found communities. With the help of these shock-troops Bocskai defeated the Imperial armies under the Italian Belgiojoso, while his allies the Turks returned to the offensive against the Empire too.

In the Ecsedy branch of the Báthory family, loyalty to the Habsburgs was traditionally stronger than in the senior Somlyói branch with its aspirations to royalty, but Elisabeth's brother Stephen sided with Bocskai in 1605 because he lived close to Transylvania. If Elisabeth had openly declared for Bocskai, she would have risked losing her estates as her western lands were so near the Imperial capital, so she remained nominally loyal to Vienna but, as Thurzó and the Austrians well knew, she was also maintaining close links with her nephew Gábor Báthory, whose mentor was the new Prince. Bocskai ordered the Hajdúks to leave her estates alone.

The whole country was on the edge of civil war and, even when Elisabeth wished to travel through the southern and western regions in late August 1605, she was obliged to send to her son-in-law Count Zrínyi, who supported Bocskai, for a safe pass before setting out from his castle of Monyorókerék. 'I have invited My Mother, My Right Honourable Lady, together with her servants and chattels, and I will not impede her . . .' it read.[6]

On the first of July 1605 George Thurzó, the stalwart ally of the King, had written to his wife:

I have received from Bocskai the document guaranteeing the protection of my estates. But do not you show it to anybody, it is only for a case of emergency should the Hajdúks wish to enter into my possessions, because he writes in his letter that I have accepted his authority, but it is not the truth, and I shall never accept him, I need only his protection to defend myself against his soldiers, so it would be most unfortunate if other respected persons were to see this letter.[7]

During the continuing unrest following the rebellion in the latter part of 1605, Hajdúk troops burned and looted the town of Bytča and the village of Čachtice. They tried to occupy George Thurzó's castle in the middle of Bytča, but were bought off; Elisabeth Báthory's castle they left untouched. It is not known whether local people were given shelter by their master and mistress in the fortified castles, but it is known that around fifty commoners died in Bytča and an unknown number in Čachtice. We can try to imagine the feelings of those whose family members were slaughtered while the neighbouring aristocrats went unscathed. The fragmentary *Chronicles of Csejthe* record cryptically that as late as 27 March 1606 'devils carried András Vajda from the town':[8] the devils in question being, in all probability, from among the Hajdúks who had been left out of the land-sharing, and were still running amok in search of plunder.

Elisabeth's brother Stephen, Count of Ecsed, although a reclusive

man, wielded great influence in the kingdom. He was Chief Justice
of Hungary and was besides the guardian of the two children of the
more exalted Somlyói branch of the Báthorys, Gábor and Anna. When
Stephen died on 26 July 1605, Gábor Báthory was considered by many
to be the strongest candidate for the throne of Transylvania, should
it become vacant – and Prince Bocskai was in poor health. With his
uncle no longer alive to promote his cause, the young Count was at a
disadvantage, and a group of the most powerful aristocrats, including
George Thurzó and his new ally, the former fugitive Stephen Illésházy,
opposed Gábor's nomination. There were good political reasons for
this as well as the family jealousies and dynastic rivalries which
permeated the world of the senior nobility: Báthory would provide
a spectacular focus for those who aspired to independence from the
Habsburgs, and once in place he might well re-establish a hereditary
Magyar royal line which would be virtually unchallengeable. Bocskai
himself wished Gábor Báthory to succeed him, but somehow Thurzó
and Illésházy managed to prevail upon him to name their candidate
Bálint Homonnay Drugeth as his successor in his will (some say they
simply forged the document with the help of their many agents in the
Transylvanian court).

Bocskai died on 27 December 1606, and by January 1607 his
chancellor Kátai, who supported the Báthory cause and had already
been slandered and politically isolated by Illésházy, was cut down by
a group of Hajdúks in the pay of Thurzó's faction. After Kátai's death
rumours spread that he had poisoned his master. It is much more likely
that Bocskai died of natural causes, but the coincidences were too
much for seventeenth-century chroniclers, who treated their readers
to another lurid set-piece, masquerading as history, which became the
version of events that everyone remembered, including those who
later testified against Elisabeth Báthory:

> *1606 die 29 decembris hora 5 matutina* His Majesty the Prince
> Stephen Bocskai, the liberator of the Hungarian nation, died in
> Kassa, having been administered poison by Mihály Kátai some
> months before at a garden feast.[9]

After Kátai had been betrayed in turn, according to the folk-tales
by his young envoy's talkative mistress, the stage is set for the Grand
Guigno resolution:

Then at dawn, Mihály Kátai was brought forth from his detention by the Prince's men of court, so he said, 'What are you doing, men-at-arms? It was Ferenc Gymes who first slashed him, and then the crowd cut him up into small pieces for poisoning the Prince. Afterwards, around nine o'clock, his wife had the several thousand small pieces swept up, put into a blanket and, bringing the remains out of Kassa the same day, had him buried in Misle.

Popular legend adds the detail that dogs carried off some of the pieces and ate his liver and lights.

Before his death, Bocskai had succeeded in mediating between the Turks and the Habsburgs, represented by Thurzó, and forcing an accommodation which effectively ended what the German-speakers called the Great Turkish War and awarded the disputed Seven Counties to Transylvania, whose status was finally recognised by the Empire. As part of the 1606 Peace of Vienna the great reconciliation between the Hungarian nobles and the Habsburgs was belatedly arranged under the auspices of Rudolf's successor Matthias II, who, although as poor a soldier as his brother, knew that essential allies could not be persecuted or snubbed indefinitely. He overlooked, officially at least, the actions of the many nobles who had sided with Bocskai (among them Elisabeth's brother, Stephen), restored the mediaeval office of palatine, giving the Hungarians back their own viceroy while he retained the crown, and reluctantly recognised the Lutheran and Calvinist faiths. The treaty, which seemed to guarantee Hungarian independence and the rights of its aristocracy for the future, was signed on 23 September. On 9 December the Treaty of Zsitvatorok formally ended hostilities with the Turks.

One month later, the Transylvanian Diet approved Sigmund Rákóczi as the new prince, and, although the Drugeth family's ambitions were thwarted, Thurzó was content, knowing that Rákóczi's large landholdings inside Hungary would prevent him from severing the alliances with the kingdom that were now in place. This reassurance lasted only as long as Rákóczi's tenure – one year and one month – before he resigned and the golden youth, Gábor Báthory, succeeded him. Although he had managed to carry Bocskai's crown in triumph to Vienna, this was not at all what Thurzó had hoped for; the Báthorys were long-time rivals of his patrons the Habsburgs in the international arena and the main obstacle to his raising his own family to pre-eminence in Hungary. The Báthory family, in the shape of Elisabeth, allied by marriage to the Nádasdys and Zrínyis, owned more square miles of the country than either he or the King; their dependencies were so extensive that if they changed allegiance it could once again destabilise the Kingdom – and not just its eastern fringes.

Against this background of political turmoil and seething intrigue, the messages which passed between Countess Báthory and the man who masterminded her downfall are evidence of an increasingly tense, precarious relationship, masked by the demands of written protocol.

On 11 December 1606, when the worst of the political crisis was over, Countess Báthory wrote to George Thurzó from her castle at Keresztúr:

> I have received your letter and I understand its cause, that you wish me to give the abbacy of Csorna to Peter Kálli. Regarding this matter I can write to you that it would be a great pleasure for me if I were able to do this, but I cannot. I have previously been required for the same purpose before by some lords, as my lord Othkavio also has. But I have not yet decided which of them shall be given the abbacy, for there are four candidates. I shall gather them all together in the next days and I shall speak to them of this, and according to their decision the abbacy shall be granted. I will fit my order to their decision. As soon as we come to our decision, I shall inform you, so that you can give a certain answer to our friend.
>
> I serve you with pleasure as my brother[10]

This politely framed letter shows Elisabeth fully in command of her privileges and dispensing patronage confidently and, in this case, not necessarily to the advantage of her powerful and potentially vindictive neighbour. (The reference to 'Lord Othkavio' is obscure; it is possible that it is an error which should read 'as my lord also has [been petitioned] by the Octave court'.)

At the end of 1607 Elisabeth was still on cordial terms with the Thurzó family, as her polite acceptance of a wedding invitation from George Thurzó dated 16 November shows.[11]

On the same day she wrote separately to Thurzó's wife, Lady Elisabeth Czobor asking her to convey a secret message to Lord

Dersffy at Strećno. Elisabeth Báthory had been on friendly terms with her, also writing to request that Czobor send her herbs, among other things.

There are long gaps in the archive records of their correspondence, but, perhaps coincidentally with Gábor Báthory's rise to power in Transylvania (the young Gábor was the idealised – even idolised – figurehead of the 'Báthory party', the anti-Habsburg, pro-Transylvanian nationalist faction that Thurzó, the Habsburg's man, bitterly opposed), the families' former friendship became increasingly strained. On 20 October 1610, two months before her arrest, Elisabeth Báthory addressed a longer communication to Thurzó, now the Count Palatine of Hungary. After the usual greetings (and she was careful to allude to Thurzó's elevation to his new post) she writes:

> The reason for my letter is the following: A few days ago Gáspar Tatay together with my men of court went into Ujhely [Nové Mesto nad Váhom] to the market; he took drink there, and during the way home he fell out with a man of my court. He was challenged to a duel by Gáspar Tatay, and if the other men of mine had let them, and had not separated them, nobody can say what would have happened between them. They parted from each other on the way, and my men came home in peace, but Gáspar Tatay did not return to his home, in truth he went to the home of my servant and, in his anger, cut the legs of his horse. But he was not satisfied and came even to my house, where he was cursing and again challenged my servant to a duel. My servant went out of my house and they fought until my servant broke Tatay's sword and in the end of it Tatay fled. But even after the duel Tatay came again to my house and he was cursing and damning again. I was informed of the matter, I did not let my servants out, and knowing your lordship's authority and even that Tatay is said to be your servant, I wished to inform you at once. I must request you, if Tatay does not tell you the same as I have in my letter, please ask for information from my son-in-law Lord Zrínyi's men named George Zalay and Michael Baranyai; they were here in the company of my daughter and my son-in-law. If my servant had done anything against Tatay, the latter should have informed me, and I would have punished my servant by law. He would not have come to my house, nor would he have cut the legs

of my servant's horse. I can assure you that my servant is not guilty. Gáspar Tatay provoked him in all instances and I will not allow this to go unpunished. If my servant were found guilty of anything, he also would suffer punishment. Be that as it may, I beg you, please command Tatay to behave himself, not to come to my house with cursing and damning. I have never done anything against him, nor has my servant either. Otherwise, I expect protection from your honour and from your servant, too. Barring other incidents, I commend you to the protection of the Almighty, may you remain in health in your office in favour of our country.

I serve you[12]

After the greetings and preamble the letter is uncompromising. The closing phrase is curt, and, just before it, Elisabeth's reference to Thurzó's high office is not only in deference to his rank (in becoming palatine one year before, he had attained the most exalted position possible for a loyal Hungarian), but a reminder that upon accepting his office he had taken an oath to uphold the law impartially. This interesting document may simply illustrate the day-to-day tensions of life in the court, the taverns and the marketplace, but it may contain more than this. It is possible that Tatay was a provocateur sent by Thurzó to incite Báthory's entourage to commit some crime or indiscretion; against this would be the fact that the Lady's daughter and Lord Zrínyi were present as powerful – if not wholly impartial – supporters of her cause. It is intriguing that Elisabeth nowhere gives the name of the member of her household whom Tatay challenged and who fought him off. Could this have been Ficzkó, her factotum, who was accused by the squire Gregory Pásztory, testifying in the later investigation, of provoking a fight with *his* servant in very similar circumstances at almost exactly the same time?[13]

Another motive for Tatay's hostility to Elisabeth's court has been proposed by Dr Irma Szádeczky-Kardoss, who discovered that Stephen Báthory, the late King of Poland, had bequeathed large estates to the three Tatay brothers in gratitude for their faithful service, but that these estates were granted to the brothers for their lifetimes only, after which they would revert to members of the Báthory family, of which Elisabeth was one of the few surviving. Although we do not know the details of Gáspar Tatay's parentage, we can reasonably suppose that he may have resented the loss of his family's temporary fortune and held a grudge against the Countess.[14]

By judiciously arranged marriages, by petitioning the King and frequently by force, the noble Hungarian families were all engaged in a relentless contest to increase their landholdings, enrich themselves and guarantee a secure future for their offspring. If they could choose, their first priority was obviously to acquire land that was cultivable – wine was the most profitable crop, but grain and cattle could bring enormous rewards. As far as the location of estates was concerned, the ideal was that they should be as far as possible from the contested Turkish frontier and also well away from the holdings of more powerful neighbours who might move to annex a village or a few hectares of pasture at any time.

From the King's vantage point in Vienna, the priorities were different. The Austrians knew that they could not depend on the loyalty of their subjects who lived in the areas bordering Transylvania, nor could they enforce their rule in the Partium, which they had long since tacitly abandoned to the Prince, but everyone was aware that they would never allow strategic strongholds in the western parts of the Kingdom to fall into the wrong hands.

One surviving letter, hitherto unknown, confirms that after she had lost her husband, Elisabeth was subjected at least once to the usual attacks by predatory neighbours on the lands held by widows. The letter also shows clearly the uncompromising strength of the Lady's character. It was dispatched in early 1606 from her late mother-in-law's castle of Kapuvár to the Transylvanian nobleman Count George Bánffy:

Magnifice Domine Nobis Observandissime
God give you all the best. I must write to you on the following matter: My servant János Csimber arrived home yesterday evening, and he reported to me that you have occupied my estate in Lindva. I do not understand, why have you done this thing? Just do not think, George Bánffy, that I am another Widow Bánffy! Believe me that I will not keep silent, I will let no one take my property. I wanted only to let you know this. *Ex arce nobis Kapu 3 Feb 1606.*
    Elizabeta Comittissa de Bathor

P.S. I know, my good lord, that you have done this thing, have occupied my small estate because you are poor, but do not think that I shall leave you to enjoy it. You will find a man in me.[15]

Elisabeth's scathing reference is to the widow of another Bánffy, Gáspar, who was conspired against by rapacious relatives and dispossessed after her husband's death. In her final defiant flourish Elisabeth uses a Hungarian phrase meaning 'I will be more than a match for you.'

When she was placed under house arrest at the end of 1610, Elisabeth Báthory's first thought was to safeguard those of her domains which bordered on the acres of vineyards surrounding the castle of Tokaj, which had once been Bocskai's and was awarded to Thurzó in gratitude for his part in arranging the 1606 peace. With this in mind, she gave the estate of Szécskeresztúr over into the hands of her son-in-law, George Drugeth.

While Elisabeth owned the Báthory estates which were her dowry and still governed the huge Nádasdy–Kanizsai inheritance that she had acquired by marriage, she was so well endowed with land scattered all across what remained of the Kingdom that most other nobles were smallholders in comparison. Any one of her score of castles and mansions would have made an honourable seat for a family of substance. She would regularly depart on tours of inspection, visiting most of the larger holdings, but she held court only in the four or five most magnificent and left the others in the hands of factors and stewards. It has been said that the peripatetic existence that Elisabeth led in the years after her husband's death was made necessary because she had become so notorious in the environs of her castles that she had to go further afield to entice victims for her sadistic practices, but this is unconvincing: local mothers, neighbours and officials continued to send or bring girls to all the courts, and Elisabeth's constant travelling was forced upon her once she took over her late husband's role of overseeing the vast estates, the town-houses in Trnava and Piešt'ány and the many farms, and attending to the other duties of a feudal dignitary (under this cover she may also have been travelling for political purposes, too). Once again it seems that the popular imagination has misinterpreted the 'inexplicable' behaviour of the aristocrats and the fact that Elisabeth had stepped outside the normal bounds of feminine custom.

The closest property to Čachtice, situated about halfway between Nové Mesto nad Váhom and the free royal town of Trenčín was the village and castle of Beckov. Sited on the summit of a rock which rises perpendicularly from the flat valley floor and overlooking the fields which open out towards the Danube lowlands, Beckov is today a picturesque pile of ruins. Placed where Bohemia, Moravia and Hungary meet, it had been a point of great strategic importance in the constant wars of the preceding centuries.

The valley of the Váh is famous for the romantic stories that have grown up around its landmarks, many of them concerning the mediaeval Polish warlord Duke Stibor, who was given tracts of land there by the Hungarian King Sigismund. At Čachtice, Stibor built the first chapel hard by the castle walls and was reputed to have lured travellers into the fortress by offering sanctuary from brigands, then robbing his guests himself and tossing them from his battlements.

Not far north-west of Sárvár lies the village of Deutschkreuz, in Elisabeth's day called Creitz by the German-speaking locals, but known to her as Németkeresztúr (the *német*-prefix, meaning 'German', is important to distinguish this possession from the eastern estate of Szécskeresztúr – *szécs* is an ancient Slavonic word for a clearing – which also belonged to the family). There among low hills lay a vast fortified palace adjoining a lake and abutted by paddocks and an ornamental garden. Not far away another of Elizabeth's castles, Léka (now Lockenhaus in the Austrian Burgenland) was built on a dramatic hilltop site. It contains a crude iron maiden in which the evil Countess is reputed to have shut her enemies,[16] its secret wells were said to penetrate the solid rock down to the valley floor far below, and the Nádasdy crypt beneath the castle is still haunted by Elisabeth herself, who, local people say, will reach out of the darkness to clutch at the arms of visitors.

On a more massive peak near by in Burgenland stands the impregnable fortress of Forchtenstein, once the property of Elisabeth's mother-in-law Ursula Kanizsai and today still in the hands of the Esterházys, whose ancestor Count Nicholas, the nemesis of the Thurzós, received it in 1610. Elisabeth is reputed – anachronistically – to have stayed there as Esterházy's guest and to have indulged in her satanic hobbies in the dungeons whose upper vents can still be seen at the base of the inner walls. Turkish prisoners-of-war laboured for long years in unspeakable conditions to tunnel Forchtenstein's 142-metre well and it was there, the folktales say, that Elisabeth disposed of her horribly maimed victims when she had tired of them. Forchtenstein's foundation myth is especially apt in that it prefigures our later drama. The tale tells that the castle, known to the Hungarians as Frakno, was built by a prince named Giletus who had Rosalia his wife thrown into its deepest dungeon as a punishment for ill-treating her serfs while her husband was away.

North-west of Ecsed and close to Szécskeresztúr was another of Elisabeth's possessions, the spectacular twelfth-century gothic fortress of Füzér. Füzér castle, which was destroyed during the anti-Habsburg Rákóczi rebellion at the end of the sixteenth century, stood on a rock butte atop a steep rise covered with pines and birches. Below in the flat meadows, small village houses covered in vines were scattered among orchards where animals foraged and villagers lounged, lulled by the benign, almost freakishly tropical climate, the beauty of the landscape and potency of the local wines.

Memories of Elisabeth's notoriety cling to other stately sites, now mostly in ruins: Buják, where within living memory the occupying Russians took over the maze of underground passageways, the pinnacle at Strečno, and Fogaras in Romania, which had passed into the hands of the princes of Transylvania, but whose name was always attached to the male Nádasdy heir's titles.

Even while her husband Lord Nádasdy was still alive and known despite his misgivings to be their faithful subject, the Imperial strategists in Vienna must have looked in consternation at their maps, musing on how they could secure these territories if the shifting allegiances settled once and for all in favour of their enemies. Elisabeth's brother, the judge Stephen Báthory, died at the very moment when a quarter of Hungary had joined Bocskai's insurrection and challenged the dominance of the Habsburgs. Among other bequests, the pro-Bocskai Stephen left Elisabeth the fortress of Devín, which stood on a promontory in the Danube, dominating the city of Bratislava and guarding the threshold to Vienna itself, the 'Red Apple' coveted by the Turks. It was quite unthinkable that a woman, a widow of questionable loyalties whose late brother and young nephew were in the enemy camp, should be allowed to take possession of this prize, and when Elisabeth at the head of a detachment of her own soldiers rode from Sárvár to lay claim to the citadel, the German burghers of Bratislava, either under direct orders from Vienna or loyally anticipating the King's wishes, barred her way. The garrison commander refused to let the Countess and her entourage cross the Danube and the ferries at Bratislava were the only means of approaching Devín. Elisabeth had no option but to turn back. There was no question of defying the wishes of the Empire and risking charges of treason, but Elisabeth was furious; she had been deprived of her inheritance illegally and had been personally insulted by the Bratislava authorities. 'If the Germans can behave thus towards me, they can do this to anyone!' she stormed to a Transylvanian relative.

Unquestionably part of Elisabeth Báthory's offence in the eyes of her peers was that she had too much property, more than the Palatine himself, and too much power, and this would in itself be justification in those times for the confiscation of her land and fortune. The other strongly held view was that property and wealth should be devolved quickly and efficiently to the male children or children-in-law who had need of it to support them in their political duties. The widows had no official responsibilities in society, and so were held not to deserve the possessions they retained. It was only a matter of time before someone – a member of her own family, a rival aristocrat more formidable than Lord Bánffy or an agent of the King – made their move against her.

CHAPTER SEVEN

A Notorious Dynasty

Protected in your boundless infamy,
For dissoluteness cherished, loved and praised
On pyramids of your own vices raised
Above the reach of law, reproof, or shame

John Wilmot, Earl of Rochester, *Valentinian*

King Stephen Báthory and Prince Sigmund ~ family scandals ~ Count Stephen of Ecsed ~ two literary wantons ~ the events of 1610 ~ the Widow Nádasdy's testament ~ a letter from the Prince of Transylvania ~ collusion, conspiracy and pleas for mercy ~ the mystery of Megyery 'the Red'

To comprehend Elisabeth's haughtiness, it must not be forgotten that by the time of her birth Báthorys had been holding the highest offices in Hungary and Transylvania for 300 years. They had been warlords, counts palatine, *vajdas* and *voivodes*, senior prelates and judges, and they were the richest landowners in the Kingdom. Infamy and glory has been allotted to the Báthorys in equal parts, but much of what was written about them has been a sensationalist or sentimental travesty,

142

the documented events festooned with colourful ribbons of untruth and rags of wishful folk conjecture.

Of the generation that preceded Elisabeth, Count Stephen (one of many to bear the name), a gifted soldier and later Chief Justice of Hungary, had been instrumental in crushing Dózsa's peasant crusade, Christopher was made the ruler of Transylvania and Nicholas, an influential humanist, became Bishop of Vác – but there is one Báthory whose name is still displayed today above the doors of universities and charitable foundations in central Europe, whose tomb in the Wawel castle in Craców is piled with fresh flowers and covered with school emblems placed there in his honour by successive generations of students. The object of this veneration is Elisabeth's uncle, another Stephen Báthory, the King of Poland.

The Polish Diet, the Sejm, chose this Hungarian nobleman as the country's first elected monarch after the Jagiełłon dynasty died out and he has been celebrated for presiding over a glorious period in Polish history during which he consolidated the Polish position in the Baltic, defeated the Russian Tsar, Ivan the Terrible, and conquered the key port of Gdansk with the tacit support of Elizabeth I of England, with whom he corresponded and whose merchants he allowed freedom to trade in the region.

An English report sent from Vienna in 1576 mentions that a certain Baron Swendius 'thinks much of Báthory's education, talent, prudence, industry, vigilance'[1], and Swendius was in the enemy camp. Stephen had studied at the University of Padua, where he was steeped in the spirit of humanism; he also knew the Habsburg court well, as his family had sent him there at an early age, as was the custom, to gain experience and influence. After the Battle of Mohács, however, he sided with the Hungarian successor King John Zápolya against the Habsburg claimant, Archduke Ferdinand, the brother of the Holy Roman Emperor Charles. Báthory became a diplomat in Zápolya's court, often travelling to Vienna for discussions and negotiations, later serving Hungary's next ruler John Sigismund, who also became the prince of the new state of Transylvania. When John Sigismund died, Báthory was the logical choice to succeed him, and he was given the Transylvanian crown. Needless to say, the Habsburgs tried to oppose him and he was able to enter his principality only at the head of an army, in 1572. When the Polish throne fell vacant four years later it was again the Habsburgs who were his rivals.

Talented though he was, the Poles did not choose Báthory for his personal qualities. Many of the Polish aristocrats did favour the Austrian claimant Archduke Maximilian, but not quite enough to force the issue at the parliament. Even after the French Prince Henri de Valois had been elected and had then abruptly abdicated, the anti-Habsburg faction remained the stronger, so Báthory's relative obscurity actually aided his claim. The Habsburgs stepped down, consoling themselves with the thought that a weak ruler on their eastern borders was better than one of their stronger western neighbours. The Turks, with whom Poland and Hungary were officially at war, also welcomed a weak and malleable king in Poland. Both the Austrians and the Ottomans regarded Transylvania as their personal fiefdom; both courts knew Báthory personally; and both thought that, once open hostilities had died down, they could pressure him into doing their bidding. In particular the Turks had supported Báthory in his claim to Transylvania, and hoped to collect their debt in the form of influence in Poland. A report in the Foreign State Papers in London says: 'The Turk was never more peaceful than now, since he has gained the kingdom of Poland, which seems to open to him all the way to Saxony and Silesia.'[2]

As is often the case, the compromise candidate proved to be a resolute leader and an expert tactician, playing the Turks and Austrians off against each other and making overtures to France and England. His wars against the Russians and the exploits of his generals were celebrated even in English broadsheets. Stephen also showed a trait which other members of his family, particularly Elisabeth's nephew Gábor, shared – a limitless ambition that was tinged with megalomania. He dreamed of creating a central and eastern European empire which would not stop at Transylvania, the Romanian Principalities and Poland, but would ultimately absorb all of Hungary, the Baltic States and Russia itself. Although such a vision may seem on the face of it impossibly grandiose, in the violent flux of international politics at that time it was a scenario that might have come about despite the Habsburgs and the Turks, providing death from disease or assassination did not intervene. A version of this picture – of a new dynastic European empire with the Báthorys at its head – tantalised the family members who came after Stephen as well as their supporters and protégés, and it may have sustained Elisabeth Báthory as she intrigued on behalf of her nephew Gábor.

King Stephen Báthory was an undoubted success as a statesman and as a military leader, and, almost uniquely, the stories told of his exploits from the seventeenth century to the present reflect the approval of those who decide the reputations of historical figures. For the Báthory princes who followed Stephen and tried to emulate him, neither fate nor remembrance was as kind. The tragicomedy of the career of the great King's nephew, Sigmund Báthory, was just as characteristic of the family and the time. This 'handsome, stalwart weight-lifter and swordsman'[3] ruled Transylvania between 1581 and 1597, when his regime collapsed in ignominy and confusion. Sigmund was the son of Christopher, the younger brother of King Stephen of Poland and Transylvania, and much, perhaps too much, was expected of him – the curse of all the Báthory males. The late King had died childless (his consort, Anna Jagiełłowska, the Hungarians said had been ugly, old and barren) and the family had decided that of the new generation Sigmund was to be the ruler, Balthasar the soldier and Andrew the diplomat and man of God.

In the event, the dangerous morass of Transylvanian politics, the machinations of his domineering ally Bocskai and the pressure of an arranged marriage to Maria-Christina, a Habsburg princess, were too much for Sigmund. He abdicated four times and reclaimed his throne three times in eight years; having turned over the Principality to his warrior cousin Balthasar Báthory, he was pushed back into power by Bocskai and forced to execute his kinsman and wipe out the pro-Turkish faction which Balthasar had led and which had included two of his most faithful counsellors, his confidant Paul Gyulai and his tutor John Gálfi. He avoided his wife, who complained in letters to her family ('those things have not yet taken place . . .') that Sigmund had not consummated their union; he was henceforth branded by history not only as capricious and sadistic, but as impotent, or bisexual, or a pederast, or all three. In fact Maria-Christina was suspected of frigidity by many Hungarians simply on account of her nationality; more charitably, she may have been under orders not to yield to her husband's advances for fear of giving birth to a new royal dynasty which would combine the prestige of the Habsburgs and the Báthorys and prove more powerful than either. At the same time, Sigmund seems to have been impressionable and highly strung and may have been persuaded by his Spanish confessor, Carrillo, that celibacy would spiritually ennoble him.

While he was in power Sigmund pursued a policy of terror against many of his subjects, so that when he abdicated for a second time in 1599 in favour of another cousin, the peaceable Andrew Báthory, a cardinal who had spent most of his life in the humanist atmosphere of the courts and cloisters of Italy, the latter stood very little chance of holding on to the throne. On 9 November 1597, this Andrew, whose spies had been sheltered in Hungary by his cousin Elisabeth,[4] was trapped in a Székely village while on the run from the Voivode Michael the Brave. The Székelys recognised him as a kinsman of Sigmund, who had bribed them to fight for him, then cheated them of their reward. They cut Andrew into pieces, some of which were reassembled later so that his body could be exhibited to his subjects in the capital, Alba Julia. The cardinal's head, bearing an axe wound above the right eye, was portrayed in engravings resting on a cloak before being sewn back on to the rest of the remains.[5]

Sigmund returned again to the imbroglios, and his subjects had little to choose between the cruelties perpetrated by his enemy, the Habsburg General Basta, and his own forces' excesses. After Sigmund temporarily abandoned his followers in 1602:

> The people of the region were forced to flee to the forests, to the high mountains – in the horrible cold. But they could not hide! They were tracked down in the woods, dire cruelties were committed, many were burned with fire, many had their heads twisted, so that their eyes started out from their heads – many of them were later seen begging, who had been men of property beforehand, carrying themselves well; many were burned with hot iron, their stomachs and backs were burned with live coals, thongs were cut from their backs for merriment, many were hanged by their hair and straw-fires were lit under them – they [Basta's men] laughed at it. What they did to women, I will not relate, as it was such an infamy. Those Magyars among Basta's troops were alike, women's breasts were cut through, their hands drawn through the wounds, and in this way they were hung up on nails.[6]

Finally pushed aside and into exile and obscurity in Poland, Sigmund was, much to everyone's surprise, still alive in Silesia when in 1613 the last member of his family to achieve a temporary glory, Gábor Báthory, was murdered.

★   ★   ★

When we turn to the more obscure corners of the family, history even more quickly becomes confused with fabulation. Father Revický's 1900 life of Countess Báthory provides examples in the form of quasi-scholarly cameos: 'One of her uncles was a very lustful man, and his sinful passion destroyed his health early on in his life. But he did not care: when his wife died he married one of his wife's former maidservants, which brought great shame on his family in those days.'[7]

Lady Klára Báthory, Elisabeth's aunt on her father's side, has been remembered in the histories as an insatiable bisexual adventuress – 'that madwoman, who picked up lovers on all the roads of Hungary and bounced chambermaids on her bed . . .'[8]

The nobly born pastor and man of letters Bornemissza was the first to mention her, when he referred to his own sins and those of his contemporaries in his sixteenth-century work, *The Temptations of the Devil*, a polemic against suicide which reveals the prevalent attitudes to sin and abnormal behaviour among the Hungarian elite.[9] Bornemissza cites Klára as a sinner, simply stating that she had a lover and that the lover killed her husband. The popular version of Klára's story is that her first husband, Stephen Drugeth, died after a few years of marriage and she had her second husband, the bedridden Lord Anthony Losonczy smothered in his bed. In the words of Revický, the priest of Čachtice, who is retelling nineteenth-century stories:

> Klára Báthory, the wife of Michael Várday [sic], became the murderer of her husband because she wanted to enjoy her sinful passion of love with her husband's best musician, who was a violinist. Her lustful passion – according to the letter from Cardinal Forgách – had grown so much that even in the prison where she was confined as a murderess, she made sinful love with her guards and with other prisoners.[10]

Her other husbands and lovers included John Betko and Bálint Benkő of Paly. Then the story lurches into the fantastic. Klára was said to have taken up with a very young lover and made him a present of one of her castles. The amorous pair were taken captive by a Turkish pasha, who had the young man skewered and roasted on a spit. Klára's punishment was to be raped by every member of the Turkish garrison in turn, before being put out of her misery by having her throat ceremonially cut.

The notorious aunt was reconstructed for the 1995 novel in English by Andrei Codrescu. In this version she is, perversely, unmarried, but the voracious sophisticate serves as one of the young Elisabeth's many initiators into the carnal mysteries.[11] But little is known of the real Klára's character, and her sins must be partly mitigated by the fact that most historians confused her with Elisabeth Báthory's younger sister of the same name, adding that lady's husband to the list of the older Klára's victims. She has also provided a useful element otherwise missing from the myth: the decadent, worldly mentor who might have initiated Elisabeth into a life of sin. There is certainly no hard evidence of her lesbianism, which was in any case an abomination that was literally indescribable with the words available at the time. She seems more like a headstrong English noblewoman of the nineteenth century whose contemporaries could not forgive her for living openly with her secretary – a commoner – whom she later took as her third husband. If Klára had been younger and less sure of her status, a family court would normally have been convened and she would have been put under trusteeship. But the message that infuriated squires and plebeians alike was that, in her rarefied world, a Báthory again went her own sweet way in proud disregard for the conventions that the rest lived by.

What Klára's case does reveal is the sixteenth century's obsession with family honour and public propriety, which were taken more seriously in aristocratic circles than occasional lapses such as the manslaughter or rape of a commoner. Remarriage was common, even necessary to protect inheritances, but multiple marriages by a woman could not be condoned, and all Europe thrilled with indignation at the exploits of adventuresses such as Jeanne d'Aragon, the wayward daughter of the King of Portugal; rumour invented melodramatic explanations – poison or suffocation – for the non-violent deaths of husbands. One sort of sinful behaviour implied another, and religious or social lapses became elaborated, particularly in the black propaganda of the Catholic pamphleteers, into sexual perversion and incest.

The nineteenth century's concern was to build a convincing and, if possible, exciting narrative out of the mixture of fragmentary documentation and outright rumour that it had inherited. From that time on it became necessary not only to marvel at the Báthorys but to analyse and make sense of them. Eccentricity and deviancy were cited: 'Most of the Báthorys in both family branches shared extreme character traits. Many of them leaned towards tyranny, complacency, pride, cruelty, carnality and sexual perversion.'[12]

Elisabeth was much closer to her elder brother than to Klára. Even during his lifetime Stephen Ecsedy Báthory's strange behaviour was misunderstood by his bewildered servants, and their gossip became the substance of later tales in which he is reconstructed as an alcoholic, a lecher and a probable lunatic. The unfounded charge of alcoholism seems to be an attempt to explain his reclusive nature, and the lechery is simply guilt by association with his scandalous relatives. Stories of lunacy are more revealing of the wonder which the workings of the cultivated imagination provoked in simpler minds. Stephen was excessively devout and recited his own poems and probably also sang religious songs late into the night; the noises were taken to be the ravings of a man possessed. To travel on the waterlogged causeways which crisscrossed the marshes surrounding Ecsed castle, he put his carriage on ski-like runners; the legends record that he was so thoroughly demented that he rode on a sleigh in summer. If we search Stephen's surviving writings for dementia and dissipation, we find only piety and lucidity.[13]

There was also a strong element of religious prejudice in the gradual composition of a family mythos. Catholics later condemned Elisabeth as an agent of Calvinism; yet, although she was praised in her lifetime for her understanding of doctrine, there were no signs in her letters of fanaticism, or even deep devotion.

Literary authors have even more licence to rearrange and embellish the residue of past lives and use the results for their own ends. Elisabeth plays a central role in the 1925 novel *Ördögszekér* (the literal translation is 'Devil's Wagon', but the meaning is 'Tumbleweed') by Sándor Makkai. The writer, a noted theologian and historian and a Calvinist, like Elisabeth Báthory herself, was elected Bishop of Cluj in Transylvania (now Romania) the year after the book's publication. In the book, Elisabeth ('of wondrous beauty') instructs her niece Anna Báthory – aged fifteen and 'awakening to the magic of her beauty' – in the ways of the world:

> The chief pleasure for some, to love and to sacrifice oneself, is absolutely nothing for us. For us the pleasure of love is the pleasure of conquest. We enjoy the burning of those who wither in our embrace more than the fire in our own blood.

When the Emperor's envoy arrives, Elisabeth 'bewitches' him, and Anna also applies what she has learned to a member of his retinue, a noble officer:

Elisabeth and Anna laughed long at the Emperor's men, of whom they had made fools. They sat together for quite some time, and finally, Elisabeth proposed that Anna should sleep with her, not go back to her own quarters.

'You are a wonderful apprentice!' Elisabeth said, embracing Anna. She held her tight, passionately, did not let go of her. Her embrace grew hotter and hotter, more and more overwhelming, her face distorted in the dark. The beautiful beast embraced and kissed her till dawn.[14]

For Elisabeth Báthory, 1610 was the year in which the events of her private life and the political manoeuvrings taking place beyond her walls came together, culminating in the transformation of the country's most formidable woman into a prisoner without a social identity or any hope of salvation.

As the new year began, Countess Báthory was still in firm control of the family's business affairs: she personally negotiated the loan of 400 gold pieces and a plot of land to one Andrew Orossy in January.[15]

At the same time from Vienna King Matthias was anxiously trying to extend his control over the senior Hungarian nobles with the help of George Thurzó, the newly appointed Count Palatine, whose first priority was to deal with the anti-Habsburg elements who were gravitating towards Gábor Báthory just as they had towards Bocskai. Among the key figures who had to be brought under the Habsburg wing at all costs were Count Nicholas Zrínyi, Elisabeth's son-in-law, and a powerful twenty-seven-year-old grandee whose family had supported Bocskai but were themselves pretenders to the Transylvanian throne, George Drugeth of Homonna. George Homonnay Drugeth has been described – in the dismissive shorthand favoured by old-fashioned historians, as 'a notorious adventurer' and was accused by the seventeenth-century essayist Máté Szepsi Laczkó (whose writings tend to the sensationalist, as in the case of Chancellor Kátai) of poisoning his cousin and his son for the inheritance. The year 1610 was a momentous one for Drugeth, too; on 6 January he celebrated his wedding to the younger daughter of Countess Báthory, Lady Kate Nádasdy. Later in the same year he converted to Catholicism and declared for the Habsburg cause.

The north and west of the country was now in a state of uneasy peace, and there was nothing but the winter weather to prevent guests from attending Lord Drugeth's nuptials. During the festivities the village of Čachtice would have been lit with torches and bonfires and hung with evergreen branches and the small square crowded with well-wishers. Inside the manor, according to the witness Török and others, the corpses of two girls were concealed in the private apartments of the Countess, after which, the priest Fábry claimed, they were secretly buried without his permission in his parish of Kostol'any. Whatever had gone on in that closed world was not allowed to disturb the celebrations, but the court of justice at Nové Mesto recorded the news of the deaths. No action was taken; no official dared interrupt such a glittering occasion, although Elisabeth's enemies, the Lutheran priests, were well aware – indeed may have reported the news – and would have informed their patron, George Thurzó. The cabal of local squires around Daniel Pongrácz kept the rumours on the boil, and these cases could have been the immediate pretext for the judicial hearings which started two months later.

Elisabeth began her annual progress around her estates by travelling to Sárvár some time in March. In the meantime the new Palatine was determined both to move against his enemies and to increase his personal wealth as decisively and as quickly as practicable, but did nothing about the widow Nádasdy for the time being for the very good reason that he was waiting on the outcome of the plot, which he and his circle had covertly encouraged, by Chancellor Kendy and his associates to murder Gábor Báthory in Transylvania.

On 5 March, Thurzó initiated an investigation into crimes alleged against Countess Báthory by ordering the secret examination of witnesses from the counties of Györ, Veszprém, Pozsony, Trenčín and Nitra, in western and upper Hungary.[16] The wording of his letter of instruction is important as it set out for the first time the accusation that was being made, for the time being in private, against the Widow Nádasdy: 'several maids and virgins and other women have been killed by various means, who were in her apartments'. The interrogations began on 22 March. Shortly afterwards the second phase of the inquiry opened, with witnesses summoned from the west and south-west.

On 10 May, Palatine Thurzó was forced to travel east to the Seven Counties to deal with unrest caused by Hajdúk bands who were looting and burning the estates of the lesser gentry and killing the proprietors. Thurzó was still in that region on 7 June when Elisabeth's sons-in-law joined him secretly for discussions. Also in June Thurzó met with Prince Gábor Báthory at Majtény and tried to persuade him to declare formally for the Empire against the Ottomans. Gábor refused.

On 19 August, Countess Báthory accompanied a widowed gentlewoman named Hernath to the Vasvár-Szombathely county court near her Sárvár estates, and a voluntary deposition was formally lodged with the local justices.[17] The lady stated on oath that her late daughter, Susanna Ungváry, who had been in Elisabeth's service, had died of natural causes and that the marks to be found on her body after death were the result of disease and not of violence, her employer being wholly innocent of her untimely death. This document, which has been mentioned in passing in some recent accounts of the case, deserves closer attention. It proves firstly and beyond doubt that Elisabeth Báthory was aware of the accusations that were being laid against her elsewhere (although the investigation was proceeding in private and in secret) and was ready to move decisively to defend herself. Had she been guilty of causing the death of a servant and had wished to admit it, there was a course of action that was open to her at almost no risk; this was the private negotiated payment, a later version of the old Anglo-Saxon *wergild*, whereby a killer could compensate the victim's family in cash or in kind and avoid further punishment. But there is no evidence that Elisabeth ever contemplated this strategy, although, as we shall see, it was employed by a noblewoman in circumstances very similar to hers.

Just as Pastor Ponikenus said, the Countess thought that the county courts would be her salvation. The statement given by her maidservant's mother shows that Elisabeth was aware of the sort of evidence that could be brought up in any trial – the same evidence that was indeed being put forward at the secret sessions. An important part of the information lodged against Countess Báthory and her senior domestics concerned the signs of torture visible on the bodies of the many young girls carried out for the informal burials that so provoked the local clergy. Although the descriptions taken down are too sketchy to allow a proper analysis, it is possible to offer a sceptic's explanation for some of the marks that witnesses claimed to have seen.

Livid red and blue patches on the skin, so easily identified as bruises from beatings, can be caused by blood settling in certain parts of the body after death. It was also standard practice to tie the hands and feet of corpses, both to help in moving bodies before rigor mortis froze them in less manageable poses, and to make it impossible for the dead to escape from their coffins and wander abroad. This combination of practicality and superstition extended in some cases to piercing the bodies so that a build-up of gases would not swell and perhaps burst the coffin; at the same time the post-mortem wounding would ensure that the deceased was perfectly dead.

The widow Hernath's statement was never referred to at the trial of Elisabeth's servants, or in the later phases of the investigation.

In the meantime, Thurzó had convened the Diet, not in Bratislava but in Bocskai's old fiefdom of Košice, the centre of the mutinous eastern counties. He intended to coerce the nobles and the representatives of the other powers in the Kingdom to give a unanimous declaration of opposition to Gábor Báthory.

On 25 August, Thurzó travelled to Vienna, where he closeted himself with his spies and his Austrian advisers to plan the next stage in his campaign to subvert the Transylvanian Prince.

On 3 September, Elisabeth was in residence at her castle of Németkeresztúr, where she drew up her last will and testament. The original of the will, a five-page manuscript, can still be inspected in the Hungarian National Archives in Budapest:

I, the Honourable Lady Elisabeth Báthory, the widow of the Most Honourable Lord, Francis Nádasdy, thinking of my weak health and being at an advanced age [she was fifty] . . . for I wish to be free of all my duties in the material world, I order, according to this, my last will, that all of my estates, including those inherited from my husband, should be given to my son, Paul Nádasdy. However, my much loved children have not until this time decided to divide the estates among themselves, as my daughters are far from here, but I ask them that if at any time in the future they will gather together, they will find a way to divide the estates peacefully and in harmony, but until that time that my son, Paul Nádasdy, should not be disturbed in his inheritance. The estates of Kapuvár, Léka and Kanizsa should be given to one of them, these must be kept intact and undivided, on condition that if the inheritor should die, the surviving inheritors may divide them among themselves. The remaining estates, wherever in the country they be, should be divided between the three. The estate that was my wedding gift [Čachtice] should be given to my three children with each having equal rights to it.[18]

This was to be the public settlement, but in private Elisabeth was even more carefully specific in her instructions: she was especially concerned about the estate of Szécskeresztúr, which bordered the famous vineyards of Tokaj. The castle of Tokaj had been given to Thurzó, and in 1610 he was extending the borders of his demesne there by his usual methods. When she was arrested later, one of Elisabeth's first concerns was to give the eastern Keresztúr lands into the hands of George and Kate Drugeth with immediate effect so that they could safeguard them from the attentions of predators and use their revenues to support Elisabeth in her captivity: 'Those properties that I shall inherit from my family in the future should be divided equally between my children, as I bequeath them my castles and houses. The property documents will be kept together with one of my children in accordance with the law.'

The will was the recording of a decision, but it was not the end of the matter. She still had to make sure that all the land certificates, leases and records of debts were safe in the hands of her son – or rather of her son's protector, Megyery:

> My gold and other jewels from my treasury should be given to Paul Nádasdy, as I have already given to my daughters their shares of the jewels in the usual form as wedding presents. The arms and the horse furnitures should be given to Paul Nádasdy. I desire only to be allowed to keep for my lifetime my wedding dress and jewels.
>
> This is my last will and command, which I have completed freely, being of sound mind.

The will is almost certainly written in Elisabeth's own hand, but looks like a rough draft, rather than the will of one of the richest noblewomen in the kingdom: its format is as prescribed by the laws of the time, but its appearance is poor and simple. The list of witnesses at the end of the document is written by the same person in much larger letters and the signatures of the witnesses and their seals are on the reverse of the paper. Elisabeth's signature is in a much less firm hand than the rest of the text, and this has led to speculation that the will was not signed at the time of writing, but was kept unsigned as insurance until much later when Elisabeth felt that her death was imminent. Some believe that the will was drawn up hurriedly in 1610 so that the witnesses (who included her court officials Deseő and Pásztory who later testified against her, and the priest Piterius, whom Zvonarić and Magyary had consulted before condemning her eight years before) could leak the contents, indicating that her property had been disposed of before her arrest (as the Royal Treasury later claimed in its letter to the King). It is known that Elisabeth, not her son, still had a part of her treasure in her possession in 1612, and we know that the final dividing up of the property between the male heirs was not completed (according to the eighteenth-century *Chronicles of Čachtice*) until just before her death in 1614.

It is questionable whether a hidden unsigned will would really have deterred anyone bent on grabbing part of the inheritance, in an age when property was often annexed by force and when oaths and documents could easily be falsified. (Another explanation is that she drew up the will under duress, and refused to sign it until her own wellbeing was assured – she signed it only in 1614 when she knew she was going to die: Thurzó, Zrínyi, Drugeth and Megyery needed the will to safeguard the estates, and would have produced it if the Royal Treasury had been ordered by Matthias to examine it.) Nevertheless, it seems that Elisabeth kept this copy of the will (which may of course not have been the only one) in her private casket which she took with her into captivity and which remained with her until she died. Her son Paul wrote an undated note on the document: 'I gave this letter to Mister Megyery [his tutor and guardian] from the box which was my mother's box for letters. *Comes Paulus de Nadasd, manu propria* [in my own hand].'

The will may have been a ruse to forestall the ambitions of George Thurzó, and it may have been written as a reaction to a visit from Elisabeth's two sons-in-law who came to Németkeresztúr in September 1610, perhaps to tell her that the Palatine's machinations against her were nearing some sort of climax and to press their own claims on the properties that were all still in her name. At the same time, there was good reason to confirm her son's inheritance at that particular moment: the boy was now twelve years old and therefore officially of an age to take up the rulership of the county which Elisabeth had been occupying on his behalf during his minority. Her daughters were now safely married off and their dowries settled.

Although there is nothing in the provisions of the will which go against normal practice, it neatly postpones the actual carving up of the estates until some unspecified future and ensures that there will be proper negotiation between the heirs. It also frustrates any immediate ambitions on the part of the sons-in-law by securing the lion's share in the hands of the best claimant, her young son. But once again, as so often in the case of Elisabeth Báthory, there is yet another explanation for the timing and the wording of the will. In the text itself, Elisabeth states that she is in poor health, and we know that she visited Piešt'ány spa with her daughter Anna Zrínyi just after the date on the testament. It is quite possible that the terms of the will in a first draft had been decided for some time and that Elisabeth signed it on the day indicated, in a hand shaking from rheumatics, palsy or ague, because she really did fear for her survival, but it seems even more plausible that she signed it after her arrest in a state of despair and near-collapse. Whatever the truth of it, the will seems to be, as it claims, the work of someone 'of sound mind'.

Meanwhile, in Bratislava Thurzó looked over the first set of depositions from witnesses, and the documents, still secret, were formally entered into the legal records.

At the beginning of October Count Zrínyi brought his wife Lady Anna to Čachtice, probably intending to leave her in her mother's company while he joined the other lords for the Octave, the October sitting of the national Diet at Bratislava (in the event something mysteriously prevented him). Elisabeth entertained her daughter and her attendants in the manor-house while most of the household were moved out into the high castle. It was in mid-October, if there is any truth in what the witnesses later asserted, that several of the banished maidservants came close to death, either through disease, neglect or deliberate ill-treatment by Dorothy Szentes, who had been put in charge of them. After Elisabeth had taken her daughter with her to their town-house at Piešt'ány spa, where they both bathed in the thermal mudbaths, between five and eight girls died and their bodies were clumsily disposed of around the estates. Witnesses later described how parts of corpses buried at the manor were rooted out and carried about by Lord Zrínyi's dogs, a gruesome anecdote reminiscent of the Kátai story which had been circulating three years previously. The most alarming rumours must have spread through the towns and villages of Upper Hungary, and Thurzó, who was reading through the second collection of confessions, would soon have heard of them, if not from his spies in Elisabeth's court, then from his agents in Nové Mesto and Bytča.

Towards the end of October, Elisabeth travelled west to the castle of Sárvár, where her son was living under the supervision of Imre Megyery, and gathered together her jewels, other valuables and movable furnishings, loading them into coaches and transporting them to Čachtice before the winter roads became impassable. Renovation work was going on at Sárvár throughout the period from Francis Nádasdy's death up to 1615, when the plaque set in the castle courtyard wall by Paul Nádasdy proclaims its completion, and this may have been the reason for the removal of Elisabeth's treasures. It may also have been connected with the arrangements for the disposal of her wealth that were contained in the will drawn up a couple of months before. Nevertheless, it is not surprising that the most popular interpretation has been that the Countess was preparing to flee, fearing that her enemies would make their move some time early in the coming year. She would not have expected anything to happen during the midwinter festivities, and she expected to be warned, either by her agents or by a formal summons, if a trial was to be convened. It is very unlikely that she would have tried to cross into Transylvania before the early spring if she intended carrying more than the lightest baggage. The high passes and even the local roads were usually blocked by snow from December well into February.

There is another reason why Elisabeth would not have fled unless she was absolutely sure that her life was in imminent danger: her leaving the kingdom of Hungary to join the Transylvanian Prince without royal permission would have been construed as treason, allowing Thurzó and the Habsburg authorities not only to confiscate her lands, but almost certainly to condemn her to death *in absentia* and take steps to pauperise her heirs – in such grave circumstances the ruse of the will would have offered no protection and all her plans to safeguard her children's futures would have been for nothing.

On 20 October, as Thurzó was about to put his seal to the collected papers of the second stage of questioning, Elisabeth wrote to him complaining of the outrageous behaviour of his servant, Tatay. In the same month Vienna received copies of letters sent by Prince Gábor to nobles in eastern Hungary, requesting them to supply him with troops to bolster his forces.

On 6 November 1610, Gábor wrote privately from Gyulafehérvár (Alba Julia, the capital of Transylvania) to Elisabeth, his aunt:

Your letter was given to me in which you ask me and my good brother [Andrew Báthory] to send you a legal certificate. For my part I shall send it at once, but our brother is not here at present. I have sent for him and as soon as he has come hither he will send to you his letter as well. Therefore, as I have said here, I have had this document taken from the convent and from our chancellery and it has been sent to you. Only ask of us and we shall help you in whatsoever you wish. With love from your family and God grant you long life and health.

He added in his own extravagant scrawl the affectionate words:

I serve you with love and with joy, your brother
    Gábor Báthory[19]

This communication, which has never been mentioned before, nor published, is an exciting find since it proves that Elisabeth was in touch with the Prince only weeks before her arrest and that, judging by his warm and respectful salutation, their relationship was close. It would be more exciting still if the letter was firm evidence of a conspiracy among the Báthorys. Gábor's message to his aunt alluded to an important document, the *procator* – a legal certificate or deed which she required – but he did not specify its purpose. Nevertheless, we can be sure that if she had wanted a safe pass to allow her to escape to her nephew's court, or a certificate protecting her from his invading troops like the one which Bocskai had given her, Gábor would not have sent word through normal channels and his secret note, once read, would have been destroyed. The fact that the signature of his younger brother Andrew Báthory was also necessary means that this was almost certainly a question of property rights and ownership, rather than part of a political plot. Elisabeth, resolute and efficient as always, was putting her affairs in order following the broadcasting of the will.

On 12 November 1610 Nicholas Zrínyi wrote to the Palatine.[20] He said that he had only been able to get as far as the place called Veb, and he had not after all been able to attend the Octave. It is apparent that a parallel secret message was being sent with a trusted servant, but the pretext for the official letter is to mention his own poor health – his reason for not meeting with Thurzó, who must have summoned him. Zrínyi states in his note that now that he has recovered he intends to comply with the Palatine's personal instructions, and promises to set out on the following Saturday to be in Bratislava to offer his humble service to his 'uncle' the Palatine there. It seems that Zrínyi had been hanging back, reluctant to speak face to face with Thurzó and pleading ill health as an excuse. But Thurzó was insistent.

Count Nicholas Zrínyi at thirty was the oldest male member of Elisabeth Báthory's family circle and the scion of one of the few dynasties of a rank equal to her own. His grandfather of the same name had been a hero of the Turkish wars whose renown eclipsed even that of Francis Nádasdy and who is still remembered today as the tragic hero of the siege of Szigetvár. This Nicholas was possessed of lands, wealth and political influence in abundance, as well as the inherited glory of his ancestor, but he was as yet untried in war and still undecided in his private political allegiances. The young Zrínyi had sided with Bocskai during the latter's insurrection and, although his own power-base was far from Transylvania, may have secretly sympathised with the pro-Báthory faction, but if he wanted to protect his material prospects and ensure that his head remained on his shoulders he had little choice but publicly to protest his loyalty to Thurzó, his relative by marriage (Thurzó's mother was his aunt) and to the King.

A demonstration of loyalty in the form of an oath of allegiance was precisely what Thurzó was demanding on behalf of his master from each of the one hundred most powerful families in Hungary, and it was to sign a letter incorporating this oath that Zrínyi had been summoned to Bratislava. There were rumours in Vienna that Zrínyi was entertaining treasonous thoughts, and that his links with the Prince of Transylvania were closer than they should have been. On 11 December, Gábor Báthory's troops took the Saxon town of Szeben, which had appealed to the Habsburgs for help, and on 16 December Zrínyi appeared before a specially convened court to clear himself of slurs against his character by persons unknown (the papers giving details of the affair have not survived).[21] Having dealt with this difficulty, which may have been part of a campaign of pressure by the pro-Habsburg group, Zrínyi addressed a letter the following day to Thurzó's agent, Egyed Nagy.[22]

The text – the words were dictated to a scribe (Zrínyi's own handwriting, in which the closing words and signature appear, is clumsy and ill-formed, suggesting that he was barely literate) – confirms the machinations that were taking place just before the denouement of Elisabeth's drama, and proves, as does Elisabeth Czobor's letter, that Thurzó's stumbling upon the murderess 'in action' was carefully pre-planned:

> I have sent my most trustworthy servant with my letter to Čachtice as your lordship required me to do, according to our agreement. I desire a peaceful conclusion to that affair, and I hope that Lady Nádasdy will remain in that place in peace, and that the property will remain intact – that even the Fiscus [the Royal Treasury] will not confiscate the estates, but most importantly for the whole family that the gravest punishment, the loss of the fortune and the losing of one's head shall not be applied. We have both been in agreement that the case should be resolved in this way; my confidential servant has been sent to Čachtice for this purpose. In truth your lordship must remember our agreement; when we spoke face to face at that time we came to no agreement concerning the estates, and now you wish to divide those estates, but I am not prepared for that to be done, it is too hasty. I do not know your lordship's mind in this matter, therefore I may not help you, I must even gainsay you in this proposal. I am myself related to the family, therefore I want my portion, both on this side and on the far side of the Danube, too. I know full well that your lordship is my benefactor and a loving brother to me, what is more, in my soul I have the hope that you will also rejoice at my advantage and most certainly would not wish my misfortune.

Zrínyi refers to a message he has sent to Čachtice on Thurzó's instructions, and this must be part of the manoeuvring in preparation for the forthcoming arrest: one possible reason for such a message would be to refuse an invitation to join the Christmas celebrations at his mother-in-law's home (where very possibly she was hoping to conclude some manoeuvres of her own in the company of her advisers and confidants), and to leave Thurzó a free hand in the matter of the actual attack on the mansion. There is, then, an agreement in advance of the raid that Elisabeth should be shut away to spare the family shame. The letter from Zrínyi is coolly businesslike and self-seeking, and, despite the polite conventions, it is forthright, even defiant. There is no mention at all of the Lady's alleged crimes, no expression of horror or pious disapproval: his reference to the risk of beheading and dispossession could more easily apply to a case of high treason than to the murder of a few servants, noble or otherwise.

The letter shows that George Thurzó had pressed for the sharing out of the estates to take place immediately, and this could have been in his interest only if he hoped to receive something himself. Could it be that it was the manor of Čachtice and the movable treasures that Elisabeth had taken there that were to be the price of Thurzó's collusion?

Having warned the Palatine that he would not be allowed to share out the huge prize according to his own whim, Zrínyi crossed the Danube *en route* to his seat of Monyorókerék, leaving a detachment of his soldiers at Thurzó's disposal. In December Elisabeth settled down with the ladies of her court to celebrate Christmas. There was great tension in the air in Čachtice, as Ponikenus' account of the confrontation in the church confirms. Perhaps the Countess did, as her enemies stated, summon her wise-woman, Erzsi, the wife of the Myjava farmer, to bake her magic cakes and cast her spells against the forces that were gathering to destroy her.

On 29 December, the Countess was surprised 'over the evening meal'. The Palatine's secretary George Závodský recorded the incident in a brief entry in his journal: 'She and her lackeys inflicted butchery and torture upon the female sex for long years, and cruelly tormented nearly six hundred . . .'[23] He specifically exonerated the other dignitaries who were closest to the Countess: 'neither Zrínyi nor Homonnay knew of it, nor even Imre Megyery knew . . .'

On 30 December Thurzó arranged his macabre display before the assembled household, then carried off Elisabeth's assistants to his stronghold at Bytča and to their deaths.

In the last days of January 1611, Count George Homonnay Drugeth, who had done nothing to oppose Thurzó, but who had stayed away until the arrest and trial had been concluded, rode into Čachtice at the head of a band of armed retainers, who accompanied him up the frozen track through the woods to the castle. He was admitted and spoke to his mother-in-law, who instructed him to arrange for funds to support her in her captivity.

★   ★   ★

The next letter from Lord Nicholas Zrínyi which was carried to Thurzó on 12 February 1611 was very different in tone from his previous note; it was couched in the most respectful terms as befitted a plea for mercy which would no doubt be transmitted to the King himself:

> May the Lord bless your highness and all your relatives. I understood the copy of your highness' letter and also the letter from the King which your highness sent to me. My heart is aching now, which is natural in such circumstances and in such shame that Mistress Nádasdy my lady mother finds herself, as I have heard. And I suffer very much for that, but nevertheless, though it is terrible to hear and horrifying to learn of her activities and deeds, and how your highness has punished her, of the two evils, I think, I needs must choose the lesser one. And besides, what your highness has done with her, this was for our greater good, and for our self-respect and the future of our honour, and for the putting away of the shame which might have befallen. In his Royal Highness's letters I could likewise apprehend . . . it would be better to die and to be nothing, with her relatives and children, too, than to hear of her brazen and horrifying executioner's work and torture, but your highness as a benevolent and truly loving brother, willing to prevent these shameful things from coming about, found the right means and solution whereby she should be imprisoned for ever and for our good name and our good memory she should be punished. For your highness's benevolence and your piety and brotherliness, and we would desire to serve you until our death and we will do our utmost to show our gratitude towards yourself. And now we request your highness that your highness should intercede with his Royal Highness on our behalf, so that his Majesty might reconsider his punishment that he wished to inflict upon her, and that his Majesty be content with the punishment that your highness has given her . . . After God our hope lies with your highness, that your highness shall intervene and mediate with his Majesty in the interest of our case . . .[24]

Zrínyi expected this letter to be passed on to others, as evidenced by his feigned surprise at learning of his mother-in-law's misdeeds – 'her brazen and horrifying executioner's work'. Even if the contents of the earlier secret letter were disregarded, the words do not ring entirely true.

Zrínyi's missive was followed by a letter from Paul Nádasdy to Thurzó dated 23 February 1611:

I have understood what your lordship has written, what his Royal Highness commanded for your lordship, and as concerns my miserable lady mother. I not only understood, but I myself have also experienced likewise in other affairs many times and in this affair, too, the goodwill of your lordship towards me and towards my sisters. May the Lord grant you, with all my female relatives and also my family with our whole hearts we wish to serve you all our lives. As your lordship wrote to his Royal Majesty with good reason, that first the summons to appear should have been issued, but that it is now too late, as your lordship as the judge of the country has already carried out the necessary examination, and it is not now necessary to repeat this, as the punishment of my poor mother now is much worse than death, and according to his Royal Highness's order, the taking of her life should be effected, and in what concerns her property, although we have no fears in this respect, since according to her own decision, we three have all received it before her incarceration. But otherwise, we wish with our relatives to entreat with our prayers and we ask his Majesty that with the assistance of the law, because of my mother, for our line and our nation he should not bring eternal shame upon them. But we did not wish to act without news from your lordship, nor without your advice, as this is not meet. It is not customary to act against the will of his lordship the Palatine. I pray and I beseech your lordship, as my lord and as my loving father, that you should give me your agreement and whether you approve or not, [as to] how I should with my sisters proceed [so as] not in any manner to cause trouble or commit harm for your lordship at his Majesty's court or with his Majesty himself. As per your lordship's letter, which we have kept always secret, we have understood your intention. I await a good answer from your lordship, as from my loving father and my lord. May God keep your lordship in good health for many long years.[25]

Paul was seeking the Palatine's permission to petition the King directly: he knew that the gist, although not the text, of this letter would also be conveyed to the King. In writing as he does, 'the goodwill of your lordship towards me and towards my sisters', he recalls that on his deathbed Francis Nádasdy had entrusted his children into Thurzó's care. He earnestly hopes that there will be no need for a further investigation and possible trial – 'your lordship as the judge of the country has already carried out the necessary examination' – even though the Palatine has dispensed with all the other usual legal requirements. The reference to 'your lordship's letter, which we have kept always secret' prove that confidential negotiations with the family had taken place; 'not in any manner to cause trouble or commit harm' – the situation was delicate and unprecedented: Thurzó was defying the King on the family's behalf.

There is no reference by Paul Nádasdy to his mother's supposed crimes, only to her current predicament. The real purpose of the letter is to underline again the fact that the inheritance had been safely disposed of and to plead for Elisabeth's life to spare the family shame.

Paul signed the letter with his firm, regular signature, but the twelve-year-old boy had not composed the text. The author was 'Megyery the Red' (the sobriquet probably referred to the distinctive colour of his beard), his tutor and guardian, the one man who in the literary versions of the story of the Blood Countess figures on a par with Lord George Thurzó as Elisabeth's *bête noire*, a conspirator against her who, it was said, she blamed above all others for her misfortunes and tried to kill with magic.

This was Imre Megyery, who on Francis Nádasdy's death had been appointed tutor to the young heir, Paul, and who referred to the boy, actually his cousin, as 'my young brother'. Megyery was the Nádasdys' representative at the Hungarian parliament's lower house when it met at Bratislava. He was a familiar at the Sárvár court, that is, someone of lesser but still noble rank who was bound to the family by feudal allegiance and a blood relationship. Imre Megyery's mother, Lady Agatha Nádasdy, was a cousin of the former Palatine Thomas, Elisabeth's father-in-law. Through his wife, Megyery was also related to the junior branch of the Nádasdy line. He was a relative too of Theodore Syrmiensis, who presided over the investigation of Elisabeth Báthory, and of Caspar Ordódy, the Deputy Governor of Trenčín county, who assisted at the trial of Elisabeth's servants in 1611. Several Megyerys performed the function of assistants to the most powerful personages of the time: Sigmund Megyery, for instance, was secretary to Palatine Nicholas Esterházy in the mid-seventeenth century.

Although he and his family lived beyond the confines of the castle, Megyery dealt with the Countess on a day-to-day basis during all the time she spent at the Nádasdy seat at Sárvár. Whatever their feelings for each other and whatever Megyery's links with George Thurzó and his circle (he must have maintained cordial relations with the man named as benefactor, virtually a godfather to his charge), there was ample reason for him to turn against his master's widow and plot her downfall if he was simply fulfilling his duty to the late Count Francis and to his heir. The 'tutor' in the great houses of Hungary was much more than a poor pedagogue: his role was closer to that of mentor and guardian and carried a great deal of power. Perhaps like many in his position, Megyery relished the power that his role as regent gave him while the young Paul – heir to the still intact family honour as well as its vast fortune – was not of age. But he must have been alarmed for himself and for his protégé at the thought of the rogue termagant Elisabeth forfeiting the good name of her late husband and risking the entire legacy. Megyery was a perfect candidate for the role of evil mastermind – the organiser of the subterfuges that hid the investigation from its subject, the orchestrator of the household officials' betrayal of their mistress – and it was not only later legend but the lady herself who cast him in that role, if Ponikenus is to be believed. It would be satisfying to be able to confirm Megyery in his part as villain – or, if Elisabeth was guilty, as protector of the young heir's name and fortune – but not enough is known about the man. There is no portrait, no journal that would bring him to life for us. What is known and is surely significant is that when Paul Nádasdy attained his majority, Megyery continued to serve him faithfully in the capacity of chief steward of the family estates.

CHAPTER EIGHT

The End of Elisabeth

I would find grievous ways to have thee slain,
Intense device, and superflux of pain.

Algernon Charles Swinburne, *Anactoria*

The Palatine defies the King ~ the 1611 hearings ~ further exchanges ~ a letter from the Fiscus ~ the last twelve testimonies ~ strange consistencies ~ the judicial aspects of the case ~ family relations ~ the Chief Justice upbraids the Palatine ~ the rise and fall of Gábor Báthory ~ Elisabeth's last declaration ~ death and silence

If the followers of Luther had been entrusted with the Hungarian Palatine's spiritual wellbeing, we can still see in his character a struggle between the enlightened humanism of Erasmus and the cynical *Realpolitik* of Macchiavelli. In his correspondence with Matthias, the absentee King of Hungary during the year 1611, Macchiavelli is to the fore, but there is another tension running through George Thurzó's half of the exchanges between the two men: the need to strike a balance between, on the one side, his loyalty to the holy crown and the Habsburg cause, strengthened by a personal regard for Matthias, and on the other, his patriotic duty as Palatine and as a Magyar noble to protect the remains of Hungary from disintegration or annexation by the Empire to the west. No less than this was at stake while Countess Báthory's right to life was still in question and the Nádasdy–Báthory inheritance at risk.

Once Elisabeth had been shut into the castle at Čachtice and the bodies of her servants consumed on the pyre, Thurzó sent word to the King. The sovereign Matthias of course had his own agents in Upper Hungary and knew that steps had been taken to isolate Francis Nádasdy's widow, but he was relying on Thurzó to deal with the matter and keep him informed: communications were slow and the King was preoccupied with strengthening his position in his own Imperial court and with formulating a policy to cope with the aggressive resurgence of Transylvania under Gábor Báthory.

The draft of Thurzó's message to the King still exists, and it hints that at this point the Palatine was improvising rather than working to a carefully scheduled plan.[1] He reports the arrest of Countess Báthory for the murder of up to 300 maidens and asserts that the Lady was caught in the act, prompting Thurzó in his righteous anger to pass his own sentence of life imprisonment on her there and then. The letter includes a brief account of the confessions of the servants, but, intriguingly, in the description of their interrogation by his legal assistants the phrase 'et tortura' – 'and [by] torture' – has been struck out, probably by Thurzó himself. This would have the effect of adding credibility to the charges, but in reinforcing an accusation of mass-murder would make it even more likely that the King would intervene.

If Thurzó hoped that Matthias would meekly accept this *fait accompli* and endorse his decision, he was quickly disabused. On 14 January the King responded by issuing a letter which contained the substance of Thurzó's report, but emphasised the noble rank of some of the murdered girls.[2] On the basis of the information he had received, the King decreed that fresh investigations should be carried out in Čachtice, Újhely, Beckov, Kostol'any, Sárvár, Keresztúr and Léka – the family estates in the north and west – in preparation for a full-scale trial.

On the same date in a separate letter the King requested the Palatine's advice on how to deal with another member of the Nádasdy family whom he suspected of treasonable sympathies. The noble in question was Count Thomas Nádasdy, cousin to the late Francis, and the suspicion of disloyalty was not unexpected, given that Thomas was living in Gábor Báthory's court in Transylvania at the time. In his letter Matthias asked Thurzó whether in his opinion there were grounds for putting Lord Nádasdy on trial.[3] It is known that Thomas had sought and received permission from the crown before going to Alba Julia, and Hungary was not at war with Transylvania: even if Thomas had not signed the oath of allegiance demanded by Thurzó at the end of the previous year, any trumped-up charges made against him would remind the Hungarians of the blatantly unjust attempt by the Habsburgs to destroy Count Illésházy and would undo all Thurzó's attempts to keep the Magyars loyal and their estates out of Habsburg hands. Thurzó's reply has not survived, but he seems to have persuaded Matthias against another show trial.

Where Elisabeth was concerned the King was adamant and Thurzó could not openly defy him, so in response to the demand for a new and thorough inquiry followed by a formal trial, the same Andrew Keresztúry presided over a further stage in the investigations during the first half of 1611. Two hundred and twenty-four new testimonies were heard from witnesses coming from the communities bordering the Váh river including Kostol'any, Čachtice, Beckov and Vrbové.[4] The resulting evidence was officially certified on 26 July. Many of the new informants simply confirmed the testimony of fellow-witnesses or stated that they were aware of the Lady's cruelties and nothing more, but some went into more detail, and a consistent set of accusations emerges.

Michael Fábry, the Kostol'any pastor who gave evidence during the first round of interrogations, appeared again, and amplified his previous statements, saying that he knew that many maidens had been tortured and that the Countess ducked naked girls in icy water in wintertime. In his previous deposition he had said simply that two girls were buried in his parish in secret: this time he affirmed that they had been murdered at Čachtice at the time of George Drugeth's marriage to Kate Nádasdy. His statements were confirmed by the magistrate at Kostol'any, Thomas Jávorka, who further testified that Elisabeth Báthory put a hot iron into the girls' genitals. This detail was confirmed by the manor clerk, Michael Horváth, who added that two other girls had been buried at Lešetice 'even during the sitting of the Lord Palatine's court [the Diet] at Bratislava' – in other words, as late as October 1610, after the investigations had begun.

A gentleman named Michael Hervojth, an administrator at the castle at Čachtice, said that the Countess tortured girls daily by putting hot iron bars into their vaginas and by whipping them. When the Lady's daughter, the wife of Lord Nicholas Zrínyi, had come to visit her (in the autumn of 1610), the Lady had had five girls buried in the grain pit. Two other maidens had been buried at Lešetice and one body was buried in a little garden by the manor-house, where dogs had discovered it and dug it up.

Paul Horváth stated that Ficzkó had used planks of wood to construct the coffins for the two girls who had been buried at Kostol'any. These two facts – the burials and Ficzkó's involvement – were the substance of most of the following testimonies. Matthew Lakatjártó, whose brother had testified in 1610, mentioned the death of the 'Sittkey girl' at the hands of (or on the orders of) the Countess.

Nicholas Barosius, the priest of Vrbové village, said that he had seen girls suffering from injuries both at the castle and at the manor-house in Čachtice. He also asserted that Countess Báthory had threatened that, if she was imprisoned, Gábor Báthory, the Prince of Transylvania, would come and rescue her.

The next to give evidence was John Sl'uka, a member of the minor gentry, also from Vrbové, who had been named the previous year as the person sent to obtain poisons from the pharmacist at Trnava. He confirmed this and said that the substance was antimony, and that the supplier, Dr Martin, had asked him what such a large quantity was needed for because it could kill many people.

The name of the ninetieth witness is already familiar to us from the secret letter sent by Pastor Ponikenus at the time of Elisabeth's arrest:[5] this was Andrew Priderović, who was listed as a squire from the village of Čachtice. Priderović said that he had been present at the manor-house when the Countess had been taken away to the castle to be imprisoned. He also said that he had seen for himself the body of a young girl being loaded into a coach. He had heard from others, and the doctor could verify, that one girl's corpse had been seen with traces of rope marks around the neck and marks of mutilation on the rest of her body. A woman had also been bound because she had refused to allow her daughter to be taken away, and another girl had wounds in her body so deep that a whole fist could be placed in them. The injuries looked as if they had been made by the tongs used in torturing.

John Jeleň, also a squire from Čachtice, said that he had seen three young girls who had been carried to Lešetice for burial and two others who had been buried at Kostol'any. One of these two maidens was from Trnava and the other was from the Nitra region (he did not name them). John Andačy, one of the Čachtice castle wardens, repeated the story of the murders at the time of George Drugeth's wedding. He added that a girl who had been mutilated was treated by the surgeon from Nové Mesto nad Váhom. Another of the castle wardens, a second Michael Horváth, referred to the occasion on which dogs dug up bodies from a small garden near the manor-house: he asserted that seven maidens had been buried there.

The ninety-seventh witness to be examined was the target of Andrew Priderović's anger, Jan Abrahamides Ponikenus himself, the priest of Čachtice who had supplied details of the Lady's atrocities in a letter to his superior in the last days of the previous year. On this occasion Ponikenus, after giving his age as thirty-eight and stating that he had been in his post at Čachtice for eight years, said that during his incumbency he had heard many dreadful things concerning the Widow Nádasdy. He said that he had heard from a servant who had been 'in the place where the doomed girls were sent to recover'. This servant had spied on the goings-on in these quarters through a crack in the wooden panelling and had seen a group of crones holding lighted candles 'gathered around the stomach of a naked woman'. Ponikenus' informant had no inkling, he said, of what the old women were up to.

It was the following witness who supplied details of cannibalism: the squire Martin Čanády stated that Elisabeth Báthory murdered the sister of squire John Belanský when the young woman was at her court. She also murdered squire George Tuchinský's daughter. He knew also that she put a hot iron bar into the genitals of a girl who was the daughter of Benedict the barber–surgeon, the brother of John Čápový (referred to elsewhere as Čáfordý and Čápodý), the castle warden at Beckov. What is more, he had knowledge that the lady had sausages made from the flesh of dead girls and served them at meals. George Kéry of Beckov confirmed the cruel murders of the daughters of Belanský and Tuchinský, as did several other witnesses, and George Szombathy of Beckov, one of Daniel Pongrácz's administrators, declared that Tuchinský had told him that Báthory had cruelly killed his daughter and buried her at Kostol'any.

Dorothy, the wife of George Stankovský of Beckov, said that she knew that one Anna Velika had brought the daughter of Benedict

Barbel, the sister of Čápový, alias Szabó, the Beckov castle warden, whom she had tortured. The victim was named as Anna by a later witness, the magistrate George Tarnócy, who also said that Báthory had used a heated iron bar to torture.

Peter Szabó, a local official from Beckov, said that he had seen with his own eyes a number of girls suffering from many wounds and bruises. He had heard that Nicholas Kardoss' wife (someone mentioned by several other witnesses) had brought two girls for the Countess. John Kun, who served Francis Mágóchy at Beckov, said that his kinsman Sándor Kun, who was the court master at the Nádasdy manor-house in Čachtice, told him that girls were made to sit in baths of scalding water and that the Countess tore their flesh from their shoulders and dislocated their arms.

Several other women testified, among them Dorothy Jezernická, wife of Francis Bárdy, a squire. She claimed that in 1590 she sent her own daughter Elisabeth to Countess Báthory's court and that Báthory cruelly murdered the girl. Frusina Latkócy, another squire's wife, stated that she had frequently seen with her own eyes young women suffering from weakness and wounds and covered with bruises at the Nádasdy court. All the remaining witnesses either referred to or repeated the information given by others.

Several questions immediately arise in connection with this evidence. Why, if they were still living (which is not certain), were the bereaved fathers, the nobles Belanský and Tuchinský, not called to testify in person? The answer may be that they both lived in Liptov county, which was not wholly under George Thurzó's direct control. Additionally, it is vital to remember that only the lesser nobility could be called upon to appear before a court without an order from the King himself. If these men were of the rank of Pongrácz, Mágóchy or Megyery, for example, they, like those notables and like other named aristocrats – Zichy, Sittkey and the rest – could never be summoned.

Why was Dorothy Jezernická allowed to accuse the Countess of murdering her daughter without being required to go into more detail about the circumstances? And why did Pastor Ponikenus, who in his letter had been so prolific in describing the horrors inflicted by the Lady, say so little, giving only the second-hand account of the women hovering over a naked body (explained by Elisabeth's defenders today as a healing or gynaecological process), leaving it to his fellow-witness Martin Čanády to make the only mention of cooking and eating human flesh, and to his fellow-priest Barosius to impute disloyalty to the crown?

Two other points have been overlooked by previous commentators. Andrew Priderović is one of the only witnesses in all the hearings whose name has come down to us in another context.[6] He was the person who angrily disrupted the Lutheran sermon given by Ponikenus in December 1610, a man whom the priest characterised as 'an instrument of the Devil'. It seems certain that Priderović was close to the Countess (he may have actually been dining with her at the manor-house when the raid took place) and had been intimidating her enemies, the local Lutherans, on her behalf. Yet now her own man was prepared to echo the accusations against his Lady, quoting hearsay but even adding his own eyewitness account for good measure. Of course Priderović may have been a craven liar or even a double agent, but a more plausible explanation is that he, like so many other witnesses who had formerly been part of her circle, had been coerced by threats, torture or bribes into testifying against Elisabeth.

The last comment to append to this batch of testimonies is to note that Pastor Ponikenus spoke no Hungarian, which means that interpreters or translators must have played a part in the transcription of confessions. As well as proving that not all the citizens of Upper Hungary were multilingual, as is sometimes claimed today, this goes some way to explaining the many inconsistencies and confusions in the written records of the proceedings.

It was during February that Count Zrínyi and Paul Nádasdy wrote to Thurzó with their pleas for a resolution which would combine mercy for Elisabeth with the least shame for the families.[7]

On 26 February 1611, King Matthias again wrote to Thurzó to insist that a proper trial be held; he wanted a formal arraignment and a properly constituted interrogation.[8] On 5 March, Thurzó promised that 'the affair of great importance concerning Mistress Nádasdy' would be brought before the justices of the country in the following spring, between 8 and 22 March, suddenly agreeing disingenuously that 'it should be brought to a conclusion and examined according to the legal regulations of the country'.[9]

Matthias sent a new message on 18 March in which he ignored the Palatine's assurances and inquired about Thurzó's compliance with his (Matthias') previous letter, instructing Thurzó to bring Countess

Báthory before the tabular court in Bratislava forthwith.[10] It is quite clear that the King was still not prepared to be worn down by Thurzó's delaying tactics and pettifogging, but if Thurzó did not dare to countermand the King's decrees, Matthias knew that to brush aside his vice-regent's arguments and overrule him would bring him into open conflict with the Magyar lords. The Palatine did not reply at once, but on 23 March he sent a letter in which he discusses the threat from Prince Gábor Báthory without mentioning the case of the Prince's aunt at all.[11] He returns to the case in a letter written on 30 March in which he admits that, despite previous reports, the formal trial proceedings had not been initiated for several good reasons, which in his opinion were not profitable to debate (he nevertheless went on to discuss them).[12] Thurzó – a man well versed in law and holder of the country's highest legal office – suggested that he had done his best in accordance with the customs of the land in managing the affair and was in agreement with the treasury counsellors, who themselves had agreed with the justices of the country, arguing that he had foregone 'proper' procedure and had not formally summonsed the accused because, once in custody, the prisoner should be considered as legally dead, and thus could not be arraigned. Thurzó added that the court had recessed for Easter, that not enough evidence had yet been collected and in addition that crimes of this nature were so rarely committed by women that it was not clear under whose jurisdiction they fell or what the proper punishment was. With all this in mind he respectfully pressed the King to accept his pronouncement of permanent loss of liberty upon Elisabeth.

Some of these novel and contradictory interpretations were set out, only slightly more coherently, in the letter from the Hungarian Royal Treasury (the Fiscus) in Bratislava to the King in Vienna, dated 31 March 1611:

Taking into consideration the several obstacles from the point of view of common law and the customs of the land, we have determined that this trial does not belong simply and properly within the jurisdiction of the Royal Treasury. And the reasons for this are the following: From the examination which was commenced by the notaries, of which they report that they have begun but not yet concluded, nothing of obvious guilt can be ascertained, and for this reason the work of the Treasury would be in vain. In any case, regarding the simple homicide [the killing of a commoner or commoners] that she had committed, an act meriting punishment, and also in the murdering of noble persons, which should be punished in your Highness' courts by the loss of one's head, this is not the affair of the Treasury but of the parties concerned to debate and to commence a trial, and it is possible we fear that a possible compromise between the relatives of the murdered person would be much simpler for the accused than with the Treasury's representative, and that is why the Treasury would have been excluded from the negotiations and from such a compromise.[13]

In practice the punishment meted out to nobles in serious cases usually consisted of the loss of one's properties or of one's head, rarely both, and might even be a question of choice by the accused. Not mentioned by Thurzó himself or by the Fiscus is the fact that anyone putting a senior aristocrat on trial on such grave charges would risk ruin or even conceivably execution themselves if the case were lost and counter-charges brought.

Even if the Treasury became involved in this affair, it could not hope for any great gain. The Treasury would receive the third part remaining after separating the part to be given to the sons and daughters according to the second part of the Sixtieth Article from the wealth of the person who is condemned to lose their head, and because the remaining two parts should be given to the judge who is his excellency the Palatine himself.

It seems likely that at this stage George Thurzó still had hopes of grabbing some of Elisabeth's wealth for himself, either by way of an eventual trial, or by blackmailing the family members into giving up some of their shares. The first option was risky, and hopes of the second option must have faded after the heirs had stood firm. But the threat of a trial would still bring the sons-in-law to heel, and Thurzó could offer to let them keep the properties in return for acquiescing in her neutralising.

However, it is probable that even this small gain would not be granted to the Treasury as the above-mentioned Mistress Nádasdy, her ladyship, as it is said, some years ago resigned from her estates and wealth and gave them to her son and all her rights she also gave to her son. Now as a prisoner and in captivity, she possesses nothing and in reality she does not enjoy the income from her estates, which means that even if she were declared to be guilty, she could forfeit nothing, but the Royal Treasury would likewise have no advantage of it. Thus the effort and labour invested in this matter and all the other expenditure and monies devoted to the matter would be quite in vain. Nonetheless, besides, it is within the power of your Majesty to decide the further fate of the accused person, but even regarding this we could not achieve a more favourable outcome, even if his Majesty were to order that the accused, who is in any case in the custody of her judges, should be brought before the Diet and after the consideration of her guilt and the sentence of the Diet, should be punished after arraignment according to the second part of the Seventy-fifth Article. For until now we have not had the opportunity to arraign her before a court, in part because of the lack of time, partly because the notaries have not publicly announced the interrogation, and of course, have not concluded it. As all those judges and persons in your Majesty's court are of the opinion that the Royal Treasury have nothing to gain, it is up to your Majesty's favour or desire, whether the process be advertised and commenced against the above-mentioned lady, with the aim of pronouncing the punishment of beheading, and it is likewise your choice to decide whether to let stand the punishment according to which she should be kept in close captivity in perpetuity, in appreciation of the great deeds of her late husband, who was a great and useful servant of your Majesty, and also taking into account the great service of her sons [actually sons-in-law] and daughters . . .

Thomas Viskelety
Francis Loránt

Counsellors of the Chamber

The letter from the Treasury, which, if not actually dictated by George Thurzó, would have been drafted according to his wishes, amounts to an attempt to browbeat the King into acceding to

Thurzó's unilateral sentencing of Elisabeth. The barrage of reasons put forward to explain why a formal trial would be futile is at least partly specious; the claims that there had not been time formally to summons the accused is particularly absurd – Matthias knew well that Thurzó had been gathering evidence for more than a year. Likewise the legalistic assertion that no guilt had yet been determined, when the Palatine had already condemned the lady, whom he claimed he had caught in the act.

The document's intention is clearly to bolster the Palatine's arguments as set out in his letters and to persuade Matthias that proceeding against Elisabeth will be far too troublesome, for little guaranteed reward, and will in any case risk upsetting powerful and – for the time being – loyal subjects of His Majesty. The letter incidentally confirms that the terms of Elisabeth's will had been broadcast; it also suggests that none of the victims' families had yet called for a trial and that no private deals had already been struck with aggrieved relatives.

On 17 April 1611 Matthias replied from Prague, saying that he understood the views of the Palatine and of the judges.[14] In recognition of the services performed by the late Francis Nádasdy, and in view of the pleas for clemency that had been lodged by his widow's relatives, the King was minded formally to consent to the Palatine's verdict of incarceration for life. This was the decision that the family had prayed for and that Thurzó had schemed to achieve. But, having made this concession to his trusted ally, the King was not prepared to let the matter drop. He still insisted that proper proceedings should be started from scratch, partly because of Mistress Nádasdy's rightful complaint (presumably Elisabeth had managed to transmit an oral or written protest from her prison, but there is no record of this), partly because of the astonishment expressed by certain (unnamed) noblemen at the violation of the rights of the nobility, and partly because the disapproval of Prince Gábor Báthory of Transylvania could be anticipated. The King refers to the improper arrest, investigation and imprisonment without trial as an 'unspeakable, unheard of and abnormal case', and a 'process contrary to law'.

At this point the to and fro of official missives stops and there is a long interval while the Palatine's investigations followed their unhurried course. With hindsight we can see that, even if his obstructions had come perilously close to *lèse-majesté*, he had managed thus far to pre-empt a political trial directed from Vienna, with all its attendant threats to stability in Hungary. At the same time it was not in Thurzó's personal interests to bring things to a conclusion; he had gambled that his own outrageous behaviour in seizing Countess Báthory would be eclipsed in the eyes of their fellow-peers by the scandal of her brutalities, but they would need time to get over this provocation. The estates had been saved, but the Palatine might still be able to stake a claim if the family showed signs of changing their loyalties.

On 17 December 1611, nearly a year after the execution of Elisabeth's trusted servants and the start of her imprisonment, the last round of the investigation that we know of was closed and the confessions of the final witnesses were certified. This time only twelve witnesses had been questioned, but these were mostly people of good social standing, some of whom were Elisabeth's most senior courtiers: they came from the town of Sopron and the county of Vas, in which the western Nádasdy–Báthory estates of Sárvár, Léka and Keresztúr were situated.[15]

The first witness was a widow from Sárvár of about thirty-six years old, Elisabeth, wife of the late John Sidó. She said that Elisabeth Báthory had had three girls beaten to death after cutting their noses and lips, pushing needles under their fingernails and personally heating a key and a laundry iron with which she burned them. The girls were named as Miss Kate Birinyi or Perényi, Miss Szabatkay and Miss Draskóczy. The witness knew no more, except that wicked rumours of cruelty emanated from the court.

The second to testify was the young Susanna, wife of John (other sources have Stephen) Eötvös, also of Sárvár. She knew that the younger daughter of Gábor Sittkey died at the court after prolonged beating. She does not know the girl's first name because she was always referred to simply as 'Miss Sittkey'.

The third witness was Helena, the wife of Paul Gercsey, a noblewoman of about forty-five from Sárvár. She knew that Kate Fekete had been chained and died in Keresztúr. She witnessed girls being beaten and burned on the hands by Countess Báthory, and being 'bathed' in stinging nettles. Girls had needles pushed into their shoulders and their breasts were beaten by their mistress.

The fourth testimony was from the doctor, Ambrose Borbély, giving evidence for the second time. He claimed that Elisabeth Báthory often asked him for curing plasters, but that he knew no more, as he rarely visited the court.

The fifth witness was Anna Szelesthey, a fifty-year-old widow from Mihályfalva. This woman stated that she took Susan, her own daughter, to Elisabeth Báthory's court, and she heard from certain persons that her daughter was beaten and tortured and that her flesh was torn from her body, and she died without hope of a cure. The witness heard of the torturing of many others, but did not see for herself, as she never entered the court.

Witness number six is one of the key figures in the affair, the court chamberlain at Sárvár, Benedict Deseő, who had been named by the first accused as someone deeply implicated in the crimes of his mistress, the Countess. Deseő, a man of around fifty, said he was very familiar with her cruelty and had seen some of the barbarities with his own eyes. But he had heard more about her actions from others. In his words, 'the lady is so wicked that it is impossible to account for her actions and cruelties'. Among many other instances he saw the Lady force a girl called Helena to stand nude before her, and the Lady took a knife and cut her arms, beginning at the fingers and then going higher: the girl was then burned on both hands with a candle until she died. He also saw a young woman (he could not remember her name) whose lips were stitched together by the Lady, who also stitched her tongue. He saw a number of girls who were made to stand naked before the Lady and were beaten by her. She hurt their hands so badly that the wounds became infected and they could not work, but the Lady pressed them to work and, if they did not work with their mutilated hands, the Lady scolded them roundly and called them whores. And she took the needle again and pricked their fingers and arms. She deprived the girls of water and when they were standing nude before her and suffering from thirst, they would drink their own urine, if they had any.

Deseő had heard, he said, that the Lady would heat the smaller round laundry iron and push it into the girls' vaginas. He knew for certain that two German girls were taken into her court, and straightaway they accompanied the Lady to Bratislava. On the way she gave them two 'Slovak cakes' to look after, which had been given to her by Francis Zempscey, but one of the maids ate one of the cakes, so the Lady had the remaining cake heated up and forced the girl to eat it, punishing her in this way. She later tortured the two German girls to death. There was a young bride called Modl, and the Lady cut off the flesh of her bottom and forced the girl to eat it raw. The girl died after torture at Sárvár. During the time that the Diet was sitting at Bratislava a young girl was tortured and died in Cseklész. One of the maidens' bodies was buried near the privy by a certain Helena. The body was discovered and pulled out in pieces by dogs.

Deseő told the investigators that Báthory's accomplices who had been hanged (sic) in Bytča could have added much more, and other officials of her court, in particular Jacob Szilvássy, Matthew Nagy and Gregory Pásztory, could say more about her cruelty, because they spent all their time at her court. 'God knows what else she might have done! . . . We were only her servants and we constantly asked her to cease her terrible activities,' Deseő claimed. The Lady had replied that she was not afraid because she had good advisers and supporters all over the country, and that a person of noble birth could not be detained without first receiving a formal summons to appear before a court. Deseő claimed that her staff had wanted to leave her service, but that Imre Megyery (her son's tutor and supervisor of the Sárvár estate) had asked them to stay on until she moved to Čachtice.

The Gregory Pásztory (described as a squire of around forty, living on his own estate) named by Deseő was the next to be called. He claimed to know little, as his duty was to supervise the cultivation on the Sárvár estates, and he rarely attended the court. When he was there, he saw nothing himself, except for the slapping of girls' faces, but he heard tell that many maidens were beaten and that many perished as a result. The Lady took him with her to Füzér when she held court there. At this point Pásztory repeats the story of the Modl girl suckling the log, adding that he heard that her breast was later cut off, but did not see it with his own eyes.

Pásztory then told how Elisabeth Báthory's manservant Ficzkó had assaulted one of his servants, who had wanted to thrash him in return, causing Pásztory to complain to Ficzkó, who ran to his mistress and lodged complaints about him. The Lady had summoned Pásztory to her court and asked him about the quarrel between them. He had replied that his servant had been chastised for no reason by Ficzkó, and that Ficzkó was anyway a bad man, who gossiped about many strange and wicked things that he had seen in the court, including the fact that five dead girls were hidden there. The Countess promised to investigate the matter, but did nothing.

Pásztory also saw a large wooden box at Sárvár, which he was told was used to carry corpses out of the castle. A gentleman named Sebastian Orben told him that once he had asked the woman Helena what was in the box, but she refused to answer. On another occasion, he noticed a pair of chains and locks in a bag and asked Helena what she was carrying them for. She said that the maids were put in chains every night. He knew no more.

The eighth witness was thirty-seven-year-old Jacob Szilvássy, the bookkeeper and administrator of the castles of Léka and Keresztúr. He said, in words which echo Deseő, that it was impossible to account for all the Lady's cruelties, because it would take ages. He could only attempt to summarise what he himself knew.

When she was holding court in Ecsed in 1606, an old soldier who was entrusted with the care of a thirteen-year-old girl took her to the court. The girl was sweet-tempered and always smiling and it seemed that she was loved by the Lady. Shortly afterwards she became pale and sickly (one version says that her guardian or father asked for her return, but that the Lady refused), and, when she was leaving the castle in a carriage which Szilvássy shared, he asked her about burns on her hands. She said that pieces of paper had been put between her fingers and that these had been lit. She was very thirsty, she said, as she had not drunk for five days. The witness gave her a cherry, but her condition worsened and before they could reach their destination she died in a village called Szedikerte. He was told, although he did not see it, that Elisabeth Báthory stood on the girl's throat when she died. Her body was buried, but he did not know where. At the same time two other girls died, and their bodies were carried for days before being buried along the way to Prešov. Báthory, he added, also tortured with frost (another version says that on a frosty day she told the serving-girls to hold her dripping nose, then slapped and beat them).

The young daughter of the cobbler died at Füzér, and he had been told that before she died she said to Báthory's face that she was a whore and would go to hell for her bestial crimes, whereas she, the bootmaker's daughter, would go to heaven. The Countess asked the girl why she abused her, and the girl urged her to hurry up and finish her brutal work. He had heard that two other girls had died in her court, and a maiden called Dorica and another called Margaret were beaten and tortured and later died in Keresztúr. He saw that the Lady punctured Dorica's belly with a great (some versions say rusty) needle, and in the very early morning he saw the bodies being removed, rolled up in a mat. He also heard that five girls had been buried in the grain pit; another girl died while the Lady was taking the waters at Piešt'ány. Szilvássy had also seen maidens standing quite naked in the presence of their mistress, and their bodies showed signs of injuries. At the time of Lord Homonnay's wedding two German girls died at Čachtice. He himself saw Báthory thrust a dagger into one of them by the ferry at Bratislava.

Szilvássy also said that the executed accomplices could have added more details.

The following witness, a castle warden, Stephen Mártonfalvy, simply said that he did not know much about these things, although he had seen girls slapped. When he had heard about brutalities, he had no longer wished to serve the Lady.

John Dezső, the warden of Keresztúr, was the next to be questioned. He said that his cousin Katherine Berény had been living at the court and he had heard that she was being beaten by the Countess. He went to see her but was prevented from doing so by one of the old women. He later asked the Lady if he could speak to his cousin, but was told that he could see her only when she was leaving in the carriage for Čachtice. On the following day he came face to face with Katherine, who was crying and appeared to be very weak. He asked that she be allowed to return home with him, but this was refused. The Lady told him that she was going to kill his cousin and he had never seen the girl again.

The penultimate witness was John Zamobothny or Zambotny, a gentleman of about forty years of age. All he knew was that about twelve servants and girls had died and were buried. He had been ordered to have coffins prepared, but did not know how the victims had died.

The last person to testify was Mistress Barbara Bix, who ran one of the farms at Sárvár, a married woman of twenty-five. She had seen that girls were tortured and beaten by those who were burned at the stake in Bytča. The maidens were often made to sit on stinging nettles. She did not know their names. John Ficzkó had told her that they collected girls from all over the countryside. She had heard that they were burned with the laundry iron and she saw their wounds. The dead girl who was found in Čachtice when Báthory was arrested was called Szalai (another version has 'was from Zala').

If we look at these new statements in turn (and we must keep in mind that these are once again 'confessions' or depositions obtained without torture as far as we know, and without any further charges having been brought against anyone), there are interesting features in all of them.

The first witness, the widow Elisabeth, specifically names three of Báthory's alleged victims. Of the names she gives, 'Perényi' and Draskóczy are those of noble families, indeed, the tenth witness in the same round of questioning confirms the death of his cousin, Katherine Berény, which is certainly the same person. The tortures that this Elisabeth mentions are among those already listed by previous witnesses.

The second witness refers to the death of one girl named Sittkey, a name mentioned by several earlier witnesses, who also were ignorant of the victim's first name. Some other testimonies claimed that two Sittkey girls had been murdered.

Helena, the third witness, names a certain Kate Fekete as one of the victims: this name has been mentioned before by Andrew Lakatjártó. Helen also claims to have witnessed with her own eyes beating, burning and 'bathing in nettles', but the rest of her testimony seems to be hearsay.

The curious fact about the doctor Ambrose Borbély's testimony is that he actually says less than he did at a previous hearing,[16] whereas the natural tendency at this stage of the investigation, with the Countess safely incarcerated, would be to say more. Borbély's reticence would make sense if, for instance, he was fearful of saying too much about his own real role in Báthory's business. The fact that the Countess asked him for healing plasters is not in itself incriminating, but does show that amateur healing was being practised at the court.

Anna Szelesthey's statement is maddeningly brief; she accuses Báthory of murdering her own daughter, but gives no details (at least, none was taken down by the transcribers) of where and when, or whether she ever saw her daughter's body before burial. The form of words she uses 'died without hope of a cure' might suggest that sickness or disease was implicated; perhaps this had been the official explanation. This witness's brother, Squire Adam Szelesthey, had testified previously and it is odd that the couple's statements do not seem to complement each other – Adam had not even mentioned the death of his niece.

Benedict Deseő provides much fuller testimony about Elisabeth's crimes, and well he might. The accomplices who had been burned nearly one year before had referred to him by name and suggested that he must have been more intimately involved than they in the atrocities committed by their mistress (to quote Ficzkó, 'Deseő knew everything but did not warn the Lady'). Deseő's evidence is a patchwork of stories told by earlier witnesses with several notable additions: he elaborates the affair of the insolent German servant, Miss Modl, by stating that she was forced into eating her own flesh by the Countess, a detail not mentioned by any other witness, but which comes, perhaps significantly, after the priest Ponikenus had first introduced the notion of cannibalism into the inquiry. The second novelty which Deseő relates is the story of the greedy German girl being forced to eat the 'Slovak cake'. This has the ring of truth, but taken in isolation just confirms the picture of Báthory inventing punishments to 'fit the crime'. Deseő extends the standard repertoire of abuses with his descriptions of the drinking of urine and the stitching of the victim's tongue. (He does not explain how he, an ageing male, who implies that he did not spend all his time in her court, came to be present when naked girls were being tortured, presumably in the women's quarters and in the laundry.)

The other interesting aspects of Deseő's deposition are his eagerness to implicate his fellow-officials Szilvássy, Pásztory and Nagy, and his claim that Imre Megyery had urged the servants to remain with the Countess *until she moved to Čachtice*. This proves that Elisabeth's journey at the end of 1610 to Čachtice, where she was arrested, was not a spontaneous attempt to flee the country, but a planned change of venue for the end-of-year celebrations, which those at the court in Sárvár were already aware of. It is even possible that they persuaded Elisabeth to go to Č-achtice where she would present an easier target – the little town with its small complement of guards was isolated between the estates of the Palatine, those of his ally Illésházy and the hostile town of Nové Mesto.

Deseő's reference to the tutor Imre Megyery disproves the entry in the diary of Thurzó's secretary and prosecutor, Závodský, where it was noted that 'even Megyery knew nothing [of the lady's crimes]'.[17]

Pásztory, who was the next to testify, played down his involvement in the Countess's affairs, although he had been named as one of her confidants. He tells the story against Ficzkó perhaps to devalue Ficzkó's own statements, but it gives a picture of feuding servants that we know to be generally true, whatever the ins and outs, from Elisabeth Báthory's letter to Thurzó complaining of Gáspar Tatay's violence.[18] He is, interestingly, the only witness to use the word 'gossip', although a great many of the testimonies imply that gossip was rife in and around the court.

Pásztory brings a new element to the developing theme of secret containers: we have had home-made coffins and incriminating

183

documents in locked caskets; now we have the sinister accessory, the bag of chains and locks. A modern cynic might feel that Pásztory is slipping into place one of the missing pieces needed to build a convincing overall picture. No one had yet explained why none of the maidservants, some of whom must have been girls of spirit, had managed to get away: the chains, put on each night, provide the answer. But were they individually manacled, in which case a large number of chains would be required, or was the door of their dormitory simply padlocked shut? The records are silent, of course.

Jacob Szilvássy seems to be one of the most voluble of the witnesses, and we can imagine a man of some education who is, perhaps, more articulate than some of the simpler gentry who testify, and is also desperate to acquit himself of any suspicion (Helena Jó had stated before she was burned that 'Szilvássy and the court steward Deseő both saw how the Lady tortured naked maidservants'). Szilvássy mentions again the practice of putting burning paper between the fingers, Lord Francis Nádasdy's novel revival technique which understandably aroused the curiosity of the servants. This witness's evidence is spiced with detail and pathos – the cherry given to the dying girl, the stabbing at the Bratislava ferry and the use of the giant needle, and, most affecting of all, the bravado of the doomed cobbler's daughter. We are in no position to dismiss this exchange as a fantasy, but it is remarkable that the heroic girl's last words had not passed into local folklore and were not mentioned by any other witness. Furthermore, it is interesting that Szilvássy, Deseő and an earlier witness, Sir Francis Török, who lived in the same county, use almost identical phrases in their testimonies, each of them exclaiming, 'It is impossible to account for all her horrible deeds!', 'Only God could enumerate her crimes!' and 'Her wickedness is as boundless as the sea!' This proves nothing – these may have been common forms of words – but it could suggest that the witnesses had been coached, or simply that they had prepared their testimonies together.

Szilvássy was a senior and trusted servant who offered vivid eyewitness descriptions of his mistress's sadism as well as the usual hearsay; the modern reader is bound to want to ask, as the examining authorities seem never to have done, 'Why did you do nothing, tell no one?' (The earlier witness, Deseő, had provided an answer to this unasked question. He claimed, like some others who testified, that he had wanted to stop serving the Countess and that Imre Megyery had asked him to stay on. This hints at a promise by Megyery to protect Elisabeth's attendants if they gave evidence against her, but it does not excuse them for remaining silent in the past, in some cases for years.)

One more loose end is left untied by Jacob Szilvássy's deposition in this round of hearings and it concerns the book that the woman Susannah claimed Szilvássy had seen, in which Elisabeth Báthory had recorded the number of her victims as 650. How Szilvássy was supposed to have stolen a glance at this most secret document was never explained, but by the time he came to give his evidence the inquisitors and most of the population of the family estates must have heard of this little book and its shocking contents. According to the record, when Szilvássy had his chance to speak he said nothing about it at all. If we decide that the existence of the book was a fantasy or a fabrication, it is still easy to see where it might have come from. The servants must have been fascinated by the locked cabinets, chests and travelling trunks that filled their employer's private rooms and into which they would never be permitted to pry. When the Countess was sent to the high castle in disgrace, she was allowed to take with her a little box, perhaps the same box that Ficzkó had said was part of her magical paraphernalia, or the box containing her will and her private letters that her son Paul took possession of when she died (perhaps they were one and the same).

The remaining witnesses add only incidental detail to the evidence already collected, with the exception of John Dezső who, like Anna Szelesthey, accuses the Countess of murdering his relative – and even announcing that she would do so – but frustratingly fails to explain what steps, if any, he or the girl's immediate family took against her.

Modern legal experts who have considered the conduct of the trial of the accomplices – foremost among whom is the Hungarian judge Dr Irma Szádeczky-Kardoss, whose distant ancestor, Caspar Kardoss, was co-presiding in 1611 – have declared it a travesty, and have pointed to the similarities between the whole investigation with its accumulation of unproven and often contradictory accusations, followed by a hasty trial before a hand-picked court, and the show trials of the communist era in which names were systematically blackened, guilt was imputed, then assumed.

There are certainly many unusual aspects to the gathering of testimonies and the trial, not the least being that the principal accused was not present. But there was method in the Palatine's bending of the rules and precedents. Firstly, it seems clear that the arrest and the trial of the servants had been carefully planned well in advance, and was not put together in response to the dramatic 'discoveries' at the manor-house in Čachtice. The examining authorities were all present and ready to start the proceedings one day after the arrests, on New Year's Day, and the jury took only days to assemble. This accelerated timetable not only allowed the key personalities in the case to be disposed of without interference, but, given the season, would prevent news reaching the outside world until the case had been decisively closed.

The only permitted circumstances in which a nobleman or woman could be condemned without a formal summons being issued first were if the accused was caught red-handed in the act of murdering someone of equal status. The status problem was never clarified in the case of the girl found dead at the manor-house, but, by stating that he had come upon Báthory in the act of torturing, Thurzó was able to justify his instant sentence upon her. Even in such a case, precedent demanded that there be at least seven persons of high rank on hand to pronounce judgement. There were not. Thurzó's secretary, George Závodský, claimed in his journal that his master had been in the company of Zrínyi, Drugeth and Megyery at the scene of the crimes, but this is not so. Although all three had probably supplied men for the raid on the village, the sons-in-law did not arrive until after the Countess had been removed to the castle. So it was Thurzó alone, or Thurzó and Megyery, who dispensed summary justice to her.'[19]

Such irregularities were not unknown in seventeenth-century Hungary: there were recognised traditions of 'alternative' forms of justice, two of which Thurzó may have had in mind at different stages of the Báthory affair. The first was the so-called 'family court' whereby the senior members of noble families gathered privately to deal with offences committed by relatives that threatened the honour or prosperity of the whole dynasty. Although unofficial, this method of judgement had been sanctioned at the highest level, since it was the way in which the Habsburg family were thought to have persuaded the eccentric Emperor Rudolf II to abdicate in favour of Archduke Matthias. In the case of Hungarian noble families, the objective was usually to isolate and neutralise the offending family member. If the person concerned was female, she would often be placed in a convent, and Thurzó is said to have considered this fate for Elisabeth Báthory. The other type of case in which normal legal processes were often sidestepped was where sedition or sorcery were involved, and in many ways the trial and condemnation of Elisabeth Báthory's manservant and confidantes most resembles a witch-trial, although it was she, and not they, who were accused, almost in passing, of practising black magic.

By royal decree, the trial documentation for capital crimes had to include a medical certificate relating to the victim or victims, and this was not done in the case of Báthory's accomplices, although a medical report was attached to the papers at a later stage. It was not an official coroner's report, but a deposition made by a bonesetter named Thomas Borbély who declared that he had cured a girl named Anna who was a member of Elisabeth Báthory's court, almost certainly the same person who was displayed to the people of Čachtice immediately after the raid. He detailed the wounds that the girl had exhibited: there were four deep lacerations, two on her shoulders, two on her buttocks, and another serious wound on the back of her hand. There was pus in the wounds when Borbély attended the girl, but after two months in bed she recovered and the doctor was paid 56 florins and 15 pounds of corn by order of Count Thurzó.[20]

Other oddities which have been pointed out are the obvious ones: potential star witnesses such as the surviving maids and seamstresses – the 'little Cseglei' mentioned by Helena Jó for one – were never called. Those who did testify were not cross-examined about their own guilt or complicity. The many cadavers were not exhumed, even though it was known where they were supposed to have been buried – in the village churchyards of Lešetice and Kostol'any, for instance.

Why were all the investigations focused on the west of the country closer to Vienna, when torturing girls would have been so much easier in the more remote and lawless east? Even though witnesses mentioned murders which were carried out at Füzér castle in eastern Hungary, none of the castle staff from there or from Szécskeresztúr or Ecsed were interviewed as far as we know. Could this have been because they would have been less easy to intimidate? They might have felt that their interests lay with the Báthory rather than the Nádasdy patrimony; they were living beyond George Thurzó's ambit and were probably weighing up the prospect of declaring for his rival the Transylvanian Prince if the chance arose.

When we look at the choice of witnesses, there are definite criteria being applied: although both lowly peasants and members of the minor gentry were called and heard, no senior aristocrats were summoned – to do so would have been a serious slur on individual families and the ruling class as a whole. But, if it was unthinkable for the country's elite to appear in person, there was nothing to stop them sending their familiars to speak on their behalf; no servant of the Sittkey family came forward to corroborate the death of their relations, and why should the Zichys have remained silent, if their daughter had been killed? (It was Count Zichy, not a simple country squire, but a man of influence, who had written in admiring terms to Elisabeth four years earlier.)

Some of the witnesses and the supposed victims – and the Nádasdy–Báthory family themselves – were interrelated by blood and marriage, which casts more doubt on the objectivity of the investigation. Imre Megyery, the familiar of the Nádasdy family who was appointed as Paul Nádasdy's tutor, was related by marriage to the Szép family who were in turn related to the legal official Caspar Ordódy and to the witness Katherine Dömölky. Megyery was also related to the Szelesthey family, one of whom was a victim of Elisabeth and another a witness testifying against her. The Szelestheys, the Megyerys and the Nádasdys were all related to the Sittkeys, two of whose daughters were alleged to have been killed by Elisabeth. The presiding investigator Syrmiensis was a familiar of the Thurzó household and was also related to Daniel Pongrácz, the part-owner of Beckov, whose serfs provided so much damning testimony in Nové Mesto nad Váhom.

In a painstakingly thorough review of the judicial aspects of the case, the Hungarian legal expert Irma Szádeczky-Kardoss appointed herself counsel for the defence and after considering the whole body of written evidence and the personal and family connections between witnesses and prosecutors, exonerated Elisabeth in her conclusions. When this author asked her to assume the prosecuting role and asked her whether she would have had enough evidence to bring a case, she said she would not have.

But we must not expect the citizens of seventeenth-century Hungary to conform to modern notions of legality or fairness.

There is another letter in the Thurzó family archives which no one who has written on the Báthory case seems to have commented on at any length. Yet it is one of the most surprising and revealing of the few documents that have come down to us, and it draws together more than one strand of the complex network of events and personalities that we have to contend with. It is a letter dispatched by Count Sigmund Forgách, the Chief Justice of Hungary, to the Palatine,

George Thurzó. Forgách was an ardently pro-Habsburg Catholic who was related to Thurzó through his stepfather and a man who hated Gábor Báthory and his supporters inside Hungary (Forgách in his parallel role as captain-general of the armies of Upper Hungary had invaded Transylvania the previous year to try and unseat the Prince), so this was someone with no reason to side with Elisabeth Báthory. Nevertheless on this occasion, 16 February 1612, just over a year into Elisabeth's captivity, Forgách wrote from Bratislava:

> We should have hoped not to have written this letter to you regarding an affair of this kind, but as the subject calls in question your honour and your reputation, we have no other choice but to inform you of it.
>
> In the last few days you have gone to Čachtice and your beloved wife has gone up into the castle, and there she had the treasury opened by force and removed a larger number of objects and money, too. We have registered all the articles that have been taken away by her. However, your wife then went to the manor-house below, where she did the same; had the treasury opened by force and took away with her a large quantity of valuables. We were informed of this matter by Lord George Homonnay and the young orphaned Lord Nádasdy, both of whom resented the fact that your wife could act thus against their family. However, rumours are spreading among the people that she would not have done this without your knowledge and permission.
>
> As we are entrusted by our office to defend all the helpless and the orphaned throughout his Majesty's Kingdom of Hungary, and as we, together with yourself, are charged with upholding justice; therefore I warn and solemnly require you, not only as my brother, but in the authority of my office, to hand back in full all the goods and monies which were taken from Čachtice by your wife as soon as possible. We can promise and assure you that we will call together certain wise and well-skilled men of law even from the Council of his Majesty to examine the said case, and if they should find something from these goods belonging lawfully to your wife, she will have it. But, if you will not accede to our advice, we will pass legal sentence upon you, and you will suffer more damage for the goods taken than their worth to you.

Because we must account for our duties before Almighty God, therefore we cannot desert the young orphaned lord in his need for justice. I am bound to advise you of this matter.[21]

This startling development and the document that records it illuminate some murky corners of the affair. The letter firstly proves that Elisabeth really was closely confined at Čachtice, and not in a position to stop Elisabeth Czobor from seizing her valuables – her detention was no mere sham to appease the King or the public. It also makes very clear that Elisabeth Báthory still had some of her treasures intact, not only in the manor-house in the centre of Čachtice, but also in the high castle where she was detained. It is unthinkable that the Palatine's wife, who may have wanted to use some of the Báthory treasure as gifts, or to finance her daughter Barbara's wedding later that year, would have attempted this crude manoeuvre on her own initiative, as Forgách well knew. Once again, as she did just prior to Countess Báthory's arrest, Thurzó's wife assisted him in his persecution of the Báthorys.

The incident underlines the helplessness of the isolated widow, but also proves that Thurzó's actions were not inspired, as has been claimed, by friendship for the Countess or by aristocratic solidarity. As in his dealings with other less powerful neighbours, he was quite ready to use force to get what he wanted – in this case jewels and cash – and to risk the offence to the honour of his fellow-lords Paul Nádasdy and George Drugeth into the bargain (one wonders, too, what Lady Anna and Lord Nicholas Zrínyi, by now a loyal pro-Habsburg Catholic, made of this incident: there is no mention of their protest). The letter is also quite remarkable for the fact that it directly challenges the Palatine himself and calls him to account. Forgách, carefully speaking from within his official remit, is warning Thurzó that, in the great ruthless dance of the contending dynasties, even he cannot act with impunity.

There is no record, unfortunately, of the outcome of this affair, but we can be fairly sure that on past precedent Thurzó would try every stratagem, legal or otherwise, to avoid returning his booty to its rightful owner. As a footnote, it is interesting that on 30 September 1612 Elisabeth Czobor and George Thurzó hosted a celebration in the painted wedding-house (the finest in the Kingdom) in the grounds of their castle in Bytča. The feasting followed the marriage of their favourite daughter Barbara to Count Christopher Erdődy, and among the names of the guests are those of the lords Nicholas Zrínyi and Paul Nádasdy.[22] It may seem strange that the relatives of a woman who has just been stripped of her valuables should pay their respects at a wedding hosted by the robbers, but this incongruity illustrates an essential difference between modern attitudes and the codes of the seventeenth century. Life was indeed ruled by codes, which were observed in spite of personal feelings and which served to prevent a slide into anarchy. The relationships between the aristocratic holders of high office were of crucial importance, and individuals might work together in government while struggling to best one another in the savage and unceasing game of self-enrichment. It was universally understood that power, and skill in exercising power, were the beginning and end of public life – of all social interactions, in fact. If an opportunity presented itself, it was normal to take it, whether it was the annexing of a parcel of land or the emptying of a neighbour's treasure-chest. Paul Nádasdy and Nicholas Zrínyi were bound to George Thurzó by family ties, by their duties to the nation and by traditions of honour: they could not lightly break with their 'uncle'.

On 24 January 1613 the King wrote again from Vienna to the Palatine in Bratislava ordering the start of the trial. His renewed interest in Countess Báthory's fate coincided with peace negotiations between Gábor Báthory and the Habsburg court.[23]

It is conceivable that Gábor could have tried to enforce his own claim on Elisabeth's lands, had they been confiscated after a political trial; if he had succeeded, this would have been disastrous for Thurzó and the Hungarian aristocracy. The Habsburg inner court had been weakened by the conflict between the Archduke Matthias and the Emperor Rudolf, and the occupation of Elisabeth's properties, so near Bratislava and Vienna, would also have been a strategic catastrophe for them. The next Prince of Transylvania, Gábor Bethlen, did succeed in occupying land in Royal Hungary, but not enough to destabilise the Kingdom. It was unthinkable for Gábor Báthory to risk an invasion of Hungary west of the Tisza just to free his aunt, but while she languished under house arrest without trial he had a pretext for subversions and an opportunity for making propaganda.

To understand fully the political backdrop against which the arguments over Elisabeth's fate were conducted, it will be necessary to make one more excursion into the history books to consider the brief and frenetic career of 'Crazy Gábor' Báthory, the family's last hope.

When the handsome, wild and arrogant seventeen-year-old was elected to the throne of Transylvania, the unanimous view was that, although he possessed virtually no land there, he was someone born to rule. Behind Prince Gábor stood his mentor and supporter, Gábor Bethlen, who understood the realities of the region's politics and understood the ways of the Turks and was instrumental in getting the Sublime Porte's agreement to Báthory's enthronement. Within recent memory there had been terrible years in Transylvania; in 1603 and 1604, 'indeed man had become a wolf to man, and reduced by pestilence, famine and spoliation to the utmost misery, those who could afford it bought human flesh sold openly on the market . . .'[24] But the rule of the 'Fairy Prince' began with the very highest expectations. From 1608 onwards the economy prospered and harvests were good, and after the frozen anxiety of the previous years, the people easily put away their recollections of Prince Sigmund and Cardinal Andrew's shortcomings and let themselves believe that the return of a Báthory would restore the splendours of King Stephen's reign. The new Prince based his administration in Alba Julia, a city which had itself been renovated and restored to latinate luxury, and the court that he and his favourites created quickly became celebrated for its gaiety and swashbuckling vitality.

Back in Hungary, however, the pro-Habsburg faction led by the Catholic Forgách was determined to frustrate Gabor's rise to power. The Calvinist Gábor chanceller, Stephen Kendy, leader of the Catholic aristocracy in Transylvania, was already in secret discussions with Catholics inside Hungary, and Radu Sherban, the Voivode of Wallachia, a protégé of Basta (the murderous Habsburg general who had laid waste the Principality) and inheritor of the pro-Habsburg policy of Michael the Brave, was tentatively putting out feelers in Vienna, offering to stab Báthory in the back. Oblivious to all this, the merry Prince was travelling from feast to feast on a progress around the country which he hardly knew.[25]

From a time, Gábor was forgiven for courting beautiful women while hiding his ugly wife, but it quickly became apparent that his noisy feasts and flagrant promiscuity were not simply the pardonable and transient indulgences of a golden youth, but were all the governance he was going to offer. The first job of any ruler of Transylvania, even if he had been properly elected and was personally popular, was to secure his possessions and crush any dissent among the different *nationes* and the many factions. Gábor preferred hedonism to strategy from the start, behaving like a gleeful child who had been handed a kingdom as a playground. Not satisfied with the courtesans he was offered, Báthory awarded himself *droit de seigneur* over the wives of his counsellors, and before long everyone believed the rumours that he had also pursued an incestuous relationship with his younger sister Anna, who was later tried for witchcraft and murder. It was not only women he was drawn to, if the romances can be believed. In this extract from a set text for Hungarian high-school children, Gábor is toying with his favourites in the midst of the campaign in Wallachia: 'Come here, my darling,' and he seated the young Hajduk, Pal Szilassy, by his own side, put the girl [a young Wallachian noblewoman] on his lap, and began to teach the boy how to kiss the girl. He embraced them both, and now he kissed and fondled the boy, then the girl . . .'[26] Sitting in retrospective judgement on Gábor, Anna and their aunt Elisabeth, historians declared ringingly that 'The last scions of this once great family were being consumed in the flames of their unbridled passions.'[27]

While Anna and Elisabeth were judged and condemned by their contemporaries, Gábor was forgiven, not least because he was a man, but even a ruler of an absolutist state was taking a risk when he breached feudal codes of honour, and those whose family pride he had trampled upon hated him. When Gábor forced his lustful attentions on the wife of a senior Catholic aristocrat, Balthazar Kornis, this provided a good excuse for the Chancellor Kendy, who had suffered no personal slight himself (and who was given one of the most profitable manors of Transylvania) to take advantage of the popular discontent for his own purposes. He approached those nobles opposed to Gábor, who then met to orchestrate a conspiracy to murder the Prince. Assassins were sent to kill him, but the plotters were betrayed, Kornis was arrested and his brother George was killed; the rest of the conspirators fled. In his first rage Gábor had János Kolosváry, a high judge, whom Kornis had named as a fellow-conspirator hanged without trial. He also confiscated the estates of the Kornises, the Kendys and other Catholic nobles.

After the failure of the Kendy plot, the Jesuits who were spearheading the Counter-Reformation fled the country immediately. The Diet then invoked an old law banning their activities, and although nobles were allowed to keep a Catholic priest on their properties, they were forbidden to try to convert their serfs.

The country was restive, and the Prince and his entourage were resentful after the attempt on his life. His first meeting with the new Hungarian Palatine George Thurzó on the Kiralydaróc field between the two territories was not a success. The purpose of the negotiations should have been the strengthening of ties between the two Hungarian states, but Thurzó, who Gábor knew had given the would-be assassins his backing, delivered his far-reaching demands bluntly: he wanted Transylvania to have a representative in the Royal Hungarian Diet, which would have meant acknowledging the sovereignty of the Hungarian crown, and he and the Habsburg monarch wanted the renewal of an alliance with the subordinate partner, Transylvania, supporting the Empire in its anti-Turkish policy. The Prince considered this a provocation, and abruptly departed. He took out his rage on Balthazar Kornis by peremptorily executing him.

Twice during the summer of 1610, Gábor met with Thurzó again. On both occasions Thurzó's arrogant intransigence, which matched the hot-tempered pride of the Prince, led them into a personal confrontation which scuppered the talks. On 15 August it was a question of precedence. George Thurzó refused to address Gábor as prince (*fejedelem*) and insisted that in the eyes of Royal Hungary he was a mere provincial governor (*vajda*), a rank lower than that of count palatine. Gábor left immediately.

Letters discovered by this author in Vienna show that Gábor was trying brazenly to recruit troops from within Hungary in late 1610 – at the very moment that Thurzó decided to arrest his aunt.[28] Later, after Thurzó had succeeded in establishing an understanding with Báthory, the Palatine wrote to Elisabeth Czobor, his wife. 'In Vienna they should give me their thanks, for if I had not succeeded in making peace, the entire country as far as the Fatras would have fallen and been lost to his Majesty. His Majesty should offer thanks to the Almighty for this peace!'[29] This revealing private note is the only admission of how grave the situation was. It proves beyond doubt that there was a real danger that a combination of anti-Habsburg and pro-Báthory feeling in Hungary and a military uprising or invasion inspired in the east by Gábor himself could have ensured that not only the disputed territories of the Partium and the volatile Seven Counties, but the entire eastern third of Hungary (separated by the Fatra mountain chain) would go over to Gábor and his Hajdúks. This in itself was sufficient reason for Thurzó to incapacitate Elisabeth, to prevent her rallying supporters or subsidising mercenaries and to destroy the reputation of her family in the eyes of the undecided nobles.

Although he was headstrong to the point of folly, Gábor was not stupid. He began to sense that circumstances could quickly rearrange themselves very unfavourably: there was news that Kendy was in touch with the Voivode of Wallachia and was recruiting Cossacks in Poland for an attack on Transylvania.

Gábor occupied the Szeben Saxon cities which had refused to acknowledge his authority (violating the Saxon leaders' wives too, it was said), and took Wallachia, but could not keep it. Radu Sherban fled to Poland. If Báthory had managed to explain the Wallachians' pro-Habsburg machinations, the Turks would probably have supported the Voivode's deposing and the state's annexation, but by the time Báthory's envoys reached Constantinople, the Porte had mobilised its pashas in the occupied zone to attack the Hajdúks' towns and villages in eastern Hungary while the men were fighting on Báthory's behalf in Wallachia. When they heard that their settlements had been burned, the Hajdúk regiments withdrew.

Gábor had far-reaching ambitions. Hoping to create an empire consisting of Transylvania, Wallachia and Poland, he requested the Turks' support for an attack on the pro-Polish Voivode of Moldova, followed by an invasion of Poland itself. He hoped to forge a Russo-Turkish alliance – not a completely outrageous conceit in that the Poles had just occupied Moscow. Báthory did not take account of the recent compromise between the Polish nobles and the Swede Sigismund III and the internal problems of the Ottomans. The Turkish Porte's diplomacy became ultra-cautious and the Habsburgs put diplomatic pressure on Constantinople. Báthory had to withdraw and was left without even Wallachia.[30]

It was now June 1611, and Sigmund Forgách's Hungarian forces chose this time to intervene. The Saxon cities of southern Transylvania had asked for aid from the Habsburgs but could not get either money or soldiers. Although he hated and despised Gábor, George Thurzó counselled caution, but against his advice the Habsburg court gave Forgách permission for an armed attack on Transylvania. Before they invaded, the deposed Voivode attacked with Polish Cossacks and Moldavian troops, first ousting his replacement in Wallachia and then entering Transylvania at the behest of the Brasov Saxons.

Báthory had now resorted to his drinking companions for policy-making. He was flaunting his scandalous life, appearing in public with his illicit lovers and appeasing the cuckolded husbands with large estates. He was morose after the failure of the Wallachian campaign and did not send his tributes to Constantinople on time. The Hajdúk Andrew Ghyczy, a flamboyant and dashing figure but a criminal and fraudster too, became Gábor's favourite, but soon began to plot against him. The disaffected parties in the Principality sent Ghyczy as their representative to ask the Turkish Sultan to depose Báthory in favour of Ghyczy himself, and the pretender entered the independent city of Brasov as a prince, while the legitimate ruler was distracted by the pleasures of the flesh. The Voivode of Wallachia would not support this coup, however, and neither Ghyczy nor his patron, Weiss, the chief magistrate of Brasov, had any military expertise. When Báthory's soldiers moved decisively against them, they were quickly defeated and Weiss was killed. The legitimate Prince, now in a constant state of intoxication, began to issue contradictory commands and indulge his tyrannical fantasies, first by executing Andrew Nagy, the leader of the Hajdúks. Alienating the fanatical Hajdúks was an act of utter folly, but his next impulse was yet more dangerous: it was to make an enemy of his patron, confidant and most able political tactician, Gábor Bethlen. The two quarrelled when Bethlen attempted to restrain the Prince. Báthory's response to the man he began to see as a rival was to draw his sword in Bethlen's presence – a mortal insult to a Renaissance gentleman – and, worse, to put a lighted candle to his beard. Bethlen left the court and found shelter with his associate, the Turkish Pasha of Timişoara. Gábor Báthory came partially to his senses, and sought a rapprochement with Royal Hungary – but doing so, astonishingly, with the assistance of Ghyczy. His misfortunes were an unexpected gift to the Habsburgs, and the price of peace with the Germans of Brasov and with Hungary was Báthory's agreement to abide by Hungarian policy, to lend troops to campaign against the Turks, to restore religious freedom to the Transylvanian Catholics and to pardon the Brasov Saxons.

Gábor Báthory's outrageous personal immorality and disregard for the traditional rights of the nobility in Transylvania made another plot against his life an inevitability. The Reformation had focused on the need for moral codes – the Popish way or the Protestant way. Gábor's way was a profligate personal abandon that flew in the face of both. The feudal knight and satyr was a figure out of time, and now without friends.

In Constantinople Bethlen was urging the Turks to support his own claim to the throne, a claim supported by the Szeben Saxons, whose territory Báthory had refused to give up. Once again Gábor

The End of Elisabeth

Báthory's envoys belatedly left for negotiations with the Turks when the latter's armies were already *en route* for Transylvania with Gábor Bethlen at their head. Báthory fled westwards with Ghyczy and a troop of Hajdúks, only to meet Forgách's invading force at Várad in the Partium. Ghyczy betrayed his friend yet again, inducing the Hajdúk bodyguard, who had not forgiven the killing of their leader, to murder the Prince. The Nero of the *Siebenburgen*, the Transylvanian Casanova, the last feudal hero – and, as it transpired, the last hope of glory for his line – was dead at twenty-three.

In February 1613 all the protocols were assembled to allow the formal trial of Countess Elisabeth Báthory finally to start. With nearly 300 depositions, the comprehensively damning contents of the letter from Ponikenus and a medical certificate for appearance's sake, Thurzó had all he needed to have Elisabeth brought to trial on a charge of his choice: mass-murder, treason or sorcery – they were all capital crimes. But nothing happened. There is no record of any further moves by the family on behalf of the widow in the castle or any reference to her in official correspondence during the time that remained to her.

Gábor was shot down in October 1613, and once he was dead the 'Báthory faction' in Hungary ceased to exist. The 'Transylvanian party', after initial disarray, regrouped around the figure of Gábor Bethlen, who now saw himself as a rival to the Báthorys, though at that time he held no significant estates inside Hungary. There was no reason for King Matthias to pursue the case: Elisabeth was powerless; her estates had officially been disposed of; George Drugeth was scheming to promote his own pro-Habsburg coup in Transylvania; and the other heirs had, despite earlier suspicions, remained loyal to the crown. The Royal Treasury could gain nothing from reopening the investigation. While Elisabeth was alive, for instance, the powerful Lord Zrínyi could be accused of proximity to the Transylvanian party, so she was useful for political blackmail, but once Gábor was dead her value to the Palatine and to the King dwindled to nothing. She was now an unperson, legally if not physically dead, with no hope of rescue and nothing left to bargain with for her freedom.

The heirs of the Widow Nádasdy had first come together to discuss the division of their inheritance on 8 October 1611, and on that occasion Nicholas Zrínyi was given a share of the Čachtice estate, which he appointed one Matthew Teöteössy to manage on his behalf.[31]

197

In the one strange sequence in her will of the previous year, Elisabeth Báthory had asked to be allowed to keep her 'wedding dress and jewels', so she had not in fact disposed of all her property, and it was certainly those jewels that Elisabeth Czobor had succeeded in seizing.[32]

On 18 August 1614, Counts Nádasdy and Homonnay Drugeth met again to finalise their arrangements for the estates of Čachtice and Beckov. According to the chronicles, 'Lord Nádasdy gave Homonnay his part,' but it seems that there was some sort of disagreement between the two men and the partition was not finalised: the same village chronicles record again on 9 March 1616 that 'Csejthe and Beckov were this day divided between Paul Nádasdy and Homonnay.'[33]

The idea of a continuing dispute over land, with George Drugeth agitating for more than his share, is supported by the fact that on 31 July 1614 Elisabeth herself made a declaration to two priestly scribes, Imre Egry (or Egery) and Andrew Kanpelich (or Kerpelich), members of the Esztergom Chapter in Trnava, who travelled to Čachtice castle to take down her instructions, which the literature calls her second will.[34] This short text was not an alternative will in either format or content, nor was it in the usual form of a codicil. In this declaration she says that when she was arrested there was an agreement that she should give her estates around the eastern Keresztúr into the use of George Homonnay Drugeth, so that during her imprisonment he could support his mother-in-law with the income. (This contradicts the terms written down in the earlier will, which may even cast doubt on the latter's authenticity; perhaps it was meant only to be bruited, or alternatively was actually composed by the family and Thurzó and not by Elisabeth, unless under duress.) The later declaration seeks to make clear that Homonnay's wife, Elisabeth's second daughter Kate, had no greater rights to the future ownership of that estate than the other two inheritors.

The declaration to the two priests is convincing proof that Elisabeth was still in possession of her faculties, and suggests that her final recorded act was to exercise her remaining authority to dispose of her estate as she saw fit. The timing of her move may have been dictated by the wishes of the family, but in the light of what followed it is likely that the Lady was ailing and preparing for her own death as best she could. Unfortunately her two visitors, the only ones on record, limited themselves to the task at hand and left no description of the circumstances in which they found the prisoner. The priests did not speak of any obstacles in communicating with her, and it seems certain that, although confined and helpless, she was not literally walled up as writers have liked to suggest. By the seventeenth century the mediaeval practice of immuring had all but disappeared; it had been a barbaric method of punishing recalcitrant brides in the dark ages, and King Mátyás Corvinus was said to have walled up the Archbishop of Kalocsa, Peter Vardá, in a tiny recess in Árva castle in revenge for a treaty he had drafted which granted too many concessions to the Turkish enemy.

Elisabeth had been placed outside the bounds of society and there is, not surprisingly, no record of any family visits, no accounts in the family archives to indicate who cooked for her and what she ate, no word at all of how she passed her time in the secluded fortress, looking out over the rivers and the forests. In the warm months the deserted castle must have looked imposing on its peak as the sun caught its painted walls, but in the winter the place would have been cheerless and uncomfortable behind the metre-and-a-half of stone, in the part-furnished rooms which had been designed to hold the roughest of soldiers under siege and not to act as living quarters for a gentlewoman. Deprived of her healers, her witches and her apothecaries, with no musicians to entertain her, the Countess would have heard only the sounds of the owls and ravens and the barking of guard dogs and the coughing of foxes interrupting the deep quiet below her. Although educated, she was a woman of decision rather than contemplation, and it seems unlikely that she committed her thoughts and reminiscences to paper. If she did, they are lost; the only document recovered by her son, and immediately handed to his mentor, her enemy Megyery, was her copy of the will, carefully preserved in her little box.[35]

Three and a half years after the start of her confinement, Elisabeth Báthory approached her guards and held out her hands to them. 'See my hands, how cold they are,' she said. It was a summer evening, but it must have been chill inside the thick stone walls. 'It is nothing, my Lady,' the guards assured her. 'Will you not now retire for the night?'

The next morning, 25 August 1614, hearing no movement, the guards entered her chamber and found her lying on the floor with her feet supported by a pillow. She was dead. As Stanislas Thurzó wrote to his uncle the Palatine, 'She left this world suddenly . . . there is as yet no news of the funeral arrangements.'[36]

The diary written in Latin kept by Thurzó's secretary George

Závodský was published in the eighteenth century by the antiquarian Mátyás Bél in his *Notitia Regni Hungaria*. Závodský recorded, 'the surviving widow of Francis Nádasdy, who some years before had been thrust away into perpetual imprisonment on account of her great, unprecedented and most cruel crimes, in that same place Čachtice died pitifully during night-time . . .'[37] He confirmed the date as 21 August and the year as 1614, as did the later *Chronicles of Csejthe*, which specified the time of death as two in the morning, but another anonymous account collected by the Jesuit István Kaprinai has the date as 16 August 1616 – surely a mistake – and reads in translation, 'the widowed consort of Francis Nádasdy, the servant of His Royal Majesty, died in captivity in Čachtice – a sudden passing without light and without crucifix'.[38] Stories circulating long afterwards claimed that she had been singing and praying during the small hours, others that she had starved and neglected herself. The only certainty is that Elisabeth had died of unknown causes at the age of fifty-four.

Elisabeth was not buried until November, exactly three months after her death. In those days, the bodies of nobles were preserved in underground grottoes on blocks of ice covered with sacking until the formal funeral arrangements had been completed. If she had been buried as a common criminal, there would have been only the shortest delay. As the patron of the local Protestant church, its benefactor and the owner of the land on which it stood, the Countess had every right to be interred there and, according to the official village chronicles composed a century later, she was. There is a story that the local people were so outraged by her crimes that they petitioned to have her body removed, and that it was taken under cover of darkness either to the family vault at Nyirbátor or north into Poland. On 7 July 1938 the crypt of the parish church at Čachtice was opened, but there was no sign of the tomb of the Blood Countess. A proper excavation remains to be done. In 1995 some tentative work began on uncovering the Báthory family tombs at Nyirbátor, but no trace of Elisabeth has yet been found. There are no lapidary inscriptions to meditate upon, but a paper epitaph was appended by Závodský to his diary entry. It is not one that would have appeased the Countess: 'Few kings descend to Ceres' son-in-law [Pluto, lord of the underworld] without slaughter and bloodshed, and few tyrants suffer a dry [bloodless] death'.

Count Nicholas Zrínyi's wife Lady Anna Nádasdy died on 13 August 1615, almost exactly one year after her mother. The cause of death was not recorded and there were no children of the marriage. Kate, who married George Homonnay Drugeth, gave birth to a daughter, who was named Elisabeth after her grandmother and grew up to marry László Révay, the scion of another noble family of Upper Hungary. The sons-in-law took up their respective inherited posts in the administration of the Kingdom, and led uncontroversial, unheroic lives: Drugeth failed to win power in Transylvania and Zrínyi failed to live up to his revered grandfather's reputation. Elisabeth's son Paul Nádasdy also married into the Révay family. His wife Judith gave birth to three sons, one of whom, Francis Nádasdy II, the last male of that line, was executed in 1671 for plotting against the Empire.

From Elisabeth's death in 1614 there followed an inexplicable silence lasting more than a century. No letters survive in which her fellow-aristocrats comment upon her tragedy; no songs, poems or broadsheets celebrated her notoriety; and stranger still, there is no recorded mention of her by the zealots of the Counter-Reformation, who usually seized any opportunity to exploit the real or imagined sins of the Protestant nobility.[39]

CHAPTER NINE

Posthumous Verdicts

Better than crypts and candles were my friendships,
Better than leaf and parchment was my grief.

D. M. Thomas, *Elegy for Isabelle le Despenser*

The Báthory case in the earliest chronicles ~ historians' conclusions ~
concealed agendas ~ a new consensus and some first conclusions ~
inside the court in a secret womens' world ~ punishments, cruelties
and lawlessness ~ the early Modern world picture ~ therapy, torture
and madness ~ a peculiar Hungarian heritage ~ monsters in our
collective memory

In Tewkesbury Abbey in England is preserved a lock of the red-brown
hair of Isabelle 'le Despenser', Countess of Warwick, dated 1429.
Elisabeth Báthory's biographer, frustrated by the paucity of material
remaining from her lifetime, longs for such a keepsake: something
that touched her, something that she touched. Somewhere there are
perhaps a few hanks of her hair still sticking to a dusty skull, a few scraps
of taffeta and cambric, or a shred of a winding-sheet – but they are lost.
There is no talisman for us to grasp, and, more prosaically, almost no

documentary evidence exists to illuminate the circumstances of her birth and her childhood, and even the period of the Lady's married life with Hungary's pre-eminent soldier and war-hero has little more than the handful of letters quoted here to show for it. The only extensive documentation referring to Elisabeth – and that itself is incomplete – consists of the papers of investigation into her alleged crimes, and is in no way an objective assessment: the very nature of inquisitorial justice and the fact that Elisabeth's judges were involved, whether they were all aware of it or not, in a conspiracy against her means that all that we can retrieve from the archives is partial, mediated and finally flawed and inconclusive.

In tracking the reports of Elisabeth Báthory's crimes, her persecution and her imprisonment through the earlier histories, the modern investigator searches in vain for anything other than the most fleeting reference to the case by her own contemporaries. Apart from the reports of Elisabeth's death and the epitaphs already quoted, the only other mention of the affair that has been cited is a passage in a letter from Miklós Istvánffy, the noble scholar and tutor to the Thurzó family, to Countess Pálffy in which he dismissed the confessions of Elisabeth's servants as 'horrible blabbering' or 'horrible gossip' (the Hungarian word used has both senses). Very unfortunately, because it would represent a unique dissenting voice from Elisabeth's time, the letter's whereabouts are unknown.[1]

The curiosity which was awakened in Hungary's neighbours once the Turks had been expelled coincided with the first stirrings of ethnography, anthropology and psychology as intellectual distractions for the cultivated European. These highminded interests were inseparable from a desire to know the darker secrets of an underground heritage that the Enlightenment was confronting. Learned guidebooks and the works of the Brothers Grimm rubbed up against one another in the traveller's baggage, and in their pages the lost tale of the murdering Countess appeared in print for the first time.

At first there was very little reading matter for the curious outsider to consult and the one or two texts produced before the eighteenth century perforce became the standard sources. The Bratislava Constable George Wernher's 1549 description in Latin of Hungary's thermal baths, *Hypomnemation*, was published in Basle and later in Vienna, Brussels and Zurich, sold widely and was reprinted every few years; works in French, Italian and English copied parts of it almost word for word. It was not until 1744 that the first general guide to Hungary's topography and history appeared: *Ungaria Suis cum Regibus Compendio Data* ('A Short Description of Hungary together with its Kings'), composed in Latin in 1729 by the Jesuit priest László Túróczi, provided a comprehensive survey of the Kingdom, a sort of Baedeker for educated foreign visitors or curious armchair explorers.[2]

Hidden among the geographical descriptions, historical anecdotes and sometimes tedious homilies couched in baroque rhetoric, there were a dozen pages of sensational narrative that chimed perfectly with the early stirrings of a gothic sensibility and its taste for horror.

> And I hesitate to bring the horrible crime to light, for I hardly believe that anyone will credit what I have uncovered, not only because it bloodily besmirches and brings disgrace upon the princely Báthorys who are deserving of the best from the Christians of this country, but because, moreover, the barbarity of it is so enormous, it will be a cause of eternal horror.

This was the first report of the crimes and incarceration of Elisabeth Báthory to appear since the papers of the case had been folded in parchment, tied with string and ribbon and filed away in the archives of the Thurzó family at Bytča and the Erdődy family at Galgóc 112 years before. The essence of Túróczi's story was borrowed, adapted and reprinted in the dozens of guides and anthologies which appeared in central Europe in the following decades. Until the last years of the nineteenth century, no scholar substantially expanded on, or thought to question seriously, the Jesuit father's version of the events surrounding Elisabeth, in which the blood-bathing story is presented for the first time in print.

> Elisabeth, washed in that deadly bath, appeared to herself yet more beautiful, under no other influence, no one will doubt, than diabolic mockery. This first crime, born of her wilfulness, rendered her more courageous and thus thereafter many others were committed. The wicked deeds went on year after year and, you will be astonished to learn, even after the death of her husband, the widow, now advancing in years, was responsible for a sacrilegious shedding of blood.

★   ★   ★

In 1794 Michael Wagner cited the Hungarian 'Countess B.' among his case studies in psychopathology in one of the earliest works in the field (which he referred to as 'philosophical anthropology'). His brief account of her actions was entitled 'The Craving for Beauty, a Source of Inhuman Cruelty'.[3] In 1812 the aristocratic polyglot Baron Mednyánszky wrote his own account of Elisabeth's case which appeared under the title 'Eine Wahre Geschichte' ('A True Story') in the journal *Hesperus, ein Nationalblatt für Gebildete Leser* ('a national paper for the cultured reader'), published in Prague. The story titillated the German-speaking readership and in 1817 Mednyánszky translated the transcripts of the servants' trial from Hungarian and printed them in the same periodical. In the meantime, in a fragment entitled '*Nach Einem Wiener Fliegende Blatt*' (a play on words which can mean 'a Flying Leaf', 'a Handbill' or 'a Rumour on the Wind . . . from Vienna'), the Brothers Grimm referred to a seventeenth-century folktale telling of an unnamed Hungarian lady who murdered eight to twelve maidens. It was not until 1839 that the papers of the investigation were published for Hungarian readers by György Gyurikovics, in an inaccurate and badly edited version, in the journal *Tudományos Gyüitemény*. Earlier in the year Gyurikovics had published a list of the existing sources referring to Countess Báthory and prefaced the transcripts with his own brief summary of the case: 'Elisabeth Báthory wished to preserve her youth, therefore she washed her face in the warm blood of her maids.'[4] He gave the date of her death correctly, but wrote, without offering corroboration, that she may have died of starvation.

In the meantime Alajos Mednyánszky had produced his own guide to the geography and history of Upper Hungary in German, *Malerische Reise auf dem Waagflusse* ('A Picturesque Journey on the River Váh') published in Pest in 1824, followed by *Erzählungen, Sagen und Legenden aus Ungarns Vorzeit* ('Stories, Fables and Legends from Hungary's Remote Past') in 1829, from which the Englishman Paget learned of the legends of Čachtice. A more famous work, *Die Geschichte der Ungern und Ihrer Landsassen* ('The History of Hungary and its Yeomen') by the eminent traveller and scholar Ignác Aurel Fessler, appeared in the same year and asserted that Lady Báthory washed in human blood daily and that her sinister passion had caused the death of 600 noble maidens. The girls were kept in readiness in the Čachtice cellars and bled one by one to provide the contents of their mistress's baths, after which, wrote Fessler, their drained bodies were interred in the same vaults. Parents and relations of the unfortunate girls were informed that they had succumbed to illness.

These were the principal writings by means of which the reputation of the Blood Countess was spread beyond the borders of her homeland. In all there were, between Father Túróczi's 'Tragica Historia' in his compendium of 1729 and Jozef Kočiš' *Alžbeta Bathoriová a Palatín Thurzo* which appeared in Slovakia in 1981, 136 publications which were either entirely dedicated to Elisabeth Báthory or which touched upon her story. Most were in the German language, the lingua franca of middle Europe, or in Hungarian; a handful appeared in Slovak or French. Among the many authors' names the only one apart from that of the Grimms which resonates for us today is Leopold von Sacher-Masoch, who referred to Elisabeth in several of his novellas and made her the basis of his short story, 'Eternal Youth', published in 1874. (His casting of Báthory as a dominatrix was emulated by more than one anonymous pornographer who incarnated her as an exultant Venus-in-Furs in illustrations from the 1930s and 1940s: not surprisingly, she made an appearance in Berlin during the Weimar Republic as one of the 'Titans of the Erotic'.)[5]

For most of the nineteenth and twentieth centuries the only authentic documents available to investigators were the incomplete testimonies of the witnesses at the inquiries, the confessions of Elisabeth's servants and a couple of letters from the King to the Palatine, together with the diary of Thurzó's secretary, George Závodský, and the reconstructed *Chronicles of Csejthe*. (Writings purporting to be missing trial documents were published in several Hungarian periodicals in the mid-nineteenth century, but when they were examined carefully glaring anachronisms in the language revealed them as forgeries.) With only these as their raw material, it is not surprising that there is a great consistency in most of the Báthory literature, even down to the repetition of certain turns of phrase which echo back and forth. Unable to adduce new evidence, the various writers could only offer by way of originality their opinions and their assumptions, but it is possible to detect certain changes of theme as the last century unfolded. Some works were more influential than others. It was von Elsberg who, inspired by his own knowledge of the Imperial armies, introduced the notion of a military culture in the Nádasdy household, picturing Elisabeth trying to match her Black Bey's victories by triumphing over her imagined enemies within the walls of her houses. He also introduced the element of doubt about Elisabeth's sanity, which came to replace the picture of a simple paragon of evil and vanity in search of an elixir of beauty.[6]

At the very end of the nineteenth century the eminent Hungarian historian Dezső Rexa, writing under the *nom de plume* of 'Hővér' ('Hotspur'), produced a short and elegantly written monograph which portrays Elisabeth as afflicted and not merely possessed.[7] But the veracity of the earliest accounts is still not questioned: 'Bathing in blood is not unknown in legend. Blood in ancient times was thought to be the very substance of life, and was used – according to Pliny – as a miraculous medicine. Lucrezia Borgia bathed in blood as well as our own Elisabeth.' With attention to abnormal mental states came an interest in the sexual nature of violence: 'Today it is clear that Elisabeth Báthory was neurotic and perverted. She suffered from the same illness that made insane the ill-famed Marquis de Sade, and after him this illness is called Sadism . . .' In his later life of Elisabeth, Rexa added: 'If the explorers of the human mind had known of her illness earlier, Sadism would be called Bathoryism now.'[8]

The idea of mental illness was taken up by later writers. The respected historian Kálmán Benda in a work from 1974 claimed that there was a hereditary taint, possibly syphilitic in origin, in the princely Somlyói branch of the family, which Elisabeth's mother Anna enabled to cross into the Ecsedy line,[9] and in 1978 Gabrielle Raskó considered Elisabeth's pathological behaviour (her guilt was assumed) from a criminologist's point of view, concluding that there were some indications of early 'sexual damage'.[10]

In the late 1970s there was a postscript to Dezső Rexa's 1896 monograph and the expanded life of Elisabeth which he published in 1908: the elderly historian visited a magazine editor in Budapest and announced that he wished to write an article on the case that would reveal startling new evidence. He had discovered, he said, that the allegations of murder and torture were a pretext by which a secret group consisting of influential aristocrats and members of the Lady's own family intended to dispossess her. Rexa, who was ninety-two years old, said no more on that occasion and died before he could complete the article.[11] It may be that he had learned of the correspondence which had been discovered at around the same time by the archivist Dr Jozef Kočiš among the tons of unsorted papers in the county archives, stored since 1925 at Bytča castle, which showed that Elisabeth's son-in-law, Count Zrínyi, and son, Paul Nádasdy, were privy to the Palatine's plans well in advance of the arrest. It was not until Dr Kočiš' slim book appeared in 1981 and became the standard work on the subject in the Slovak language that it began to seem that there might be grounds for absolving Elisabeth altogether from the accusations of cruelty and murder; that she might have been the victim of a conspiracy whose real purpose was not to punish a mass-murderess, but to achieve some less exalted objective. This was not, however, the view that Jozef Kočiš took then or takes now. His verdict is that Elisabeth was spared by the Palatine in defiance not only of the King, but of juridical and natural justice: 'it is obvious that the Palatine's motive was to protect the prestige of the feudal elite and at all costs to cover up her illegal acts . . . beside Báthory before the tribunal of history, we must also place the Palatine, Thurzó'. As regards Elisabeth's motives: 'The Báthory case from the medical point of view is a sadism on the sexual–pathological basis with the preservation of rational (intellectual) capabilities.'[12] Privately Kočiš suspects that the real tally of girls tormented and murdered by Elisabeth must be much higher than 650, given that evidence recorded in personal testimonies was collected only in certain parts of the country. Dr Kočiš argues vehemently that to doubt the veracity of the witnesses and the damning words of Ficzkó, Dorkó, Helena and Benecká is to dishonour the memory of the slaughtered innocents.

Writers have ground more than one axe before contending with the Blood Countess, and a former prime minister of Hungary, the late Dr József Antall, combined two contentious themes, the sexual and the religious, in a quasi-scientific analysis written with a fellow-historian of medicine, Károly Kapronczay, which appeared in 1973. The essay begins from the stated assumption that Elisabeth was 'schizophrenic and insane [sic]' and cites the interrogation statements, before concluding that 'eroticism played an important part in her mental life . . . prodding and scorching naked bodies is a sign of sexual perversity coupled with sadism. We may also take into account the possibility of an epileptoid manic state which occurred on a hysterical basis . . . there is no evidence of homosexual aberration . . .'[13] Antall was a devout Catholic and he and his co-writer accused the Countess of religious fanaticism, which they suggested might be further evidence of a hysterical personality.

Of those contemporary historians who have written on Elisabeth it was László Nagy (a military historian who published a life of Francis Nádasdy and a short history of the controversial members of the Báthory line) who most trenchantly questioned the assumptions made by his fellow 'experts'. Nagy suspected that Elisabeth had sided with Prince Gábor Báthory, who was trying to gain territory in Habsburg Hungary, an act of high treason on her part which would normally have been punished by beheading and confiscation, shaming and impoverishing her heirs, too; this would provide a rationale for the investigations and the trial-without-a-trial. He also reminded readers that at the end of the sixteenth century the right of life and death over serfs was still enjoyed by individuals of Elisabeth's rank and that the country was on a war footing during much of her lifetime; this could account for the instances of cruelty. Nagy admitted that his researches had not enabled him to settle once and for all the question of Elisabeth's personal innocence or guilt. In 1985 he summed up his position as follows:

> I posed two questions: one, was it possible for Elisabeth Báthory to have done all those things of which she had been accused? To this I answered yes, because the age in which she lived was a very brutal one. It was not impossible for a female aristocrat, especially when menopausal [!], to punish some of her maids . . .

Nagy secondly asked himself whether there was any reliable evidence to substantiate such charges and whether the official proceedings which were carried out were lawful: 'To this second question I had to answer, no.'[14]

Another Hungarian authority on the case is Professor Katalin Péter, a believer in Elisabeth's guilt who is routinely consulted by writers and film-makers on the subject. Katalin Péter considers that the affair illustrates the unfettered nature of feudal power and the lack of protection for the lower-ranking members of society. She sees the avoidance of dishonour as the key to Thurzó's prosecution of the Widow Nádasdy rather than political machinations, and Elisabeth's 'diseased sexuality' as the trigger for the systematic murder of the girls.[15] Professor Péter believes that Elisabeth's strict Calvinist upbringing instilled in her the idea that her ungovernable desires were wrong, and as a result 'her sickness – her nymphomania [sic] – overcame her'. At the same time she subscribes to the view of this Báthory as a *rara avis*, a freak.

There is no doubting the scholarly credentials of Nagy, Kočiš and Péter, and there are no signs of crude prejudice intruding into their work. But it is worth noting that they were all three writing during the last years of communist regimes – relatively liberal in Hungary, illiberal in Slovakia – under which opportunities for research and publication were limited and orthodoxies (such as the ritual excoriating of feudalism) had to be observed, and within which complex issues of nationalism were bubbling up from deeper strata. Ideologies and personal slants were not confined to scholars under socialism: in 1990 the German Michael Farin published a comprehensive collection of source material on the Báthory case entitled *Heroine des Grauens* (roughly, 'Horror-Heroine'). His work was dedicated to the surrealist 1960s experimental rock musician Captain Beefheart, and in his own commentary took for granted the guilt of the Countess.[16]

There are hints of complex motives behind the most recent treatment of the case, a work which examines in forensic detail the statements gathered during the investigation and extends its analysis to the social networks operating in and around the Nádasdy and Thurzó courts, the political changes taking place as the case progressed and the legal system which obtained in the Hungary of the seventeenth century. The author of the work, which was undertaken as a thesis, is Dr Irma Szádeczky-Kardoss, the former judge and legal adviser to the Hungarian government, now a practising solicitor. Her title is *Báthory Erzsébet – Igazsága* (the last word can be translated as 'the Truth' or 'Justice'), and is subtitled, 'The Signs of a Frame-up'. Its stance is confirmed on the first page: 'I dedicate this book to all who bear the stamp of false accusation, injustice, harassment and indignity on their destiny, their minds and their memories.'[17]

Szádeczky-Kardoss, a descendant of Gáspar Kardoss, the Bytča notary who was one of the prosecutors at the trial of Elisabeth Báthory's servants, uses her knowledge of law and experience of actual trials to demonstrate the illegality of the sentence passed upon Elisabeth by George Thurzó, and to refute the testimonies lodged against the Countess by identifying inconsistencies, possible collusion and hidden motives on the part of the witnesses and their masters. Drawing on research into healing practices by Ágnes R. Várkonyi, an authority on the early modern era in Hungary, she also demonstrates elegantly and at length how each of the tortures described in the case papers mirrors a method of healing that was in use at the time: even the more outlandish procedures – rolling in stinging nettles, smearing with honey, poking the genitals with metal rods, chaining the victims, can be rationalised in this way. Some dissenting historians have criticised

Matthias II, King of
Hungary and Holy
Roman Emperor
(1557–1619)

The Old Town Hall in Bratislava, seat of the Hungarian Diet in the early 17th century

The English cartographer John Speed's map of Hungary in the 17th century

The castle at Beckov in the 19th century

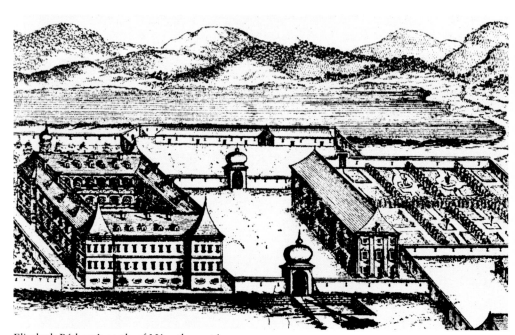

Elisabeth Báthory's castle of Németkeresztúr

Paul Nádasdy's letter pleading for the life of his mother, addressed to the
Palatine Thurzó on 23 February 1611

The Esterházy castle
of Forchtenstein
where Elisabeth was
reputed to have
tortured her victims

The castle of Devín overlooking the Danube, inherited by the Báthorys in the 17th century

Delphine Seyrig playing Elisabeth Báthory in *Le Rouge aux Lèvres*, 1971

An imaginary portrait (detail) of Countess Báthory in later life accompanied by her children, by the Dutch artist Erzsébet Baerveldt (1996)

Čachtice castle in the early 17th century (a 19th-century reconstruction)

Dr Szádeczky-Kardoss for applying modern standards of proof to a pre-modern society and others, including Jožef Kočiš, have rejected the emphasis on medical practices, pointing out that there were no explicit references to healing by witnesses. But the general thrust of her argument – that Elisabeth Báthory was unjustly condemned and possibly quite innocent – has caused many in Hungary and some in Slovakia to revise their opinions.

A younger generation of historians in Budapest and Bratislava are anxious to avoid what they see as the distractions of psychosexual theories and underlying nationalist issues which have re-surfaced to cloud the judgement of writers and to look instead for a more objective assessment. Discussing the case with them points up the beginning of a consensus view based on the facts now uncovered set against a greater understanding of the way in which early modern societies worked.[18]

All accept that the letters discovered at Bytča show an agreement between the Zrínyis and the Nádasdys (in the person of the tutor Megyery) to avoid a Habsburg-style show trial, to save the estates (vast, strategically placed and potentially providing the Habsburgs with a crippling power-base in the middle of West and Upper Hungary) and thus protect the family inheritance. That George Homonnay Drugeth was a party to this is implied by his meetings with Thurzó in 1610 and by his later actions. The plan that was formulated would not necessarily have advantaged George Thurzó personally (although at different stages of the investigation he probably had hopes of intervening to enrich himself – perhaps it was the Čachtice estate that he coveted above all), but would have safeguarded the interests of the great families of Hungary and helped to ensure their loyalty to his masters.

Comparisons suggest that Elisabeth Báthory was not treated so harshly compared to other victims of the Habsburgs, who had to forfeit their estates and flee for their lives, but this is to underestimate the overwhelming effect of the weight of shame on a personality like hers, not to mention the physical privations of captivity. Before her arrest, Elisabeth was in any case in a very precarious position. As a rich widow she was permanently vulnerable and the letters printed for the first time in this work make it clear that she had been playing an active role in family politics, and was in close contact with her nephew in the period just prior to her arrest. We can be fairly certain, although there is only circumstantial evidence for it, that Elisabeth was for a time the focus of the 'Transylvanian party' in Western and Upper Hungary, and that she was secretly funding the ambitions of the Habsburgs' arch-enemy and the personal enemy of the Palatine, her nephew Gábor Báthory. Sooner or later the threat posed by the Prince would have prompted action against her. By the standards of the time it was laudable to prevent a show trial and protect the inheritance for those who had more claim to it than an obstinate elderly woman: the children of the most illustrious Hungarian families, Nádasdy, Zrínyi and Drugeth.

The two alternatives to a private resolution of Elisabeth's case were each in its way unthinkable: arraigning Countess Báthory before the tabular court at Bratislava would both expose Thurzó to counter-accusations from her and her fellow-aristocrats (and the mediaeval *lex talionis* – like for like – could still be invoked) and give the King and his advisers a chance to commandeer the proceedings, as they had done in the case of Illésházy. Bringing Elisabeth before the county court would allow her to have her say and enable her to mobilise supporters and suborn witnesses, perhaps buy off her accusers.

Just as in the show trials mounted by totalitarian governments this century,[19] the sheer weight of allegation and incidental detail that was amassed, even if much of it is inconsistent, is very persuasive, but this was a prosecution without a defence. No counter-argument was or could have been expressed unless the Countess herself was put on trial. Had she eventually been allowed to speak and had she condescended to do so, she would have been an articulate and forceful witness in her own defence, even though she had been deprived of her most powerful potential supporters, her senior servants.

Elisabeth was never, as far as we can determine, given the chance simply to reply to the central accusation, that of the murder of servant girls. In Ponikenus' letter she is described as railing against her enemies, not denying their allegations; the letters from her relatives contain not one exculpatory plea by her or on her behalf. But to imagine Elisabeth anxiously hoping for a chance to testify would be a modern misconception; taking the stand would have been demeaning, an insult to her name. She had never in her life been required to explain herself. As the petitions of her subjects in Vas county show, she was used to sitting in judgement on others. On her own estates her right to punish those who served her as she saw fit was unquestioned, and it seems that the *lex scutari* – the right of the sword, known to the Magyars as *pallos jog* – was still enforceable: Pastor Ponikenus had written that she threatened to have her footman beheaded if he failed to bring her Majorosné's magic prayer.

Just as it would be anachronistic to imagine Elisabeth in the position of a defendant in a modern criminal process, students of seventeenth-century techniques of persuasion stress that it would be naive to blame George Thurzó for fabricating evidence against her. Of course Thurzó had to make propaganda to render the case believable, but had he not done so he could not have removed it from the hands of the court and the Habsburg state. By creating a personal scandal with sexual overtones, he pre-empted a trial for treason or political subversion, which would have been much more dangerous. In this sense his actions were quite consistent with the skilful use of black propaganda, and manipulation of opinion which was practised in the seventeenth century. Why did Thurzó choose those particular crimes? (He carefully hinted at witchcraft in case this should be needed at a later stage; also witch-trials provided a useful precedent for local, peremptory judgements.) Why were mass-murder and torture the preferred crimes? To ensure that the state would not intervene, and to cover up the illegality and the clumsy, personalised execution of the investigation, the prosecutors needed an offence that could whip up a temporary public hysteria – particularly among those whose views counted for something, the lower nobility and the townspeople. Public outrage at personal crimes precluded the Habsburgs from mounting a political trial. The exposé of the crimes also pandered to the sado-erotic fantasies then current and to contemporary notions of defiled purity, lives cut off before motherhood, and so on. Infanticide was not an option in the case of a middle-aged woman, nor was promiscuity, particularly given that Elisabeth had not married her clerk and was not living with a commoner (but Ficzkó's story of Ironhead Steve was placed on file just in case – and of course might have been true). And if one wanted to blow up minor but persistent cruelty into atrocity, where would one look for models? The visualisations of suffering by Brueghel and Bosch, inflammatory religious pamphlets, the practices of war, backroom surgery, strange healing practices, witchcraft – and, perhaps, the rumours of insanity and murder which were emanating from other courts as well as her own.[20]

The Palatine and his henchmen did not need to base their case upon fantasy, for the head women in the Widow Nádasdy's household were indeed extremely cruel, and it was common knowledge that the local priests had complained of this in the past. This provided the idea for a

213

campaign of propaganda against Elisabeth Báthory, in which the priests themselves, the link between the lords and the populace, could be used to manipulate opinion. Everyone knew that these women were ill-treating the girls in the castle, but accepted it as this was the only hope of the girls bettering themselves. As for their mistress's guilt or innocence, testimony by Elisabeth's confidantes and by other witnesses who were excluded from her private quarters is often ambiguous on the question whether it was the Lady's own hand that slapped or maimed, or whether the atrocities were carried out on her behalf. We must remember that if the real purpose of the hearings was a smear-campaign and not the death penalty, it was not necessary to prove direct guilt, but for anyone who is searching for the truth this question becomes absolutely crucial, once it is accepted that there is any substance at all in the accusations.

There was a tacit agreement in the Báthory case, not only among those intimately involved, but among the rest of the senior Hungarian aristocracy. There was no outcry, a fact which can again be characterised as a typically eastern European scenario: everyone knows that the real decisions are made behind the scenes; everyone knows the unwritten rules of the game. (The playing of a complex game with unwritten rules was an inherent part of the post-Renaissance scene and is reminiscent of the behaviour of the secretive socialist regimes of the 1940s and 1950s.) No one necessarily believed in the accusations of witchcraft, or cared whether the allegations of cruelty were true. Everyone realised that it was an extremely clever manoeuvre to isolate and neutralise Elisabeth Báthory while keeping the affair out of the grasp of the Habsburgs, who would have granted her lands to their own German- or Czech-speaking nobles. King Matthias' letters reveal that he did not want to risk a confrontation with the Hungarian Palatine on this issue; he just wanted to show that he, too, was quite aware of the stratagems that his opponent was using.

Regarding the regime within Elisabeth Bathory's court, there is a clear parallel with military colleges, orphanages and other closed, regimented institutions where the relatively powerless are exposed to the whims of the all-powerful. In such environments, domestic spite can shade into perversity, and regulations be too earnestly enforced into institutionalised sadism. It is not even necessary to direct our minds back to the Dickensian clichés of the nineteenth century to find examples of these institutional purgatories: during the preparation of this book there have been in Britain revelations of cruelty and neglect in children's homes, rest-homes for the elderly, psychiatric wards.

The regime of punishment imposed by the old women who surrounded the Countess – assisted when brute force or menial labour was necessary by the factotum, Ficzkó – must have been frighteningly harsh, even by the standards of the time. Just as medical techniques, whether carried out in an army field hospital or in a castle chamber, were hard to distinguish from torture, so the punishment of servants, sometimes public and ritualised, sometimes just the spontaneous exercise of power or spite, looks to modern eyes no different from sadism. It seems likely that abuse of servants was much more widespread than the records show and that it was seen as acceptable within the norms of cruelty of the age, not only in Hungary, but anywhere that the ruling elite enjoyed absolute power in their own domains. Whether or not such cruelty was systematic and tinged with sexual perversity would depend in a neurotic age upon the neuroses suffered by the lady or lord (or steward or governess) in question.[21]

But it would be ingenuous to see this as a feature of the seventeenth century, or exclusive to Hungary. Wherever total power is exercised within an institution, particularly by individuals who command no authority outside it, that power is abused, whether the setting is a prison, a school, a family home. Leading figures of that age and later ages advocated physical punishment: Cardinal Peter Pázmány, the most influential Jesuit propagandist of the Counter-Reformation in Hungary, wrote, 'beat your children, for it is useful so to do . . .';[22] George Thurzó mentioned in a letter to his wife that 'I beat that miscreant until the stick broke in my hands . . .'[23] Popular public entertainments of the period included bear-baiting, dog and cock fights, blind beggars set to clubbing pigs to death, and the staging of fights between village idiots or madmen. In British upper-class households and in Viennese, to name only two instances, junior servants and children were routinely beaten until the last years of the nineteenth century.

Nor is the role of women in physical atrocities unusual; the Brazilian Gilberto Freyre wrote in the 1930s of the wives of wealthy Portuguese estate owners in that country who, to avenge the ravages of age which they detected on their own bodies, tortured and blinded their beautiful young African female slaves.[24] While this book was in preparation the widespread abuse of Filipina maidservants by wealthy Gulf Arab families became an international *cause célèbre*, the wives of the households in question regularly joining in or instigating the cruelties. The parallels with feudal Hungary in terms of power, status, ethnicity do not need to be elaborated.

The women's cruelty to one another is only a reflection, a fairly pale reflection, of the tide of mayhem which the men saw ebbing and flowing outside the manor-house walls, but the men, hardened to all sorts of indignities and to the quick, casual brutalities they inflict on each other, will not conceive of physical violence by woman upon woman. Death was palatable when part of male sport, when dressed up with plumes and swagger, strutting bravado or a rapid lunge, but not when it accompanied the refined cruelty and day-by-day suffering of the secret women's world of the inner household.

By all accounts, including her own in letters and in her last testament, Countess Báthory loved her children, and fiercely protected and cherished them, fulfilling her motherly responsibilities absolutely according to custom, even without the support of her lord. It seems she could love other children, not of her blood – one witness told how she doted on a thirteen-year-old orphan girl who soon sickened and died. But the low-born were of no account. To a Báthory, as we know from the swathe her nephew Gábor cut through the ladies of his principality, even the highest-born were just playthings. From George Thurzó's own example we learn that the greater nobility could treat the lesser nobility with oppressive contempt. As for the commoners, they were literally worth less than their masters' livestock; at the end of the sixteenth century the doctor Ferenc Pápai Párisz lamented the lot of those citizens 'living in the countryside where a sick animal gets medical aid sooner than a sick man'.[25] It is quite conceivable that, just as Count Thurzó was capable of doting on his young wife, his daughters and his infant son, and executing his neighbours' servants without trial (and, come to that, of sacrificing Elisabeth's attendants without a qualm), so Elisabeth could have loved her husband faithfully and cared tenderly for her children, and yet beaten and pricked and burned and doused her maidservants with freezing water.

In the final analysis, who really suffered? The maids, the accomplices? At that time, in a Renaissance culture, their lives would be considered of no significance. Even the well-born and powerful could be poisoned with relative impunity for material gain, stabbed in a brawl. Peasants could be hanged for theft, burghers for fraud, mothers for infanticide, old women for sorcery. The inferiority of the poor was immovably enshrined in the early modern scheme of things. The various visual metaphors which underpinned the late-sixteenth- and early-seventeenth-century imagination – the ladder, the chain, the universe of concentric spheres – all took for granted the existence of an immutable hierarchy of being, in which the social order within human society was a stratification ordained by God. The right of the aristocrat to his or her pre-eminence normally went as unquestioned as the divine right of kings and emperors to rule: even the new modes of thought such as egalitarian Calvinism or Lutheranism, or social upheavals such as Dózsa's rebellion, failed to dent these certainties in the minds of the mass of people. If the serfs of Hungary could not think of bettering themselves, they could at least gaze on the noblewoman's castle and indulge their imaginations to their limits, speculating on the sinful excesses being committed behind its walls.

What Elisabeth herself saw, when she retired to her private chamber and pondered on her dependencies, may once have been a perfect world in miniature, but by the time she was in her late forties might well have been a messy microcosm, in her possession but only barely under her control. Threatened from the outside by covetous neighbours, political schemers, insolent Germans and marauding bandits and from within by ineptitude and feuding, the several communities she ruled over, with their population of stewards, soldiers, bookkeepers, domestics and serfs, must have at times come close to calamity. Even allowing that Elisabeth's wealth was enormous and her authority unchallenged, when epidemics struck, when incompetence went too far and could not be covered up, and when the feuds which erupted in the cloistered atmosphere threatened to get out of hand, the mistress of the house must have felt a sense of helplessness and panic. Whenever we consider institutions, especially those which are alien to us, belonging to other societies in other times, we tend to see them as they were intended to be, in working order. Just like their modern counterparts – the children's home, the hospital ward, the private academy for young ladies – it is quite likely that Elisabeth's health service and her system of schooling did *not* work. For one thing, Death kept on intruding.

The confessions of the inner circle of servants paint a convincing picture of mounting chaos, climaxing in the macabre farce in which Elisabeth and her daughter are left without one able-bodied maidservant to attend them, while Dorkó, as soon as the Countess is out of the way, attempts in a frenzy to cover up her homicidal blunders, stuffing bodies into hiding places all round the estate. The discovery of body parts by Zrínyi's dogs may well be true, but possibly refers to long-dead victims of earlier epidemics. It is conceivable that large numbers of such victims were buried without ceremony to avoid local panic, but of course fuelling the most sinister rumours.

From the testimony of witnesses and what we know of her court, it seems also beyond doubt that Elisabeth herself often but not always took part in the quasi-medical experiments of her entourage, and in the punishment of those girls of her household who offended her, however innocently or trivially. She personally requested curing plasters and poisons, and, like most women of her station, traded herbs with the wives of her noble neighbours. She was as superstitious as any woman – or man, for that matter – of her age, and relied not only on the imported manuals of sympathetic magic but on local folk wisdom, charms, talismans and incantations, for which she would call on Erzsi Majorosné of Myjava, among others. The principles underlying sympathetic magic were the same as those which gave the rationale for punishment at all levels of that society: the chastisement should mirror the crime, expunge the crime in all its gravity, not by rehabilitation but by the severity of pain and shame inflicted – repentance and deterrence were secondary, but important too. Elisabeth had the coins and keys heated red-hot to scald or brand the hands of the pilferer, saw the lazy or the brazen stripped naked, dipped the runaway in the brook, starved the greedy, beat the stubborn and the slow. In all this we can be sure that she was no different from other great ladies, no doubt more inventive, more resolute, but within the tolerable bounds of cruelty as they were then understood. But tearing the flesh with tongs or teeth, stabbing with knives and needles, burning the pubic hair with candleflames, inserting hot iron bars into the vaginas of the maidens, feeding them their own flesh? These torments were indeed worthy of Bosch or Brueghel or the most refined and sinister levels of the executioner's repertoire.

The attempt made recently to explain the alleged tortures away as therapeutic techniques is ingenious, but raises several questions. It does not account for the many reports of systematic beatings, which, if they were true, must refer to punishments or deliberate brutality (slapping, in contrast, could be explained as astringent therapy). If the other practices were standard healing methods, why would witnesses describe them as deliberate tortures? And if the witnesses were searching their imaginations for elaborate torments to accuse their enemies of, why not choose unambiguous examples that could not be confused with medical treatments? (Perhaps they did not have the wit – or the time – to do better.) The healing explanation stands up only if we assume that these cures were always carried out in secret by a select few 'specialists', so that an unsophisticated person who chanced upon a therapy in progress would not understand its real purpose. This may indeed have been the case, as amateur healers guarded the secrets of their craft as carefully as the orthodox doctors did theirs, and many of their practices were bizarre.

Lunacy is popularly believed to be intimately bound up with nobility, and not only in pre-Enlightenment Europe: a British writer estimated in the 1970s that one-third of the ducal families of England were affected by madness.[26] When trying to make sense of sadism and murder as described in the Báthory case, there has been an understandable temptation to bring in a retrospective verdict of 'guilty but insane'. The derangement of the senses was of course a familiar concept to our ancestors, but how madness was defined – and whether it could be publicly ascribed to an individual of Elisabeth's status – is far from clear. Gábor Báthory has been posthumously condemned as crazy, but his contemporaries, even when they were scandalised, seem to have considered his wild impulses to be the prerogative of a prince. Whether or not madness ran in the Báthory family is a moot point, but it seems beyond doubt that they saw themselves as carrying a burden of glamour and glory to which members of the clan responded in different ways: Elisabeth's brother Stephen, for instance, came to shun public life in spite of the responsibilities of his birth and retired to Ecsed to write his religious meditations. It was particularly in the nineteenth century that the 'psychological' interpretations of the Báthorys' peculiarities were developed, and these culminated in the twentieth century in a standard treatment of the family even in school history texts as tainted, unstable and immoral.

Elisabeth does not seem to have been physically or mentally abnormal in any obvious way. Had she been deranged, she could not have written the lucid business letters and will that we have in her own hand, and there is nothing to substantiate the idea of fits. If she had suffered from physical disabilities that were out of the ordinary, this would almost certainly have been mentioned at the trial or hinted at in previous family correspondence.

Regarding other instances of madness, eccentricity and excess among the Hungarian aristocracy, there was certainly widespread neurosis, depression and hysteria brought about by the pressures of the age. A noble family might contain members loyal to the Habsburgs in the west and others espousing the Transylvanian cause in the east of the country – quite apart from having to cope with the ever-present threat to psychic and physical wellbeing from the Turks. There were great tensions inherent in the noble milieu: the possibility of total self-indulgence tempered by Lutheran or Calvinist notions of sin and retribution, and a deference to the sacred crown that had become ingrained over centuries. Dealing with conspiracies by neighbours, even members of one's own family, and the need to protect oneself and one's loved ones from disease, together with the obligation to observe European values and Hungarian traditions required a sort of fanaticism, as did the charged role that the feudal Hungarian lords had to play: they were the intelligentsia, the politicians, the soldiers, the patrons of religion, statesmen and defenders of their families all at once. A man could – should – be simultaneously a poet, a chivalrous knight, a Macchiavel and a brute. Sigmund Báthory for one seems to have buckled under the intolerable burden of his private sensitivity – as evidenced by his religious preoccupations and his intense love of music – and the caricature role of warrior prince that he was required to play.

Many women went mad with grief, either gradually as their children died one by one before their time, or suddenly when, for example, the death of a spouse tipped them over the edge of despair. Those who held on to their sanity may not by any means have met the standards of normality assumed today: extremes of behaviour were – and are – for both sexes a trait that goes with privilege; hormonal influences and the effect of diet on rationality and mood were not well understood (although the doctrine of the humours was a subtle enough precursor of our science), intoxication by alcohol or drugs, poisoning by ergot, agaric or lead, the insidious progression of syphilis could all result in delusions, rages, terrifying reversals of character.

A savage hauteur was associated with those in power in Hungary at least up until the inter-war period of our own century. But tales of the cruelty of wayward and quixotic aristocrats often come in the form not of complaints but of celebrations of gruesome mischief – the strange Hungarian cult of *káröröm*.

Typical is the story told about the proud Magyar squire George Kapy, who was the *föispan* (high sheriff) of Hunyad county in the seventeenth century. Once when Székely raftsmen were rowing by on the River Maros, they caught sight of Kapy's daughters looking down from the windows of his manor-house in Arany. When they saw the girls, the light-hearted oarsmen began neighing and whinnying at them in a teasing display of lust. Squire Kapy roused the village and had the Székelys pulled to the shore, where he commanded his blacksmith to take up his hammer and nails and neatly shoe each of them in turn.[27]

Another such anecdote tells of two country gentlemen who were in the habit of paying each other occasional visits, accompanied by their servants and their prize horses. The pair were fond of practical jokes, and on one occasion one of the squires complimented the other on the spotless appearance of his horses. The latter went outside to find that they had been whitewashed. On the next visit the duped gentleman whispered to his servant, who quietly slipped away, before remarking to his host that he was astonished to see that his horses were wearing stockings. The owner dashed out to where his horses stood with their legs flayed from knee to fetlock.

Both Elisabeth and her castles were remote, hidden, unreachable. She stood – and stands – apart from and above the lives of others. She was probably intensely private and difficult to approach, features explained by her upbringing and education. She and her lairs provide an easy focus for our fantasies, just as the gaunt closed-up fortress on the top of the forested hill became in the local imagination the scene of unimaginable horrors. The standard parallels which are usually quoted are the fourteenth-century Mongol warlord Timor the Cruel, Lucrezia Borgia, Gilles de Rais and Vlad Tepes. Each of these four was an aristocrat; each abused the power their status conferred on them; but they do not offer useful parallels in other respects. Timor, known as Tamerlane or Tamburlaine, and Vlad Tepes were military leaders in times when inventive forms of mass-slaughter were a necessary part of a tyrant's repertoire; the impaling for which Vlad has become notorious in the west was in fact a common form of execution, as the British ambassador to Constantinople noted when he crossed Hungary in 1596: 'we found two men most miserably put to death, having each of them a stake thrust in at his Fundament, through his body, and so out by his neck, the stake being set up-right on end . . .'[28] Lucrezia Borgia's reputed poisonings were part of an Italian tradition of dynastic and domestic intrigue. The Italian-born Catherine de Medici, who became Regent of France at the time of Elisabeth Báthory's birth, was another high-born lady who surrounded herself with an entourage of beautiful girls and was rumoured to have used the blood of virgins in her experiments with cosmetic potions, aphrodisiac elixirs and poisons, as well as exciting her passions by watching her maidservants being beaten. Writing in 1864, in his *Notes from Underground*, Dostoyevsky observed that the Egyptian queen Cleopatra kept boredom at bay by sticking golden pins into the flesh of her helpless slaves.

The French aristocrat Gilles de Rais or Retz was the origin of the Bluebeard legend. He was entrusted with the safety of Joan of Arc and became Maréchal de France in the early fifteenth century. This immensely wealthy grandee outdid the royal family in the lavish finery of his display and the splendour of his court. He was a dandy, a libertine and dilettante who combined humanist scholarship with patronage of the arts and satanism and was said also to have practised alchemy, sorcery, necromancy and ritual murder, torturing and sodomising up to 200 young boys whom his servants abducted for him from the surrounding countryside. In his case, too, the truth of the charges eventually laid against him was obscured by political and personal motives. De Rais was hanged for murder and heresy in 1440 and his body was consigned to the fire.

All that these famous precedents demonstrate is the truism that depravity was a prerogative of the ruling elite. But there are other authentic historical characters, obscure protagonists from the margins of the Christian world, whose examples may bring us closer to a final understanding of the Báthory enigma.

CHAPTER TEN

Stories of Witches and Widows

I am in blood
Stepp'd in so far that, should I wade no more,
Returning were as tedious as go o'er.

William Shakespeare, *Macbeth*

Witches and witchcraft in old Europe ~ fairy queens and other beings
~ subterranean mysteries ~ blood myths and bloody traditions ~
the fate of Dame Alice Kyteler ~ the persecuted widow ~ Elisabeth
Czobor and the end of the Thurzós ~ a case for comparison ~ the
enchantress, Anna Báthory

The pre-Enlightenment world was permeated by a belief in the influence of the numinous and the magical on every aspect of life. While wizards concerned themselves with alchemy, astrology and numerology, mundane magic was universally accepted to be the province of women and merged seamlessly with women's other customs and duties. When, however, a whole community or a group within it turned on an individual woman and sought to destroy her, there were three standard charges which the condition of all females made it easy to bring against her: the first was sexual impropriety; the second was infanticide; and the third, the most ambiguous and imprecise, yet more often than not with a fatal outcome, was witchcraft.

For this reason it is not surprising that, among the many acts of wickedness that Countess Báthory was accused of in the course of the investigations, were acts of *maleficium* too. It was likewise unsurprising that the priest, Ponikenus, should have included black magic (something embedded in his religious ideology) and given it prominence in his highly coloured condemnation of the Lady. Even though she was never formally charged with the crime of sorcery, it is useful when looking for precedents and parallels for Elisabeth's persecution to seek them in the wider context of the trials which were instituted against other women in other parts of Europe and beyond, nearly all of which could be categorised as witch-trials.

In Europe as a whole 80 per cent of accused witches were women; in Hungary it was 90 per cent. Only about 10 per cent of the total number of trials for witchcraft across the continent took place during the 'witch-crazes' – the frenzied outbreaks of multiple persecutions. Most of the cases that were not politically motivated involved small, scattered communities, where life moved slowly and changed little, and where resentments and suspicions festered for years until a catharsis was needed and a human sacrifice, almost always a woman, was arranged.[1]

Witch-hunts could actually be carried out in 'good faith' – literally according to the moral standards of the time, by both Catholics and Protestants, or by the secular authorities. The thinking behind such persecutions followed two different paths, both ending in the stake for the accused. Some believed that dying on the executioner's pyre would save heretics and witches from the everlasting fires of hell, while others held that the shamelessly ungodly had put themselves beyond Christian redemption; society should exact retribution as decisively and painfully as possible. When the papers of the many trials are studied dispassionately from a modern perspective, however, it is certain that there were many instances in which the charge of witchcraft was used as a pretext to settle personal disputes whose origins lay solidly in the material world.

The very real witches and wizards who inhabited post-Renaissance communities were expected to play the role of the prehistoric shaman in fighting battles in the spirit world on behalf of their fellows, or of making arrangements with supernatural forces to guarantee such benefits as fertile fields and abundant children. In return for this they were rewarded and tolerated, but they would always be feared and envied. Despite their efforts, young children were carried to the churchyard in an unending silent procession, animals sickened and died, storms flattened the crops, floods carried away the seeds. Someone had to take the blame.[2]

In the world-pictures of the people of the early modern period, the spirits who lurked on the fringes of the licit Christian belief-system were confused with the real people who lived half in and half outside their own villages and hamlets, the loners, eccentrics and recluses. Witnesses at a witch-trial in 1717 reported: 'while he was dreaming at noon, he was attacked by a cold wind in the form of Mrs Oláh Mihály'. In Vas county near Elisabeth's former estates local people testified that 'Mrs Jancsó, a midwife, made the whirlwind' and she and the other spirits 'flew away like kites bringing with them the stone rain . . .' The obsession with beauty that Father Túróczi ascribed to Elisabeth Báthory is also an attribute of the godless temptress and the witch; in the year before Túróczi published his revelations, a witch-trial at Szeged had heard that 'In the assemblies of the witches nobody is ugly or old, they all seem to be very beautiful.'[3] In 1702 English visitors coming from the east observed: 'We noticed a very miserable custom in Transylvania and Hungary as well; they are all convinced that they are surrounded by witches. Several women of all ages are sentenced to death for this reason every year. The evidences for the charge are only weak rumours, e.g. the neighbours complain that their animals are cursed by the accused person . . .'[4]

The folklore of eastern Europe was full of remnants of earlier cults from the Mediterranean, the Balkans and western Asia, whose details had been forgotten, but whose archetypes lived on under local names. The seventeenth-century Romanian *strigoi* of Transylvania were the female owl-demon *striges* of Ancient Greek legend who disembowelled their human victims. The Transylvanian *prikulici* were the Slavs' *vrkolaki*, flesh-eating and blood-drinking werewolves. And the Magyar fairies were the same as the Slavonic *vile*, an amalgam of wind-spirits and the souls of real girls who had died as unbaptised babies or virgin brides before they could take their place in the human community. So female innocents were an important and universal element of the magic pantheon of the region. Elisabeth Báthory's innocent victims could easily be identified with these troops of nymphs, who in the faery world also played the role of servants to more dangerous entities.

One of the most enduring and resonant figures, appearing in every European folk myth in one incarnation or another, is the fairy queen, a personage who can be beneficent at one moment and mercilessly cruel the next. This character is invariably beautiful, her lair is a place of mortal danger to any human enticed into it, and her habits – bathing herself, concocting magic cosmetics, gazing into enchanted mirrors, are virtually those of flesh-and-blood queens and great ladies. As personified, for example, by the enchantress Morgan le Fay in the Arthurian cycle, this queen is a distant relative of the pagan war-goddesses, transmuted by mediaeval courtly romances into a feudal sorceress. Luca, the Slav devil of the winter solstice, was the leader of a band of lost souls and was attended, like the Blood Countess, by crones. The Romanian fairy queen Doamna Zineloi was both goddess and demon and, like many of these beings, was a memory of the cult of Artemis, whose rites could ensure beauty and physical health for women and whose revels brought about a state of 'nympholepsy' – an abandoned, boundless ecstasy which possessed and unhinged young women.

Elisabeth was on the one hand a Renaissance lady who dutifully and correctly observed her prescribed role in society. She was at the same time in her own eyes a princess, existing beyond and above the limits of mundane humanity. She was both a patroness of the Protestant church and, if not a witch herself, a patron of witches.

Two potent themes are united in Elisabeth's legend: pity for the vulnerability of innocent women, and men's abiding fear of the dominance and insatiability, the uncontrollable, limitless and arcane power that women could unleash; *femmes* literally *fatales* as repositories of irrational and ungovernable forces. Two sides of the coin are represented: women as many and helpless and woman as singular and all-powerful. For the educated, Elisabeth was a Hungarian rival for the monstrous ladies of Ancient Rome, a *lamia* (the female demon of classical mythology who preyed on humans and sucked their blood), a female Tamburlaine, or a transplanted Lucrezia Borgia. As for the peasants of Nitra county, they remembered the fourth- or fifth-hand versions of the court testimonies that had the feudal chatelaine tearing at her subjects with her teeth. They needed a rationale for the enormity of Elisabeth's crimes and an explanation for the multiple disappearances:

why had the widow needed so many? To keep herself young, to keep her aristocratic skin so unnaturally white. These were reasons that even simple people could comprehend. And there was something else, something remaining from Elisabeth's time that they could see with their own eyes and whisper about at the fireside.

Under the tall castle with its blind walls and gothic turrets clinging to the limestone outcrop with Čachtice on its flank and the little hamlet of Višnové at its foot, there were natural caverns deep in the white rock of the hillside. Someone, perhaps in the far-off days of Duke Stibor, perhaps in the Nádasdys' own time, had tunnelled in from the outside and built a crude network of cellars there. Local people even said that there was another secret tunnel running from beneath the manor-house in the village itself all the way under the gardens, the woods and the vineyards up to the castle, where it connected with the subterranean vaults that no one but the family's most trusted servants had ever seen. These cellars before they had been closed off or their roofs had crumbled, blocking them with rubble, had contained wine-barrels and vats, ancient wooden casks which even when the tunnels came to be abandoned still contained the traces of a rust-red residue.[5]

It is not at all far-fetched to imagine that blood, including human blood, was used for cosmetic or ceremonial purposes. Venesection or bleeding was, with bathing and cauterising, one of the most common forms of therapy, practised by all qualified doctors, barber–surgeons and most lay healers too. A basin – wooden in the peasant's shack, silver in the manor-house – full of fresh blood would have been a common sight to those who gathered round the sickbed of a family member or servant. In the countryside, vats of blood from freshly slaughtered pigs were assembled for the making of sauces and soups – the *pörkölt* blood goulash is still a favourite – in ceremonies that had come from the Magyars' pre-Christian days on the Asian plains. Both nomadic and pastoral societies based on rearing cattle and horses had in common the drinking of blood from still-living animals, either from necessity when nourishment was scarce, or in rituals of bonding with their totem animals.

The apothecaries of the middle ages kept among their stock of potions *sanguis draconis*, dragon's blood, a balm and dye once perhaps containing the real blood of a serpent such as a boa constrictor, but later made from the red resin of a tree of the East Indies, or, more perilously for their patients, poisonous cinnabar or minium. In his twentieth-century treatise on blood, Earle Hackett demonstrates that spilled human blood is no more effective as a fertiliser or as a cosmetic than any rotting animal or vegetable matter. Its value is all symbolic: 'And yet . . . and yet . . . did not roses and anemones grow from the blood of Adonis?'[6]

One of the prosaic objections to the idea of a cosmetic blood-bath is that blood quickly coagulates, making immersion in gore an excessively messy and unpleasant experience. Literal-minded supporters of a blood-bathing hypothesis have countered by suggesting that a blood-shower is a more plausible solution, with the victim–donor's blood either quickly collected and thrown over the recipient, or released directly from above, gushing straight from the interior of one body on to the surface of the other. It was this last scenario that the actress Ingrid Pitt urged the director Peter Sasdy to simulate during the making of the movie *Countess Dracula*, but it was thought too shocking for the Hammer audience and the censor.

By curious coincidence there are two proven factors which may prevent human blood from clotting in the ordinary way, and each of them applies neatly to the setting in which Elisabeth's supposed indulgences took place. First, when a victim undergoes a sudden and violent death, the extreme stress experienced just before dying may trigger an overproduction of fibrinolysin, a powerful anti-coagulant agent. The result is that, even hours after death, the blood in the victim's cadaver remains perfectly liquid, so much so that it has been possible to transfuse blood taken from a corpse successfully into a living patient. There is another anti-clotting agent which was discovered by orthodox science some 300 years after the death of the Blood Countess, but which would have been readily available to her in the labyrinthine cellars beneath her castle: the acidic deposit which collects around the tops of the wooden casks in which wine was stored.

Blood has been a recurrent subject of dreams throughout human history, and there is a wealth of literature seeking to explain the archetypal symbolism of blood in terms of fear, particularly male fear of the viscerality of sex, castration-anxiety and horror of menstruation. Conscious and unconscious blood taboos would have been a part of the worldview of the peasants of Čachtice, just as they were everywhere else until well into the early twentieth century. But it is not necessary to invoke dream archetypes and the unconscious to imagine the associations that a bloodstain on a white sheet would have triggered in the early modern mind; first menses on a girl-child's shift, consumptive blood on the apron of a maiden, a lost maidenhead, a botched abortion or a difficult childbirth, the last traces of mortality on the shroud . . .

In the sixteenth century the chemical attributes of blood and its circulation through the body were not understood, and neither were the properties of human skin, with the result that blood-drinking – introducing alien blood into the system via the mouth – and the use of blood as a cosmetic, in the hope that it would pass into or through the skin, both seemed quite plausible. The drinking of human blood was less likely to be openly prescribed, but it undoubtedly happened. By primitive logic the blood of the strong was valued for its ability to transfer strength. When the Magyars named their favourite red wine *Egri Bikavér* (Bull's Blood), they were invoking the animal qualities they had once sought from the real thing, as had the worshippers of Mithras who contributed to the Christian mystery of transubstantiation. The Romanians preserved the tradition of the 'Blood Bear', a rogue animal fed only on blood and red meat which became possessed of supernatural ferocity.

A thousand years earlier Pliny described how doctors cured the Egyptian King of elephantiasis by means of human blood. Moreover, 'Roman epileptics attended gladiatorial displays in the hope of getting a sip or two of supposedly curative strong man's gore from the unlucky ones among the contestants. Those whose fits were hysterical and not truly epileptic might well have been cured by such a dramatic and public experience, which would have reinforced the legend of this particularly well-known blood-cure.'[8] Constantine the Great had hoped that bathing in children's blood would bring him relief from leprosy; fortunately the apostles Peter and Paul appeared to him in a dream to assure him that only holy water could effect the cure.[9] It was known throughout Europe in Elisabeth's day that a doctor had offered to cure the dying Pope Innocent VIII in 1492 (exactly the same story was told of Sixtus V) by giving him blood drained from three living ten-year-old boys (all of whom subsequently died, as did Innocent, who refused the medicine). Those decadent ladies who had the wherewithal to procure this ultimate restorative and cosmetic no doubt did so, but only rumours survive: Poppaea, Messalina, Lucrezia Borgia are the names most often cited, but almost any feudal noblewoman or wealthy courtesan would have found it easy to engage in a little private collecting from donors – voluntary or involuntary – in the same way that alchemists and necromancers acquired the supplies essential for their experiments.

It is an irony that their Countess should have smeared herself with the red blood of virgins in order to render her own skin whiter, but it is no surprise that the ruddy-featured peasants of Nitra county, whose own skin would turn to copper-brown in the summer fields, would marvel at the delicacy and translucency of their social superiors, wondering if their indifference to their serfs' wellbeing was because they were literally bloodless. By the same token, the young girls who surrounded the Lady of the house would have contrasted visibly with their counterparts outside the manor: the combination of a closeted existence, the emotional tensions of adolescence, a diet poor in minerals could leave them ghostlike in appearance and prone to fainting and hysteria.

It was not only the flowing of female blood that triggered the nervous fantasies of male-dominated societies but also the cessation of that flow. In some ways Elisabeth Báthory did not fit the profile of the typical female scapegoat – she was not poor, powerless or noticeably infirm – but she was a post-menopausal widow, and a scold. Elderly women who outlived their men were an economic and psychological threat. They had accumulated knowledge and experience, acquired confidence and often came to express their views forcibly, but they were an affront to male pride and the natural order. Once these women were no longer engaged in the business of birth and nurture, they were redundant and without a niche in the hierarchy of being. The isolation and persecution of women was nothing new, and aristocrats were not exempt. Across Europe and in the New World there are striking parallels which start to suggest a pattern of social behaviour – by the women and by their oppressors – rather than a string of sensational coincidences. One particular case was the trial of Dame Alice Kyteler for witchcraft in fourteenth-century Ireland.

Dame Alice lived in Kilkenny in south-east Ireland and was a member of the Anglo-Norman elite who ruled over the native Celtic population. She was apparently possessed of great beauty and force of character. By the time the authorities moved against her she had outlived three husbands: an influential financier, William Outlawe, by whom she had a son of the same name, and two wealthy squires, Adam le Blund and Richard de Valle. From the two last she inherited their whole estates, leaving their children, the natural heirs, resentful and impoverished. Soon after Alice had married for the fourth time to a gentleman named John le Poer, rumours of poisoning and witchcraft began to circulate, coinciding with her new husband's affliction by a mysterious wasting disease. Sir John himself denounced his wife to the ecclesiastical authorities, who began an investigation, supported by her late husbands' children and other prominent citizens of Kilkenny town. The Franciscan Bishop of Ossary, an Englishman, Richard de Ledrede, orchestrated the campaign of vilification against Alice Kyteler, her son William (on whom she doted) and the senior servants of her household, citing in evidence a litany of black-magic practices which became a template for the charges repeatedly brought against the witches of the west in the centuries that followed: desecration of the host and mockery of church rituals, animal sacrifices, sexual congress with demons, and the making of potions from ingredients such as the flesh of new-born children, the hair and fingernails of hanged men, offal, insects and noxious plants, mixed and boiled, it was said, in the hollow skull of a beheaded felon.[10] The Bishop attempted to arrest the woman and succeeded in having her excommunicated, but his jurisdiction in such cases was not clear and Dame Alice, who refused to be summonsed, had her own powerful supporters. She in turn accused the Bishop of slander in the secular county court and managed to have him confined temporarily in Kilkenny castle.

In the course of a year, the relentless pressure from the church and the repetition of the terrible accusations, together with local resentment of the Dame's arrogant behaviour, began to turn official opinion against her, and eventually permission was given to put her on trial for her life.

The contrasts with Elisabeth Báthory's case are clear: Dame Alice's accuser was not as powerful as the Palatine Thurzó, and could not take her into custody or pass sentence on her without official sanction. The accused person's own husband joined in condemning her and provided evidence of her crimes (her magical paraphernalia and samples of her poisons and charms) to the prosecutors. But the similarities are also significant: by her personal high-handedness and sharp-tongued pride Dame Alice Kyteler had alienated her neighbours, terrified her servants and unsettled her male peers. Most importantly, by accumulating great wealth and protecting it for her favourite heir, she had set herself up as a target for a jealous husband and a band of greedy relatives. The prosecution's figurehead, de Ledrede himself, stood to benefit materially if the heiress was found guilty and her estates forfeited. There may have been other factors, political or dynastic, which were involved in the affair, but the time elapsed makes it impossible for these to be ascertained. It is clear, however, that there was more to the Kyteler case than the charges of spell-casting and poisoning which were set down in the prosecutors' papers.

Just as in the later Hungarian case, the only surviving documents were authored by those who had set out to destroy Alice Kyteler's reputation and who would gain from her downfall. Those documents record that, once the great lady's survival was in doubt, her servants and her neighbours were willing to offer testimonies against her. The parallels do not end there. While her enemies waited for the right moment to seize her, Dame Alice Kyteler, like Elisabeth, gathered together her movable treasures and left her family seat. Unlike Elisabeth, before the authorities could lay hands on her she succeeded in slipping across the Irish Sea to sanctuary in England, leaving her humbly born maidservant, Petronilla de Meath, to die at the stake for the crimes of which her mistress was also found guilty and sentenced to death *in absentia*. Dame Alice's son was convicted by the court, but his rank and his wealth saved him; he was pardoned and set free in return for generous donations to de Ledrede's church.

It is extremely difficult at this remove to pronounce a final verdict upon Alice Kyteler. She may in fact have been a serial murderer – her last husband's loss of hair and of finger- and toenails were possible symptoms of slow poisoning – and perhaps her maidservant was speaking sincerely when she scorned her judges and swore that her mistress was the greatest witch in all Ireland and England too. But it is no longer possible to see such sensational events in isolation. There were many other prosecutions of older women for witchcraft – notable examples come from as far apart as Estonia and Salem, New England, which may have been motivated at least in part by a quarrel over an inheritance or the coveting of land or money owned by the accused.[11]

As well as the misogyny that was universal in patriarchal societies, it has been suggested that there were deeper changes taking place in post-mediaeval cultures, with men unconsciously perceiving that women in general had gained too much power. By this theory the cult of mariolatry – the worship of the Virgin – and the veneration of a host of sympathetic female saints had begun subtly to alter the balance of power in society and undermine men's unquestioned and absolute dominance.[12] In Hungary, because of the special circumstances that arose in a country at war, women were even more in the ascendant, particularly those aristocratic women who had become emancipated by, in some cases, fighting alongside their menfolk or else by taking over traditional male roles in the family and on the estates. Deep-seated hostility to the female sex might explain not only the persecution of rich and powerful widows but why less privileged women were prepared to suffer the hardships of domestic discipline in the manor-house in return for a modicum of security and a measure of social advancement. Who is to say that the treatment they received at the hands of brothers, fathers or husbands at home was any better than the ordeals involved in a regime of servitude?

Other striking and authentic parallels to the experiences of Countess Báthory can also be found in the history of Hungary and its sister-state, Transylvania. It seems logical to look at how other noblewomen were treated, in particular widowed noblewomen, and at women who were persecuted.

One of the best-documented examples of the harassing and isolating of a widowed noblewoman occurred a few years after the death of Countess Báthory and with neat irony concerned the neighbour and former friend who had been instrumental in her capture and imprisonment and who then had robbed her. Lady Elisabeth Czobor, the wife of the Palatine, George Thurzó, once she had lost her husband and her eldest son was persecuted and ultimately ruined by the ruthlessly ambitious would-be Renaissance Prince, Nicholas Esterházy, who was assisted in his machinations by Czobor's own daughter-in-law.

The excitable and ingenuous Lady Czobor was widowed in 1616 at the age of thirty-eight. Her letters and her behaviour after George Thurzó's passing revealed that the death of her husband had shocked her very deeply. After some months she gathered her strength and began to assume some of the responsibilities of her late husband, and to cultivate his memory. In her instructing of Imre, their only son, she constantly cited George as a paragon of moral and political probity and as a model father and upholder of the true faith.[13]

Imre had fathered two daughters but was without a male heir when he died unexpectedly in 1621. The rumours suggested that he had been poisoned, but by whom was never made clear. Whatever the truth, the main branch of the Bethlenfalva Thurzós was thereby extinguished. Having lost all her close male relatives, Lady Czobor's position as heiress to the bulk of the vast family holdings quickly became untenable. She lost the estate of Tokaj with its prize vineyards and its rich tithes. The rising star of the new aristocracy and Palatine-to-be, Count Esterházy, was distantly related to Czobor through his first wife, Lady Ursula Derssfy, and he used this fact to lay successful claim to two more Thurzó castles and promised one of Czobor's daughters that he would send his private army to resolve a dispute over her estates. The threat had the desired effect. In October 1622, less than one year after the mysterious death of Imre Thurzó, Nicholas Esterházy ordered a comprehensive inventory of the Bytča estates. A valuation showed them to be worth 8,000 florins. He then impounded the properties. Two years later, in 1624, he put the final touch to his campaign of acquisition by taking as his second wife George Thurzó's daughter-in-law Lady Christina Nyáry, Imre's widow (who had always hated her mother-in-law) and removing the grandchildren from their grandmother's care. Lady Czobor tried to keep the children with her and appealed to the courts and the King, but when Esterházy became palatine in 1625 he easily persuaded the Diet to grant him custody. Elisabeth died, emotionally and physically broken, at the home of her favourite daughter Barbara shortly afterwards.

The most tenuous claim was all it took to launch a challenge against a vulnerable heiress, after which it was largely might that established right. The surviving members of the Thurzó line were not strong enough to oppose their enemies, and the powerful families to whom they were connected (as in Báthory's case, the sons-in-law played a duplicitous role) were not willing to compromise their own positions to support a widow and a dying dynasty.

There is another true story from seventeenth-century Hungary whose denouement came more than two decades after the Widow Nádasdy's lonely death, but which echoes the Báthory scandal in many ways. Not only does it concern the dispossessing of a troublesome widow, but it ends in the trial of that widow for the brutal murder of her servants.

The woman in question was a member of the senior aristocracy and a relative by marriage of the Thurzó family, at whose wedding feasts she would have met Countess Báthory, twenty-three years her senior. Her name was Anna-Rosina Liszty, known usually by the latinised form of her surname, Listhius. She was born in 1583 to János Listhius and Anna Nauhaus.[14] The Listhius family originated as burghers in Transylvania and were related to a bishop who was an influential figure in Hungary at the time of the defeat at Mohács. They were ennobled in 1554, and in 1560 and again in 1586 the family received the important benefits and estates which formed the basis of their dynastic wealth. Anna-Rosina's grandfather, the senior member of the family, first became Bishop of Veszprém, then of Györ, his sons were given the finest education and on reaching their majority were appointed regional judges. Little is known of Anna-Rosina's mother except that she was already a widow when she married János Listhius. The family strengthened their power in the prescribed manner by arranging marriages for their offspring and Anna-Rosina was duly sent to marry Lord Stanislas Thurzó in 1598 at the age of fifteen. (We should recall George Thurzó's letter to his wife revealing his misgivings about the match: 'She is no Dido, but if Stanislas likes her so much that he cannot live without her, what can I do against it?'.)

Stanislas Thurzó presided over a court that was renowned for its ostentation; he, like his cousin George, became palatine in 1625 after the interregnum of Sigmund Forgách. In the years following their marriage he and his wife had seven children in quick succession, four of whom survived to reach adulthood. According to letters between husband and wife, Anna-Rosina showed no extraordinary mental states or eccentricity until after 1610 when she became subject to hysterical or epileptic fits followed by periods of depression. In a letter of 1621 to George Thurzó's widow Elisabeth Czobor, the family wrote:

> thanks be to God, now she is much better, and as your ladyship has written, that nothing of her deeds should be spoken of and nobody should mention this before her. But now conscious, she knows herself what she has done, and what she has spoken of. She is now firmly fixed upon it that her throat should not be bound and no one should use a knife in her presence, and people should care for her and be vigilant and when the sickness comes on her – because it came upon her before – it first strikes her on her left toe with great pain, then to her heart, then goes away . . .[15]

The strange symptoms as they were described do not permit a diagnosis, but prove beyond doubt that something was dangerously amiss and was being hushed up by the family many years before Lady Listhius came to the attention of the representatives of the law. The family papers also show that Anna-Rosina's relationship with her children, particularly with the heir, the younger Stanislas, and his wife Lady Anna Czobor was fraught with tension, to such an extent that she stated that she could not bear her daughter-in-law's company any longer, because her presence 'always left her saddened'. In a letter to Elisabeth Czobor of 1624, Anna-Rosina herself wrote:

> My dear sweet lady, I cannot bear any longer not to complain about my wicked children; my son and his wife who have caused me so much pain and sorrow and bitterness that now and forever I shall never suffer so much. I hope that God will punish them, and last Sunday I sent them away in such anger and sorrow; I do not wish to set eyes upon them, I have enough bitterness in my life . . .[16]

This correspondence also refers to Anna-Rosina's relationship with her husband, Lord Stanislas, who she claimed took her side in these quarrels with her children. But examination of his will contradicts this. He bequeathed very little directly to his wife and did not allow her to handle the estates that made up the inheritance, stipulating where she could live and limiting her independence. Stanislas Thurzó died in 1625 and at the age of forty-three his widow remarried, taking as her second husband a noble of much lower station, Baron George Pográny. Pográny could not have hoped that his elderly bride would give him a male heir and must have known of her seven childbirths and her uncertain temper. His court was much poorer than that of her late husband – and the newlyweds had to face the gossip and ill-will which went with the morganatic union, compounded by a second and simultaneous *mésalliance* (in the eyes of society, at least) between Anna-Rosina's daughter, Lady Éva Thurzó, and George Pográny's brother, István. One possible clue to this may be found in George's will: Lady Anna-Rosina had important properties in Sintava in Nitra county, owned the manor of Hlohovec and farms in Seréd and could expect in time to receive a large part of the Thurzó legacy; in 1628 the couple declared before notaries in Bratislava that each would inherit the other's goods, an arrangement which would be far more advantageous to the impoverished Pogránys, who probably persuaded Anna-Rosina to make this double marriage to protect herself from, or to spite, her Thurzó relatives.

Éva Thurzó died in childbirth in her mother's house, and the scene was recalled nearly ten years later by witnesses: 'As the child reached her time in the woman's womb, and was struggling there for two whole hours, the grandmother did not allow the child to be taken out by Caesarean section, even after the mother had succumbed, saying – let him not be taken out; let him die in her. No trace of the mixture of my blood and that executioner bastard should remain!'[17]

One year after their official declaration, George Pográny rescinded his oath and excluded Lady Listhius from his new will:

> my above-mentioned partner in marriage, when I was sorely ill, left me, taking my medicine, and cursed me and all my family, which I witnessed with my own ears. She uttered foul words concerning me, took my food, drink and kitchen utensils, took the pillows from under my head and my bedclothes so that I had to sleep upon hay. She broke my travelling trunks, as I witnessed, and took my money and my letters. As I was seriously ill, I could do nothing against her. She kept not to her oath and was so cruel to me in my great sickness, and even spat into my beard. I will not permit her to inherit anything even if she bears my name until her death.[18]

But the embittered and deserted husband succumbed to his illness in 1629, leaving his widow in possession of the joint estates. István Pográny as the senior male now stood to inherit his share, but the sister-in-law who outranked him and hated him denied him the chance.

It was in 1637, some years after he had seized Elisabeth Czobor's portion of the Thurzó family fortune, that Nicholas Esterházy, now established as Count Palatine of Hungary, turned his attentions to Anna-Rosina Listhius. The ageing, twice-widowed lady now presented an irresistible target: she had outlived her two sons by Stanislas Thurzó and was about to inherit their estates to add to the considerable wealth that was already in her hands. Of the direct Thurzó line, only Esterházy's daughter-in-law, George Thurzó's granddaughter Elisabeth, was still alive. Esterházy now enjoyed the almost unlimited power of a monarch and Listhius had no one left to defend her against him. But she delivered herself into the hands of her enemy by her own folly.

Although the papers from the proceedings are incomplete, the basic facts are not in question. Following reports that Lady Listhius had murdered one of her serving-women, a member of the lesser nobility, the Palatine ordered witnesses to be summoned and interrogated to determine whether a case could be brought against her. In the course of the inquiry, the eighty individuals who were questioned agreed that in the past twelve years Anna-Rosina had caused the deaths of eight or nine of her servants by beating them or having them beaten to death. In each case the victim had committed some trifling offence which either brought on or coincided with a bout of their mistress's 'sickness'. The Lady would become possessed by an uncontrollable fury and would begin to rave, urging her assistants to harder and harder punishments (recalling the cries of '*Üsd, Üsd, Jobban!*' that Elisabeth Báthory was said to have uttered), then joining in herself until the object of her rage was lifeless. Only then would she become calmer, sometimes cradling and caressing the corpse and trying to persuade it to live again, or lamenting in a mixture of anger and remorse that her servant had deserted her.

While the domestics (both males and females) who died were merely commoners there had been no repercussions at all, but the latest victim had been of noble blood, and after her murder, which had been signalled by repeated threats that her mistress would 'kill her that very day', her daughters decided to take action. As was usual in such cases, priests were called upon to mediate, and arranged for the victim's family to be bought off with one hundred florins in coin, one hundred florins' worth of goods and a hundred butts of corn. In spite of the payment of *wergild* to the family before the case came to court, Esterházy persisted in pressing for a full trial, and this time he was fully supported by the Royal Chamber.

The charge was murder, but witnesses also accused Lady Listhius, who had long before gained a reputation as a herbalist and healer, of practising black magic. Anna-Rosina, they said, had surrounded herself with a group of powerful witches and warlocks who assisted her in casting spells, but it was known in the regions around her court that she herself was the most powerful sorceress of them all.

In 1637, when the trial against Listhius was begun, the bulk of the property was still held by her and therefore forfeit. While the remaining inheritors argued about the Thurzó estate, the case was brought against

Listhius by the so-called 'head-money' principle, which the Fiscus had claimed could not be invoked in the case of Elisabeth Báthory. According to this tradition a successful plaintiff in a trial would receive one-third of any wealth confiscated and two-thirds went to the judge(s). In this case this was probably the Royal Chamber, the Fiscus, and the Palatine Esterházy and his henchmen respectively.[19]

It is obvious that, through his close links with his cousin and her husband Stanislas Thurzó and through the correspondence between Anna-Rosina and his wife, George Thurzó must have been intimately aware of the peculiarities of Lady Listhius, although the murders that she was specifically accused of did not take place until after his death. It is equally certain that, when Nicholas Esterházy moved against Listhius, he was aware of Thurzó's earlier case against Elisabeth Báthory.

The two cases have many obvious parallels. In both cases the victims were servants tortured by noblewomen, or by their order (during the investigation witnesses alleged that Listhius had been ill-treating her servants for more than twenty years, that is, since Elisabeth Báthory's lifetime). Listhius was able to reach a compromise with the adult daughters of her victim; in the case of Countess Báthory there is no such evidence, but if she had killed young girls from the gentry, and if their relations had protested, it is quite unlikely that such an enormously rich woman could not have avoided guilt by payment. Why is there no evidence of such payments or some form of contract among the records of her case? Did the Lutheran priests try to intervene only to be rebuffed by a woman who felt herself to be untouchable? In both cases the Count Palatine initiated the investigation; in Listhius' in spite of her *de facto* agreement with the victim's family, in Báthory's before she could take any action to defend herself by due process in the county court. If nothing else, the Listhius case proves that servants, even those of good family, were handy targets on whom their employers could vent their rages.

From the legal point of view, the differences are interesting. In the Listhius case the letters of interrogation have been prepared with greater care and attention to detail and the content of the 'confessions' is more logical than in Elisabeth Báthory's case (the distinction between personal eyewitness testimony and hearsay is made clear, for example, and the chronology of events is much more consistent).[20]

The length of time taken over the investigation into Elisabeth Báthory, which began early in 1610 and was still incomplete at the time of her death in 1614, contrasts with the speed and efficiency with which Listhius, a less influential woman, was tried and judgement passed. Only the condemnation and execution of Countess Báthory's accomplices was achieved speedily. In Listhius' case the order for the trial to be initiated was given on 27 June 1637; the interrogation took place on 2, 4 and 6 July.

Of all the statements transcribed in the course of the trial it is not the by now familiar testimony of the witnesses which stays in the mind, but the words used by the priest who interceded to secure the payoff – words whose wider implications have not been picked up: 'Even should you desire to begin something, you will never get to the end of it [this must have been a common form of words; it is almost the same as the Royal Chamber's dissuasion of King Matthias in 1611], for you cannot demonstrate conclusively that the hand of the woman was the cause of your mother's death, rather than the hand of her servant.' In those days it was not possible to convict someone on the basis of indirect guilt, in other words for inciting murder rather than committing it in person. The hints in Elisabeth Czobor's cryptic note of 1610 and the ambiguity of the evidence against her mean that Báthory would certainly have used in her defence the fact that she could not be held responsible for acts carried out by other hands.

If in Elisabeth Báthory's case there is no sign of a compromise with the victims, this shows that the accusations of the murder of noblewomen are likely to be false. It also seems clear from the Listhius case that the mere murder of a commoner was not enough to start off legal proceedings; only the murder of (only one) noble victim could have this effect. The case shows that punishment of servants was the unlimited right of the lord or lady, and, if that punishment resulted in death, it was considered an unfortunate accident. Homicide was viewed as a relatively minor abuse of power or privilege, and could be compensated by money. The social rank of perpetrator and victim were of paramount importance, and, providing she limited her abuse to commoners, a high-born lady could continue for many years to exhibit bizarre behaviour or commit domestic outrages. Only when the killing of a well-born victim coincided with ulterior or exterior motives would the full weight of the law descend on the guilty party.

According to those who knew her, all Anna-Rosina's murders, like many of Countess Báthory's punishment-tortures, were the result of some insignificant breach of discipline. Could this be the way a terribly frustrated and otherwise powerless woman released her rage? Men's rages were legitimised and dissipated in military games or real warfare, or banditry or wife-beating or hunting. Noble Hungarian women had all the responsibilities of men but few of the privileges, apart from absolute power over their female domestic staff. Where better to go to vent their anger at the intolerable tensions of their lives?

With clear evidence of her guilt, and the machinery of the state against her, the result of the trial was probably a foregone conclusion, but, as often happened in those days, during the proceedings in 1637 Anna-Rosina Listhius escaped and fled to Poland. Because of her rank and because other members of her own family were respected servants of the crown, on 27 March 1638 the King issued a letter of mercy pardoning her and even allowing her to keep some of her former family estates. The portion of the Thurzó fortune to which she was entitled very probably passed into the ownership of her accusers.

The fate of Anna Báthory, sister of the murdered Prince Gábor and niece of Elisabeth, was as extraordinary as theirs and her story, too, deserves to be looked at in detail for the parallels it contains with Elisabeth's treatment at the hands of great men.[24]

Anna was born in 1594 to the still pre-eminent Somlyóis, the senior branch of the Báthory family. Such was her fall from privilege and power that the exact date of her death was not even recorded – nothing was heard of her after the year 1640 and she is presumed to have passed away in penury and obscurity somewhere in Poland or Hungary. She spent the years from 1601 at the Ecsed court of her uncle Stephen, Elisabeth Báthory's elder brother and Chief Justice of Hungary, who doted on her not least because she bore the same name as his beloved mother. Among the charges later levelled against her were that she fornicated with a local silversmith while at Ecsed and that she committed innumerable acts of incest with Gábor her brother. While this cannot be disproved, it is hard to see the pious, reclusive guardian Count Stephen allowing his eight- or nine-year-old charge such freedoms. Two years before his death in 1605 Stephen drew up a will bequeathing the town of Tasnád with its surrounding lands to Anna with the provision that she employ only Calvinist priests to minister to its population. In the same will he also instructed the fourteen-year-old Gábor to take responsibility for his younger sister's wellbeing.

On 11 November 1608 the deafening gun salutes which rang out across the city of Koloszvár in Transylvania cracked the walls and chimneypieces of many local houses: Anna Báthory was marrying Transylvanian lord Dénes Bánffy, a supporter of Stephen Bocskai, who had appointed him captain of Nagyvárad fortress and rewarded him with estates at Tokaj, Tarcal and Kereki. Almost nothing is known of the couple's life together at Kereki castle, but it seems that the strong-minded bride refused to consummate a marriage which was probably nothing but a political arrangement: Bánffy died in 1612 and after the required year of mourning Anna married again to a young noble named Sigmund Jósika, a union which may have been initiated by love (she gave birth to a son and named him Gábor like her brother) but which fuelled the controversy that surrounded the Countess for the rest of her life. Jósika was a Catholic, a fact which turned the powerful Calvinist priesthood against Anna, and he was an intriguer who several times switched allegiances during the rule of Prince Gábor Bethlen.

If not actually widowed, the headstrong and very wealthy noblewoman was living in circumstances similar to those of her aunt in the years before her imprisonment. Left alone by Jósika, who had fled to join the Homonnay Drugeth faction in Hungary, and without a male relative to protect her since the murder of her brother in 1613, Anna nevertheless presided over a flamboyant and merry court at Kereki. Public gossip was sure that she had taken her estate manager János Krajnik as her lover and had even married him bigamously in secret.

But it was not only the prurience of hostile neighbours and tavern rumours that Anna had to fear. The new Transylvanian Prince Gábor Bethlen still lacked the wealth, property and reputation that would guarantee his hold on the Principality. He needed quickly to dispossess a noble family or two, and the relatives of the former Prince presented irresistible targets. Their dynasty was in decline, their landholdings were placed in key defensive sites across the country and their only adult heirs were three vulnerable widows, one of whom was already notorious as a shameless *femme fatale*.

With Anna's enemies the Protestant pastors to help and advise him, Bethlen put Lady Kate Török, Lady Kate Iffjú and Lady Anna Báthory on trial for witchcraft. Witnesses were called to blacken Anna's name: a certain Illés Nagy testified: 'I have heard about my ladyship, Mistress Bánffy, that she gave birth to a child by János Krajnik, her estate manager, and I was invited to Kereki castle to dine and there at dinner I saw them together over the table, winking and nibbling at each other . . .' This was the quality of the evidence laid against Anna, along with the unsupported charges of incest and infanticide. As for witchcraft, it has been seen how seamlessly and dangerously the roles of aristocratic healer and sorceress shaded into one another at that time, and Anna seems indeed to have consorted with 'witches', judging by her co-defendants in a later trial. This time, the less powerful women accused with her were duly condemned and their properties seized; Anna too forfeited part of her wealth, but escaped with her life.

After getting a portion of what he coveted, Bethlen turned his attention to political matters, among them the threat from Anna's estranged husband, Jósika, who attacked him in 1616 at the head of an army of Hajdúks loyal to the late Elisabeth's son-in-law George Drugeth. By 1618 the absurd merry-go-round of intrigue and betrayal had brought Bethlen and Jósika together again, giving Bethlen a new excuse to arrest Anna, this time on the whimsical pretext of forcing her into a reconciliation with her husband. In fact, the Prince had been plotting against the Lady throughout the year. In July he had written to his brother-in-law: 'There is no negotiating with Mistress Bánffy [he still affected not to recognise her marriage to Jósika]; she is very stubborn. I even appointed my Chancellor Péchy to act as her confessor, but all his efforts were in vain. She behaves so inhumanly towards me that I must needs find another way of dealing with her.' Bethlen ordered the arrest and interrogation of Stephen Horváth, another of Anna's retainers and supposed lovers who he hoped would confess the secrets of his mistress's incest and dabblings in sorcery.

In December that year a new trial was mounted and Anna Báthory, in addition to being tortured, suffered the indignity of being accused of the murder of her own son – actually alive and being sheltered in Hungary by Nicholas Esterházy – and of bewitching Prince Gábor Bethlen himself in an incident which must have stretched the credulity of her judges to its limits. Bethlen solemnly recorded that while they were passing Anna's castle of Kereki the previous May his counsellors had seen their prince dancing naked with the accused – a vision which, the court was told, could only have been the result of an evil spell cast upon them by the Lady herself. As the trial progressed Sigmund Jósika again turned against Bethlen, this time siding with the figurehead of the Counter-Reformation, Cardinal Peter Pázmány, while rumours surfaced in Constantinople that the Turks might back the very last surviving male Báthory, Anna's young brother Andrew, against Bethlen. Seeing that Bethlen was in deadly earnest and being completely without supporters in Transylvania, Anna allowed the Prince to seize Kereki and gave up most of her movable treasures in return for the dropping of all the charges against her. Bethlen also occupied the ancient Báthory seat, the fortified palace of Ecsed in the marshlands near the Partium, but failed to get legal title to it. Within a few months his wife was serving meals on Anna's golden dishes; the Báthory family silver had been melted down to pay the wages of the Prince's mercenaries.

There is a subtext to all the letters and testimonies that record Gábor Bethlen's persecution of Anna Báthory; Susannah Károlyi, the Prince's wife, was plain and sickly and suffered from melancholia, and hated the vivacious siren whom she rightly saw as her rival for Bethlen's affections, while her husband had secretly considered divorcing her to marry the woman he had conspired against (whether his real motive at that point was love or profit is not known; the likelihood is both). Anna was probably beautiful, with the huge eyes, long nose and black hair that ran in the Báthory family, and may have enjoyed many lovers as the gossips said and as her brother undoubtedly had – although virtually any woman who flaunted her independence was assumed to be sexually insatiable. But the evidence used against her was always tainted by prejudice and superstition and almost always hearsay. One of many similarities with the case of Elisabeth, the Blood Countess, is that those contemporary chroniclers and pamphleteers who were not in the pay of Bethlen or part of his circle were silent on the subject of Anna, as if they knew that the slanders levelled against her were just that, fictions grasped at to cloak a campaign of extortion.

What happened next is just as bizarre as what had gone before and has to be pieced together from fragmentary sources, but it seems that Bethlen agreed to re-arrest Anna Báthory, who was now living in her estate at Tasnád, to force her to cure his wife's illnesses by witchcraft. When the 'curing' failed, she was accused of using her magic to try to kill Lady Károlyi. In his letters to his depressive and deluded wife, Bethlen pandered to her fantasies about Anna, describing her as 'the fifth consort of the devil'. 'We shall start a trial', he wrote, 'and if she is condemned, we will take her life. She can expect nothing more from me. The sinful must be burned! The flagrant murderous devilish whore!' And Anna Báthory was on trial for her life again, this time alongside several poor 'wise women' and 'smearers'.

The trial took place in 1621, and the defendants would almost certainly have been burned at the stake had not Bethlen been distracted by threats to his regime from Hungary and Turkey. As it was, he succeeded this time in taking full possession of Ecsed and confiscated Anna's last substantial estate of Tasnád too. The destitute and powerless woman, still only twenty-seven years old, was allowed to flee into Poland with Andrew, her young brother.

Other women had lost their minds in circumstances less formidable than those Anna had faced, but in 1634, after the death of her persecutor Bethlen, she insisted on returning to Transylvania to fight once more to reclaim the lands that had been stripped from her so unjustly. It was not to be, of course. The families who were left with the spoils from the previous confiscations simply resurrected the charges of incest, witchcraft and murder to discredit her and she was tried yet again in 1640, inconclusively but humiliatingly. Some acquaintances pleaded on her behalf for sympathy, reporting that she was ageing and ailing with swollen legs and haemorrhages from the womb. And not everyone abandoned her in her final plight. Back in Hungary in 1636 she had visited the court of the grandest of the new aristocrats, Nicholas Esterházy, the same magnate who had dispossessed George Thurzó's widow and who the following year would arrest and try Anna-Rosina Listhius. Esterházy, who as an impoverished youth had admired the glamorous Gábor Báthory, took pity on her, giving her a house and servants near his seat at Kismarton, now Eisenstadt.

At the heart of this narrative is a blank: we know even less of Anna's real character and appearance than we do of her aunt Elisabeth. All we can be sure of is that Lady Anna Báthory was comprehensively ruined and vilified at the hands of a prince whom Hungary has since celebrated as a wise and just ruler. The most important study of her ordeals, 'The Enchantress Anna Báthory', published by the historian András Komáromy in 1894, was poetic but riddled with inaccuracies. It was this article that inspired the fictional versions of the case that soon completely overwhelmed the history. A young seductress, even if she was a witch, was a more romantic and less shameful icon than a mass-murderess, and Anna became a colourful bit-part player in the nineteenth- and twentieth-century romanticising of Transylvania's golden age and the myth of Gábor Bethlen.

★   ★   ★

The few commentators who have been aware of it have treated the Listhius affair as an open-and-shut case – there is after all written proof that the woman was unstable, and her last victim's family were willing to take action against her publicly. But it cannot be coincidence that, as with Elisabeth and her niece Anna Báthory, the defendant was an isolated and self-willed widow who was the only obstacle to the disposal of an enormous inheritance. In each of the three cases the real instigator of the legal process was the person who, if a successful trial were concluded, stood to confiscate the lion's share of that inheritance. In every case the accuser, twice the ruling Palatine, once the Prince of Transylvania, was a rapacious representative of the new aristocracy, bent on establishing the basis for a lasting dynasty. Given this compelling motive and the overwhelming power of the prosecuting forces, the guilt or innocence of the women on trial was incidental, but the choice of crime with which to charge them was a crucial element. The great attraction of sorcery and bodily harm was that they were personal transgressions, and no other powerful figures need be involved or compromised. The shock effect of crimes like these was enough to distract people from any weakness in the proof. They were in any case easy to substantiate if we conclude that many if not most nobles beat their servants or had them beaten, and that nearly all noblewomen dabbled in magic, often with the help of commoners of doubtful reputation.

Epilogue

There is no feast without cruelty.

Friedrich Nietzsche

At midnight, just before Midsummer's Day, the ruins of Castle Čachtice are transformed. Here and there among the piles of stones on the escarpment little campfires are flickering. Lit by the faint light of stars and crisscrossing meteors on a moonless night, the castle seems to stand, as the phrase goes, on the roof of the world. One shooting star, passing close by, lights up the whole hillside, bleaching out shadows, as briefly and suddenly as an arc-light switched on for an instant. From somewhere inside the ruins comes the sound of a woman laughing, not loudly, but an unrestrained and unaffected laugh that continues for minutes, then minutes more; long after her clear voice should have died away the woman goes on laughing.

Now in summer, just as in the autumn of the previous year, there is nothing especially sinister about the hill above Čachtice, and straining for intimations of the past and its ghosts goes unrewarded. But still there is something. A belief in ley-lines, geomancy, *feng shui* – the 'dragon-wind' – has been a fashionable distraction in the west for

247

years now. In Slovakia it is almost unknown, yet at this site among the White Carpathians on this clear night it is possible to experience something like a concentration of pure energy in the earth and in the sky, a sense of the nearness of elemental forces that are beyond description and (*pace* the French philosophers) beyond judgement.

Just as the manor of Čachtice, beyond the reach of the Transylvanian Prince, had been the logical setting for her arrest, its isolated castle was the ideal place to imprison the disgraced Countess. Apart from the irony that it had witnessed the cruel death of the girls in the autumn of 1610, it was almost midway between the national capital at Bratislava, whence the power of the King and the Palatine was exercised, and Bytča, from which Thurzó personally ruled over the surrounding counties. The spider in the web had become the fly. Once Elisabeth was secured, Čachtice was easily policed; most of the small population were loyal to the young Paul Nádasdy and his guardian in Sárvár, the rest were intimidated by the invisible, covetous presence of Lord George Thurzó.

After the events of January 1611 the little community had settled back into its usual seasonal routines, though this was not a return to the recent past, it was a new kind of normality, for the place was quieter, more serene than it had been for more than a decade. A great catharsis had come and gone, as when the witch is at last taken out of the village, chained in a cart.

After Elisabeth had become invisible, she began to merge in the dreams of the local people and in the musings of scholars with other creatures from legend: witches, fairies, empresses. In time she became part of the topography too, infused into the cellars and underground passages where dark water and wine and blood were indistinguishable.

By 1614 Pastor Ponikenus was gone, promoted to superintendent of the whole region, Zvonarić had been made a bishop. Records examined now for the first time show that the Čachtice estate was shunned by the senior family members after Elisabeth's death.[1] Her son Paul visited the village only rarely to negotiate the transfer of parcels of land, and it was a handful of his servants who posted guards in the empty castle and sat down to dine in the manor-house in the years before it was finally destroyed by fire. In the list of retainers employed between 1623 and 1625, three names are of particular interest: Stephen Vágy, Imre Ocskai and Balint Jelen were still in the service of the

Nádasdys. All three had testified against their mistress in the hearings of 1611.

Their testimonies and the others had started cautiously. Then, when it became clear that Countess Báthory was doomed, there came a great release of tension, a flood of denunciations. The things they said were not 'true', but were the symbolic representation of their memories of living in and around her court, years spent in awe and in fear of her when she was there, in terror of her assistants when she was not. As the horrible allegations accumulated, it became less and less important whether they were truthful or not. The Palatine had the evidence he needed to make a hostage of her. The little people of the estates, assured that they were safe from the last Báthorys and promised by Imre Megyery that they would be forgiven by the Nádasdy family, were encouraged to say what they liked, allowed their own moment of triumph over their oppressor.

While she was free Elisabeth had moved regally through two different sealed worlds, each bound by strict conventions. She stalked through the hot-house below stairs and perhaps she indulged her curiosity, experimenting with the help of her assistants with healing methods and magical procedures. At the same time she attended the nobles' festivities, slightly outside the throng, watching the great game with its hundred or so players, all known to one another, all aware of the rules, jostling for land, arranging weddings of mutual convenience, plotting to dispossess a neighbour or ruin a family member.

She had been a creature of her time, but an extraordinary woman, who was generous ('like a mother I was to you . . . from the smallest to the highest . . .') and strong ('You will feel our anger!'), but who thought too much of herself and demanded too much of those who attended her. In their turn her servants feared her and tried clumsily to emulate her, substituting brutal force for the authority that had been bred into her.

The Palatine, Thurzó, could be content that he had done what was necessary, even though neither he nor Lady Czobor would ever be certain of what had really gone on in the Widow Nádasdy's court. His own feelings about the woman were probably ambivalent until the end. He had admired her strength and been in awe of her self-assurance, but he had grown up with the darker rumours that clung to her family: on the shelves of the family library when he was a pious, impressionable boy was the history by his stepfather's kinsman, the humanist Bishop

Ferenc Forgách, in which Lady Klára Báthory's spectacular vices had been catalogued in more than disinterested detail.

Girls died – perhaps more in Elisabeth Báthory's court than in any other, given the severity of her regime. Dozens or even scores may have died over the years, but it was not the deaths so much as the disdain with which she treated curious relatives and bereaved parents and meddlesome priests that incensed outsiders, just as her Báthory pride ruffled the feathers of the other nobles. Men in particular were snubbed; it was galling for Bicsérdy, Szilvássy and the other courtiers to be overruled, sidelined, while she continued on her despotic course, dispensing gifts, issuing her instructions, conferring with her wise-woman, confounding her enemies, answerable to nobody at all.

If the way in which she was treated by her male enemies was not unique but part of a larger consistency, her own actions can be seen as part of another pattern. 'You will find a man in me!' she warned, more than a century before women retreated into a pose of fluttering defencelessness. Her sarcasm, unsettling in a woman, and her splendid cruelties were talked about in awed whispers on both sides of the Danube, and she drew like the men on an ancient tradition, the peculiarly Hungarian delight in *káröröm*, in the ingenious, even witty, exercise of grotesque cruelty, a mingling of the tragic and the hilarious.

We cannot finally know if she was guilty – of mutilating and murdering with her own hands – but we can see that she was responsible, solely and absolutely, for what happened in her courts. The blood-fetishist, the insatiable lesbian dominatrix and the serial murderess are constructs of our time, anachronisms. But so, too, is the proud lady in the tower waiting with sad dignity for history to restore her tarnished reputation. From the little hard evidence available, we cannot say for sure that Countess Elisabeth Báthory was not a uniquely prolific killer, literally a she-devil, but it was not necessary that she should be these things in order to preside over multiple deaths. If they believed that she was a depraved torturer who littered the countryside with corpses, why did the churches (the Catholics in the years before her grandson Francis converted, the banished Lutherans thereafter) remain silent and miss the opportunity to preach and propagandise?

Up by the castle in the night, it becomes more and more difficult to concentrate on the questions that remain. Individual humans, named and dated, seem impossibly distant, irrelevant, neither their misdeeds nor their suffering are easy to evoke. Just before setting off down the path through the trees and past the gypsy houses to the Slovak village, the words of the English elegy return to mind:

> We are all one
> She sees the clouds scud by, she breathes your air,
> pities the past and those who settled there.

Acknowledgements

The most sincere thanks are due to everyone who joined the author in risking what became known during the preparation of this book as 'the curse of Erzsébet'. This was the malign influence that, despite the gift from a Brazilian friend of a rosary blessed in turn by a priest and a white witch, must have caused the strange attacks of lassitude and confusion which beset the writer, and led to his near-death in a Caribbean lagoon, followed by an unexplained erasing of computer files just as writing began in earnest. The effects of the curse extended to those who accompanied the writer in his fieldwork, particularly two colleagues and friends without whom the project would scarcely have been manageable. One was the eminent Hungarian historian of the early modern period Dr Gábor Várkonyi, who witnessed the unseasonal snowstorms that came out of nowhere to block the roads at Lockenhaus and again at Deutschkreuz, and who was then marooned with the author in deeper snow beneath the walls of Castle Forchtenstein, and trapped once more, this time by a vast steel shutter, in the underground car park below the Esterházy palace at Eisenstadt. The other was the writer, critic and translator János Széky, who helped to interpret the spirit of Hungary as well as its literature and language, and who found himself at dusk on All Souls' Night locked into the grounds of Bratislava castle with the author as a red sky darkened and the temperature fell.

Another friend and guide, L'uba Vávrová of the British Council in Bratislava, with Dr Tünde Lengyelová of the Slovak Academy of Science coped bravely with further near-death experiences on the highways to and from Čachtice and Bytča. In Vienna the curse conjured up the spirit of ancient female furies, the apparition in the Haus, Hof und Staatsarchiv who glaringly brushed aside a plaintive request for assistance. In the Austrian National Library, the staff could not have been more accommodating, but there, as in the Budapest and British Libraries, key texts – some which had not been consulted for years – mysteriously disappeared from their places on the shelves as soon as they were requested, reappearing magically months later.

All those mentioned above gave most generously of their time and expertise for little or no reward, as did Professor László Péter of the London University School of Slavonic and East European Studies, who provided encouragement from the outset, and Professor Susan Bassnett of Warwick University, to whom thanks for Alejandra Pizarnik. In Budapest the historians Dr Katalin Péter, Professor Ágnes R. Várkonyi, Pál Ritoók, Borbála Benda, Zsuzsana Bozai and Tibor Lukács all provided invaluable and very tangible support, details of which can be found in the chapter notes. Attempts to trace Dr László Nagy were unsuccessful, but his published and broadcast opinions on the Báthory family scandals were enormously helpful. In Slovakia it was Beata Havelská of the Academy of Music and Dramatic Arts in Bratislava, Dr Pavol Štekauer, Dr Štefan Franko and the students of the Faculty of Arts at Šáfárik University who helped translate the great volume of source material, only a small part of which could be reproduced here. Professor Henrich Pifko, the photographer Karol Kallay and the curators of the Čachtice Museum and the State Archives at Bytča deserve especial gratitude, also extended to the heirs of Jožo Nižňanský for permission to quote from his work.

Given the deep divisions of opinion on the question of the Widow Nádasdy's guilt and the disagreements – sometimes approaching acrimony – between scholars writing on the case, it was immensely gratifying that the chief proponents of the two main views and the two most important living authorities on the life of Countess Báthory, Dr Jozef Kočiš, the former archivist at Bytča castle, and Dr Irma Szádeczky-Kardoss, lawyer and defender of Elisabeth's good name, not only were willing to spend long hours answering this author's questions, but gave permission to quote extensively from their published works and even allowed materials from their private archives to be used in the making of this book. Both refused to accept payment. Neither of them is likely to be satisfied by the conclusions reached in this appraisal of the Báthory affair, but perhaps the sincere acknowledgement of a scholarly debt will go some way towards appeasing them.

The author would like to give thanks to the explorer Rob Humphreys, to the British novelist Jennifer Potter for sharing her insights and lending him her memories of Căchtice, and to the Dutch artist Erzsébet Baerveldt, who not only provided new and essential information concerning the portraits of Countess Báthory and her costumes but reminded a distracted writer of the need for emotional empathy in any re-creation of the mysteries of the past.

Thanks must also go to the publishers, Bloomsbury, for their patience in the face of a writer labouring under a curse, and to M.M., who had to live with its daily manifestations.

Tony Thorne
London, 1997

Notes

Preface

1 *Bathory Palace*, c/o Lara A. Haynes, 1618 SW 3rd, Topeka Ks. 66606–1215, USA.
2 The case was reported in the London *Daily Mail* on Thursday 9 February 1995.

Introduction

1 See Susan Bassnett, 'Blood and Mirrors: Imagery of Violence in the Writings of Alejandra Pizarnik', in *Essays on Latin American Women*, OUP, Oxford 1996.
2 Alejandra Pizarnik, 'The Bloody Countess', in A. Manguel (ed.), *Other Fires*, Picador, London, 1986.
3 Valentine Penrose, *La Comtesse Sanglante*, Mercure de France, Paris, 1957.
4 John Paget, Esq., *Hungary and Transylvania*, John Murray, London, 1839.
5 Ibid.
6 *Contes Immoraux*, directed by Walerian Borowczyk, Argos films, France, 1974.
7 *Countess Dracula*, directed by Peter Sasdy, Hammer Films, GB, 1970.
8 Gabriel Ronay, *The Truth about Dracula*, Victor Gollancz, London, 1972.
9 J. Sheridan le Fanu, 'Carmilla', in *Dark Blue* magazine, London, 1871.

255

10 Now generally spelled Szápolyai in Hungarian sources.
11   *For snow-white steed thou gav'st the land*
                      For golden bit, the grass
                      For the rich saddle, Duna's stream
                      Now bring the deed to pass.
                                 Bowring, *Poetry of the Magyars*

12 'R. C. Gentleman' in the preface to his translation of Martin Fumée's *A True Historie of the Troubles of Hungarie*, London, 1600.
13 William Lithgow, *Travels and Voyages through Europe, Asia and Africa for Nineteen Years*, 12th edn, Leith, 1814. William Lithgow was one of the earliest English-speaking gentleman-explorers, recording the opinions of a forthright Presbyterian islander as he travelled through Hungary and into Transylvania and Wallachia in 1616, descending the Danube from Vienna in the company of the Turkish ambassador.
14 Charles Boner, *Transylvania: Its Products and its People*, Longman, London, 1865.
15 Lithgow, *Travels*.
16 'Magyarfaló vasgárdista? Cioran és a magyarok' ('Hungarophagous Iron Guardist? Cioran and the Hungarians'), *Magyar Napló*, no. 24, Budapest, November 1993.
17 Jozo Nižňanský, *Čachtická Pani*, Prague, 1932.
18 Andrei Codrescu, *The Blood Countess*, Simon & Schuster, New York, 1995.
19 Frances Gordon, *Blood Ritual*, Headline, London, 1994.
20 Margaret Nicholas, *The World's Wickedest Women*, Octopus Books, London 1984.

Chapter One

1 Béla Hamvas, *Az Öt Geniusz*, Szombathely, 1989.
2 John Paget, Esq., *Hungary and Transylvania*, John Murray, London, 1839.
3 Ibid.
4 Ibid.
5 The very few artefacts preserved from the old manor-house are displayed in the Čachtice museum, which is located in a wing of the newer mansion there.
6 Von Elsberg reproduces a photograph of the house in question in his work *Die Blutgräfin. Elisabeth Báthory*, Breslau, 1894, as does Revický in his *Báthory Erzsebet*, Piešťány, 1903.
7 See e.g. Paget, *Hungary*; and *Biographie Universelle*, Paris, 1843.
8 Jožo Nižňanský, *Čachtická Pani*, Prague, 1932.
9 G. Pálóczy-Horváth, *In Darkest Hungary*, Victor Gollancz, London, 1944.
10 Istvan Werböczy, *Opus Tripartitum Juris Consuetudinarii Hungariae*, 1514.
11 Here and elsewhere the author is much indebted to Dr Gábor Várkonyi of Budapest University for his insights into the history of Hungary and

Transylvania. Parts of this summary are adapted with kind permission from his lecture 'Poland and Hungary at the End of the Sixteenth Century', delivered at the London University School of Slavonic and East European Studies, 28 November 1995.

12 P. Burke (ed.), *Economy and Society in Early Modern Europe*, RKP, London, 1972.

13 Lady Hellenbach, *Treue Ermahnung an Ihre Einzige Tochter*, Leipzig, 1760.

14 *Voivode* or *vajda* was the title given to a ruler appointed to govern a district or province; a post which was often a stepping stone on to the higher aristocracy.

15 Katalin Péter, 'The Later Ottoman Period and Royal Hungary', in Péter F. Sugár, Péter Hanák and Tibor Frank (eds), *A History of Hungary*, I.B. Tauris & Co., London and New York, 1979.

16 Dominic G. Kosary, *A History of Hungary*, Arno Press and *New York Times*, New York, 1971.

17 Jozef Kočiš, *Bytčiansky Zámok*, Martin, 1974.

18 Thomas da Costa Kaufman, *Court, Cloister and City: The Art and Culture of Central Europe, 1450–1800*, Weidenfeld & Nicolson, London, 1995.

19 The letter is in the Thurzó family archive in the Slovak State Regional Archive at Bytča.

20 Ibid.

21 Paget, *Hungary*.

Chapter Two

1 The January trial evidence was first published in the journal *Hesperus* in Prague in 1817.

2 *Biographie Universelle*, Paris, 1843.

3 Valentine Penrose, *La Comtesse Sanglante*, Mercure de France, Paris, 1957.

4 S. T. Bindoff, *Tudor England*, Penguin, London, 1950.

5 Richard van Dülmen, *Theatre of Horror*, Polity Press, Cambridge, 1990.

6 Original instruments of torture are on display for example in the castle of Nuremberg in Germany and Warwick castle in England; methods of torture are illustrated in Foxe's *Book of Martyrs* (1554, 1563).

7 Kálmán Vándor, *Báthory Erzsébet*, Budapest, 1941.

8 The original transcript and judgements are in the Thurzó archive at Bytča.

9 Ibid.

10 Although this intriguing reference to a sexually ambiguous companion is reminiscent of similar testimony given in a number of witch-trials across Europe, it was not corroborated or referred to by other witnesses.

11 See p. 185.

12 In the Thurzó archive at Bytča.

13 Ibid.

14 Jozef Kočiš, *Bytčiansky Zámok*, Martin, 1974.

Chapter Three

1 László Túróczi, *Ungaria Suis cum Regibus Compendio Data*, Tyrnava, 1744.
2 John Paget, Esq., *Hungary and Transylvania*, John Murray, London, 1839.
3 An original copy of the evidence is in the Hungarian National Archives in Budapest.
4 One of the castle guards at Beckov, Paul Rakolupsky, was required on taking up his post in 1608 to swear his oath of fealty to Elisabeth and jointly to Francis Mágóchy, his wife Ursula Dersffy, János (not Péter) Ráttkay, Daniel Pongrácz and his wife Anna Majláth. The document is in the Nádasdy archive in Budapest.
5 The connection between the families was traced by Irma Szádeczky-Kardoss in her work, *Báthory Erzsébet – Igazsága*, Budapest, 1993.
6 The original is in the Hungarian National Archives in Budapest.
7 See p. 99.
8 'Hungarians in Purgatory', a chapter in V. Kovács Sándor (ed), from *The History of Our Literature of Chivalry*, Szépirodalmi Könyvkiadó, Budapest, 1985.
9 The original is in the Thurzó archive in the Hungarian National Archives in Budapest.
10 Ibid.
11 Ibid.
12 Ibid.
13 Count Esterházy includes in his book of spells and cures an interesting formula which he calls a 'snake-curse'. This sequence of words, which is very similar in format to Elisabeth's charm, is in fact a Slavonic prayer with the addition of one or two nonsense terms. So it seems that the Hungarian ruling class often used the language of their Slav serfs and priests in superstitious ceremonies (also suggesting that they did not well understand what they were saying and arguing against their fluency in Slovak or Croatian).
14 Ibid.
15 Barton's letter is in the British Museum Manuscript Room, collection Cotton Nero B XII.
16 There are odd words of Czech and Hungarian in both the Latin and Slovak sequences. (Ponikenus' origins are not known, although he was obviously an ethnic Slav, either native to the region or one of many who had migrated north from Slovenia and Croatia to escape from the advancing Turks or to evangelise.)
17 Tivadar Lehoczky, 'Babonaság és Kuruzslás a XVII. Században', *Századok*, Budapest, 1872.
18 Quoted in Kálmán Thaly, 'Gyógyítások Ráolvasás és Babonaság Által', *Századok*, Budapest, 1883.
19 Weber and Szádeczky, 'Adalékok'.

20 From the Chronicles of Szepesség, town records from the seventeenth century, 1st published Budapest, 1910 (2nd ed., Budapest, 1988).
21 Christopher Frayling (ed.), *Vampyres: Lord Byron to Count Dracula*, Faber & Faber, London, 1991.
22 Mme E. de Laszowska Gérard, 'Transylvanian Superstitions', in *XIV Century*, July 1885.

Chapter Four

1 Béla Radvánszky, 'Lakodalmak a XVI és XVII Században', *Századok*, Budapest, 1883.
2 Letter of 1598, published in *Századok*, Budapest, 1894.
3 Quoted in László Nagy, *Az Erös Fekete Bég (The Mighty Black Bey, the Life of Ferenc Nádasdy)*, Budapest, 1987.
4 The correspondence is in the Nádasdy family archive in the Hungarian National Archives in Budapest.
5 Ibid.
6 In the Nádasdy family archive.
7 R. A. von Elsberg, *Die Blutgräfin. Elisabeth Báthory*, Breslau, 1894.
8 The celebratory pamphlet was written by Franciscus Hippolytus Hildesheim and printed by Stephan Creuzer.
9 Radvánszky, 'Lakodalmak'.
10 Ibid.
11 Paula Delsol, *Nouveau Grimoire de l'Amour*, Mercure de France, Paris, 1971.
12 Ágnes R. Várkonyi, *Connections between the Cessation of Witch Trials and the Transformation of Social Structure Related to Hygiene*, Akadémiai Kiadó, Budapest, 1991.
13 *Magyarország Története* (1526–1686 section), ed. Ágnes R. Várkonyi, Akadémiai Kiadó, Budapest, 1987.
14 The letter from Countess Báthory is referred to in the works of Katalin Péter and Irma Szádeczky-Kardoss.
15 See p. 63.

Chapter Five

1 Quoted (abridged) in László Nagy, *A Rossz Hírü Báthoryak*, Budapest, 1984.
2 Ibid.
3 Zsuzsana Bozai, 'Hungarian Aristocratic Women in the Seventeenth Century' (unpublished thesis), Budapest, 1995.
4 Quoted in László Nagy, *Az Erös Fekete Bég: Nádasdy Ferenc*, Budapest, 1987.
5 Bozai, 'Hungarian Aristocratic Women'.
6 Béla Radvánszky, 'Foglalkozás, Idötöltés, Játék a XVI és XVII. Században', *Századok*, Budapest, 1887.

7 See p. 48.
8 Béla Radvánszky, 'The Feasts of Count Szaniszló Thurzó in 1603', *Századok*, Budapest, 1893.
9 The document is in the Thurzó archive at Bytča.
10 In the Nádasdy archive in the Hungarian National Archives in Budapest.
11 Extracts from the eulogy are quoted in Nagy, *Az Erös Fekete Bég*.
12 From the Nádasdy archive in Budapest.
13 Ibid.
14 Ibid.
15 Ibid.
16 William Lithgow, *Travels and Voyages through Europe, Asia and Africa for Nineteen Years*, 12th edn, Leith, 1814.
17 Bozai, 'Hungarian Aristocratic Women'.
18 Ágnes R. Várkonyi, *Connections between the Cessation of Witch Trials and the Transformation of Social Structure Related to Hygiene*, Akadémiai Kiadó, Budapest, 1991.
19 *Pictures from the Past of the Healing Arts*, Semmelweiss Museum, Budapest, 1993.
20 Ferenc Schram, *Magyarorszägi Boszorkányperek 1529–1768*, Budapest, 1970 and 1982.
21 In the Nádasdy archive in Budapest.
22 Ibid.
23 Sándor Takáts, *Régi Magyar Asszonyok*, Budapest, 1982.
24 R. A. von Elsberg, *Die Blutgräfin. Elisabeth Báthory*, Breslau, 1894.
25 The chronicles record that two months after Paul's death on 15 October his widow held court in Čachtice; if the portraits were hung there around that time, they were perhaps rescued by the Zays when Čachtice was taken over by the Esztergom Chapter and then by the Pest Veterans' Hospital after the execution of Francis Nádasdy II in 1671.
26 Károlyi Lajos, *Ecsedy Báthory E.*, and Jónas Zaborský, *Báthoryčka*, both 1870. The former reproduces a portrait which seems to be the same as that printed by von Elsberg.

Chapter Six

1 The correspondence referred to here is in the Thurzó family archive at Bytča, and was explored by the Hungarian historian Zsuzsana Bozai in her as yet unpublished thesis, 'Hungarian Aristocratic Women of the Seventeenth Century' (Budapest, 1995).
2 Jozef Kočiš, *Alžbeta Báthoryová a Palatín Thurzó*, Martin, 1981.
3 Ibid.
4 *Oxford History of Hungarian Literature*, ed. Lórant Czigány, OUP, Oxford, 1984.
5 Denis Sinor, *History of Hungary*, George Allen & Unwin, London, 1959.
6 The letter is in the Nádasdy archive in the Hungarian National Archives in Budapest.

7 The letter is in the Thurzo archive at Bytča.
8 *The Chronicles of Csejthe*, assembled from fragments found at Humenné by András Komáromy and published in *Történelmi Tár*, Budapest, 1899.
9 Máté Szepsi Laczkó (d. 1633) in *Emlékezetül Hagyott Írások* ('Writings from Memory'), Dacia Könyvkiadó, Romania, 1983.
10 In the Nádasdy archive in the Hungarian National Archives in Budapest.
11 Ibid.
12 In the Thurzó archive at Bytča.
13 See p. 179.
14 Irma Szádeczky-Kardoss, *Báthory Erzsébet – Igazsága*, Budapest, 1993.
15 The letter is in the Nádasdy archive in the Hungarian National Archives in Budapest.
16 Unfortunately, Elisabeth's connection with this contraption, which is a long way from the intricate effigy decorated with breasts and pubic hair described by the legends, is not supported by any recorded testimonies. In any case, many experts now think that iron maidens, like chastity belts, were invariably nineteenth-century fakes.

Chapter Seven

1 This account of the career of Stephen Báthory is adapted with permission from the text of a lecture delivered by Dr Gábor Várkonyi at the School of Slavonic and East European Studies, University of London, 28 November 1995.
2 State Papers in the Public Record Office, London.
3 Denis Sinor, *History of Hungary*, George Allen & Unwin, London, 1959.
4 See p. 118.
5 The living Cardinal Andrew is portrayed in the plate section.
6 The Latin *History of Hungary and Transylvania* by István Szamosközy (1565–1612), plagiarised in Pál Enyedi's eighteenth-century *Cantus of the Perils of Transylvania*.
7 Bartolomej Revický, *Báthory Erzsébet*, Piešt'ány, 1903.
8 Valentine Penrose, *La Comtesse Sanglante*, Mercure de France, Paris, 1957.
9 Péter Bornemissza (or Bornemisza), *Ördögi Kísértetekröl*, 1578.
10 Revický, *Báthory Erzsébet*.
11 Andrei Codrescu, *The Blood Countess*, Simon & Schuster, New York, 1995.
12 Jozef Kočiš, *Alžbeta Báthoryová a Palatín Thurzó*, Martin, 1981.
13 Stephen's life is alluded to by, among others, László Nagy in *A Rossz Hírü Báthoryak*, Budapest, 1984; Elisabeth's brother's correspondence was analysed by Zsuzsana Bozai in her unpublished thesis, 'Hungarian Aristocratic Women of the Seventeenth Century' (Budapest, 1995).
14 Sándor Makkai, *Ördögszekér*, Budapest, 1925.
15 The letter is in the Nádasdy family archive in the Hungarian National Archives in Budapest.
16 The letter to Andrew Keresztúry is in the Hungarian National Archives in Budapest.

17 The document is in the records of the Vasvár–Szombathely Chapter (protocols of 1610) in the Vas County Archives.
18 In the Hungarian National Archives in Budapest.
19 The letter was discovered among the Miscellaneous Papers of the Nádasdy family in the Hungarian National Archives.
20 The letter is in the Thurzó archive at Bytča.
21 Nagy, *A Rossz Hírü Báthoryak.*
22 In the Bytča Archive.
23 George Závodský, 'Diarium', preserved in the Thurzó archive at Bytča.
24 In the Bytča Archive.
25 Ibid.

Chapter Eight

1 The letter is in the Thurzó archive at Bytča.
2 The letter in Latin is in the Hungarian National Archives in Budapest.
3 Quoted in Irma Szádeczky-Kardoss, *Báthory Erzsébet – Igazsága*, Budapest, 1993.
4 The certified evidence is in the Thurzó archive in the Hungarian National Archives in Budapest.
5 See p. 69.
6 See also p. 69.
7 The letters are in the Thurzó archive at Bytča.
8 In the Hungarian National Archives in Budapest.
9 Ibid.
10 Ibid.
11 Ibid.
12 The document was summarised by von Elsberg from the original in the Imperial Treasury Archive in Vienna.
13 As note 12.
14 The original is in the Hungarian National Archives in Budapest.
15 In the Thurzó archive in Budapest.
16 See p. 63.
17 George Závodský, 'Diarium', in the Thurzó archive at Bytča.
18 See p. 135.
19 The current interpretation of the sixteenth- and seventeenth-century legal conventions was given to the author by Dr Irma Szádeczky-Kardoss.
20 Quoted in Szádeczky-Kardoss, *Báthory Erzsébet.*
21 In the Thurzó archive at Bytča.
22 The guest list, from the Thurzó archive at Bytča, is reproduced in Jožef Kočiš, *Bytčiansky Zámok*, Martin, 1974.
23 In the Hungarian National Archives, Budapest.
24 Denis Sinor, *History of Hungary*, George Allen & Unwin, London, 1959.
25 *Magyarország Története*, '1526–1686' section, ed. Ágnes R. Várkonyi, Budapest, 1987.
26 Zsigmond Móricz, *Tündérkert*, Budapest, 1921.
27 *Magyarország Története.*

28 The letters are in the Hungarian section of the Haus, Hof und Staatsarchiv in Vienna.

29 In the Thurzó archive at Bytča.

30 *Magyarország Története.*

31 The references are from the *Chronicles of Csejthe*, published by András Komáromy in *Történelmi Tár*, Budapest, 1899.

32 The phrase from the will was probably a coded reference, for the family's benefit only, to the Čachtice estate as well as the treasury kept there. Čachtice had been a wedding gift from Francis Nádasdy.

33 Chronicles of Csejthe.

34 The document was lodged in the archives of the Esztergom Chapter in Trnava.

35 Margaret Nicholas, *The World's Wickedest Women*, Octopus Books, London, 1984.

36 The will with Paul Nádasdy's note is in the Nádasdy archive in the Hungarian National Archives in Budapest.

37 ('Elisabeth Báthory . . . Francisci Nádasdy Relicta Vidua, ante annos propemodum aliquot ob ingentia inaudita, et crudelissima sua facinora in perpetuous carceres detrusa, in eisdem Cheytae misere, tempore nocturno expiravit . . .') The sources relating to Elisabeth Báthory's death were published by Györgyí Gyurikovics in *Tudományos Gyüitemény*, Budapest, 1839.

38 Ibid.

39 Countess Susannah Lorántffy, for instance, was derided in Catholic pamphlets of 1641 as a cow pulling the wagon of Protestantism (she had merely supported the publication of a new Bible).

Chapter Nine

1 Dr Irma Szádeczky-Kardoss mentions the Istvánffy reference in a footnote in her *Báthory Erzsébet – Igazsága*, Budapest, 1993, but admitted to the author that she was unsure of its provenance.

2 One of the few surviving copies of Túróczi's work can be found in the Hungarian Academy of Science Institute of Literature, Eötvös József College Library. The selections quoted are from a new translation by the author and Pál Ritoók.

3 Michael Wagner, *Beyträge zur Philosophischen Anthropologie und den Damit Werwandten Wissenschaft*, Vienna, 1794.

4 *Tudományos Gyüitemény*, Budapest, 1839.

5 Max Bauer, *Titanen der Erotik. Lebensbilder aus der Sittengeschichte alles Zeiten und Volker*, Berlin, 1931.

6 R. A. von Elsberg, *Die Blutgräfin. Elisabeth Báthory*, Breslau, 1894.

7 'Hővér' (*nom de plume* of Dezső Rexa), *Erzsébet Báthory: Remarks on the Painting by István Csók, from Historical Sources*, Grand Hotel, Budapest, 1896.

8 Ibid.

9 Kálmán Benda, *Egy Új Forrástudomány: a Psychografológia*, Budapest, 1974.

10 Gabrielle Raskó, *A Nöi Bünözés*, Budapest, 1978.

11 Barna Marthy, *Élet és Irodalom* 51–52, Budapest, 1979.

12 Jozef Kočiš, *Alžbeta Báthoriová a Palatín Thurzó*, Bratislava, 1981.

13 József Antall and Károly Kapronczay, 'Aus der Geschichte des Sadismus: Elisabeth Báthory,' in *Die Waage. Zeitschrift der Chemie Grunenthal*, Rheinland, 1973; reprinted as 'Tükkel Szurkálta' in the journal *Magyarország*, Budapest, July 1974.

14 László Nagy's comments are taken from the transcript of *Társalgó*, a discussion broadcast on Hungarian radio on 26 May 1985.

15 In conversation with the author, Budapest, May 1995.

16 Michael Farin, *Heroine des Grauens, Elisabeth Bathory*, Munich, 1989.

17 Szádeczky-Kardoss, *Báthory Erzsébet*.

18 The author is grateful to Dr Tünde Lengyelová in Bratislava and to Zsuzsana Bozai, Tibor Lukács and Pál Ritoók in Budapest for sharing their ideas with him and for reacting to his opinions. Dr Lengyelová and Zsuzsana Bozai also most generously made available to him the results of their own researches in the form of notes and documents.

19 Hungarians are extremely sensitive to what they see as simplistic analogies with their recent regimes, but to an outsider the comparison seems broadly to apply.

20 See p. 234.

21 Many works of fiction and some factual treatments have accused Countess Báthory of nursing 'abnormal longings' and, of course, homosexuality is just as much a 'besetting vice' of closed institutions as cruelty. But concepts of shame would have prevented any acknowledgement, and perhaps even recognition, of lesbianism; and intensely intimate but platonic friendships between women were common, particularly in societies in wartime.

22 Peter Pázmány, *Sermons*, Pozsony, 1636.

23 Quoted in Szádeczky-Kardoss, *Báthory Erzsébet*.

24 Lithgow, *Travels*.

25 Gilberto de Mello Freyre, *Casa-grande e Senzala*, Rio de Janeiro, 1933.

26 Brian Masters, *The Dukes*, London, 1976. (Some critics questioned the elasticity of the author's definition of madness, which seemed to include eccentricity and even extreme idleness.)

27 Béla Tóth, *A Magyar Anekdótakincs* ('Treasury of Hungarian Anecdotes'), 6 vols, Budapest, 1899–1904.

28 Letters by Edward Barton in *Purchas, his Pilgrimes*, London, 1625.

Chapter Ten

1 A good recent analysis of witch-trials in Europe is Robin Briggs, *Witches and Neighbours*, HarperCollins, London, 1996.

2 Éva Pócs, *Fairies and Witches at the Boundary of South-Eastern and Central Europe*, Suomalainen Tiedeakatemia, Helsinki, 1989.

3 The sources of citations are, respectively, Kamocsa 1717 reported in Alapi 1914, Szalonak 1755 reported in Schram 1970, Szeged 1728 reported in Kovács 1899, collected by Éva Pócs in ibid.

4 E. Chishull, *Travels in Turkey and Back to England*, London, 1747.

5 Father Túróczi used a description of these cellars to introduce his version of the Báthory story (see Appendix). In his work of the 1890s, von Elsberg reproduced a sketch map showing the layout of the cellars as described to him by local people. Today only holes in the ground filled with rubble can be seen in the village by the site of the old château and on the hillside beneath the castle ruins.

6 Earle Hackett, *Blood: The Paramount Humour*, Adelaide, 1973.

7 *The Greek Herbal of Dioscorides*, translated into English by John Goodyer in 1655.

8 Béla Tóth, *Mendemondák. A Világtörténet Furcsaságai* ('Legends of Hearsay, Curiosities in World History'), Budapest, 1896.

9 Richard de Ledrede, Bishop of Ossary, *A Contemporary Narrative of Proceedings against Dame Alice Kyteler, for Sorcery in 1324*, published in London by the Camden Society in 1843.

10 The Kyteler case and similar prosecutions are mentioned in Anne Llewellyn Barstow, *Witchcraze*, Pandora, San Francisco, 1994.

11 These ideas are put forward by the Hungarian historian Gábor Klaniczay in a series of works on witchcraft and shamanism, including 'The Accusations and the Universe of Popular Magic', in Bength Ankarloo and Gustav Henningsen (eds), *Early Modern Witchcraft: Centres and Peripheries*, OUP, Oxford, 1990.

12 Zsuzsana Bozai, 'Hungarian Aristocratic Women of the Seventeenth Century' (unpublished thesis), Budapest, 1995.

13 John Paget, Esq., *Hungary & Transylvania*, John Murray, London, 1839.

14 Komáromy, *Történelmi Tár*, pp. 626–52.

15 Quoted in Bozai, 'Hungarian Aristocratic Women'.

16 Ibid.

17 Ibid.

18 The papers of the case are incomplete. Those surviving are in the Esterházy archive in the Hungarian National Archives in Budapest.

19 The legal aspects and the parallels between the Báthory and Listhius cases are explored in Irma Szádeczky-Kardoss, *Báthory Erzsébet – Igazsága*, Budapest, 1993, and were kindly elucidated for this author during discussions with Dr Szádeczky-Kardoss in Budapest in 1995.

20 (Largely) factual versions of Anna Báthory's story can be found in András Komáromy, 'A "Bübájos" Báthory Anna', *Századok*, Budapest, 1894, and Bertalan Kis, 'Báthory Anna Házasságai', *Századok*, Budapest, 1899. More recently, her life was neatly summarised in László Nagy, *A Rossz Hírü Báthoryak*, Budapest, 1984.

Epilogue

1 Borbála Benda, 'Menus from the Estate of Csejthe, 1623–1625' (unpublished thesis), Budapest, 1995.

2 D. M. Thomas, Elegy to Isabel le Despenser, 1976.

Bibliography

Ady, Endre, *Rengj Csak Föld*, Budapest, 1912

Antall, József, and Kapronczay, Károl, 'Aus der Geschichte des Sadismus: Elisabeth Báthory', *Die Waage. Zeitschrift der Chemie Grünenthal*, Rheinland, 1973

Baring-Gould, Sabine, *The Book of Were-Wolves: Being an Account of a Terrible Superstition*, London, 1854

Bassnett, Susan, 'Blood and Mirrors: Imagery of Violence in the Writings of Alejandra Pizarnik', *Essays on Latin American Women*, Oxford, 1996

Bataille, Georges, *Les Larmes d'Éros*, Paris, 1961

Bauer, Max, *Titanen der Erotik. Lebensbilder aus der Sittengeschichte alles Zeiten und Völker*, Berlin, 1931

Benda, Borbála, 'Menus from the Estate of Csejthe, 1623–1625', Budapest, 1996

Benda, Kálmán, *Egy Új Forrástudomány: a Psychografológia*, Budapest, 1974

Bérenger, Jean, *Histoire de l'Empire Habsbourg*, Paris, 1990

Bindoff, S. T., *Tudor England*, London, 1950

Biographie Universelle, Paris, 1843

Bocatius, János, *Chronicles of the Life of Prince Gábor Bethlen*, Koloszvár, 1620

Boner, Charles, *Transylvania: Its Products and Its People*, London, 1865

Bornemissza, Péter, *Ördögi Kisértetekről*, Sempte, 1578

Bozai, Zsuzsana, 'Hungarian Aristocratic Women in the Seventeenth Century', Budapest, 1995

Briggs, Robin, *Witches and Neighbours*, London, 1996

Burke, P. (ed.), *Economy and Society in Early Modern Europe*, London, 1972

Bibliography

Calmet, Augustin, *Treatise on the Vampires of Hungary and Surrounding Regions*, London, 1759

Chishull, Edmund, *Travels in Turkey & Back to England*, London, 1747

Codrescu, Andrei, *The Blood Countess*, New York, 1995

Czigány, Lórant (ed.), *Oxford History of Hungarian Literature*, Oxford, 1984

da Costa Kaufman, Thomas, *Court, Cloister and City, the Art and Culture of Central Europe, 1450–1800*, London, 1995

de Laszowska Gérard, Emily, 'Transylvanian Superstitions', *XIV Century*, London, 1885

de Ledrede, Richard, *A Contemporary Narrative of Proceedings against Dame Alice Kyteler, for Sorcery in 1324*, London, 1843

Delsol, Paula, *Nouveau Grimoire de l'Amour*, Paris, 1971

de Mello Freyre, Gilberto, *Casa-grande e Senzala*, Rio de Janeiro, 1933

Dülmen, Richard van, *Theatre of Horror*, Cambridge, 1990

Elsberg, R. A. von [Ferdinand Strobl von Ravelsberg], *Die Blutgräfin. (Elisabeth Báthory) (Ein Sitten- und Charakterbild)*, Breslau, 1894

Farin, Michael, *Heroine des Grauens*, Munich, 1989

Farkas, Deák, 'Magyar Hölgyek Levelei', *Századok*, Budapest, 1883

——, *Wesselényi Anna*, Budapest, 1875

'A Fellow of the Carpathian Society', *Magyar-Land: Travels through the Snowy Carpathian and the Great Alföld of the Magyar*, London, 1881

Fessler, Ignac Aurel, *Die Geschichte der Ungern und Ihrer Landsassen*, Leipzig, 1824

Foxe's *Book of Martyrs*, London, 1554, 1563

Frayling, Christopher (ed.), *Vampyres – Lord Byron to Count Dracula*, London, 1991

Fumée, Martin, *A True Historie of the Troubles of Hungarie, newly translated by R.C., Gentleman*, London, 1600

Gardonyi, Géza, *Eclipse of the Crescent Moon*, Budapest, 1899

Gönczi, Ferenc, *Somogyi Betyárvilág*, Kaposvár, 1944

Gordon, Frances, *Blood Ritual*, London, 1994

Gróf, László, *Carta Hungarica*, Budapest, 1988

Hackett, Earle, *Blood: the Paramount Humour*, Adelaide, 1973

Hamvas, Béla, *Az Öt Geniusz*, Szombathely, 1989

Hellenbach, Freifrau von, *Treue Ermahnung an Ihre Einzige Tochter*, Leipzig, 1760

'Hővér' [Dezső Rexa], *Báthory Erzsébet. Csók István Képéhez*, Budapest, 1896

Johnson, E. C., *On the Track of the Crescent: Erratic Notes from the Piraeus to Pesth*, London, 1885

Kis, Bertalan, 'Báthory Anna Házasságai', *Századok*, 1899

Klaniczay, Gábor, 'The Accusations and Universe of Popular Magic', *Early Modern Witchcraft: Centres & Peripheries*, ed. Bength Ankarloo and Gustav Henningsen, Oxford, 1990

Kočiš, Jozef, *Alžbeta Báthoryová a Palatín Thurzó*, Martin, 1981

Kósa, László, *Magyar Néprajzi Lexikon*, Budapest, 1981

Kosáry, Dominic C., *A History of Hungary*, New York, 1971

——, *Bytčiansky Zámok*, Martin, 1974

Komáromy, András, 'A "Bübájos" Báthory Anna', *Századok*, Budapest, 1894

Lehoczky, Tivadar, 'Babonaság és Kuruzslás a XVII. Században', *Századok*, Budapest, 1872

Lithgow, William, *Travels & Voyages through Europe, Asia & Africa for Nineteen Years* (12th edn), Leith, 1814

Makkai, Sándor, *Ördögszekér*, Budapest, 1925

Marthy, Barna, *Élet és Irodalom*, issues 51, 52, Budapest, 1979

Masters, Brian, *The Dukes*, London, 1976

Masters, R. E. L., and Lea, Edward, *Perverse Crimes in History*, New York, 1963

McNally, Raymond T., *Dracula was a Woman*, London, 1984

Mednyansky, Aloys von, *Erzählungen, Sagen und Legenden aus Ungarn Vorzeit*, Pest, 1829

——, *Malerische Reise auf dem Waagflusse in Ungern*, Pest, 1826

Nagy, Ivan, *Révai Nagy Lexikon*, Budapest, 1911

Nagy, László, *A Rossz Hírü Báthoryak*, Budapest, 1984

——, *Az Erös Fekete Bég*, Budapest, 1987

Nicholas, Margaret, *The World's Wickedest Women*, London, 1984

Nižňansky, Jožo, *Čachtická Pani*, Prague, 1932

Paget, John, *Hungary & Transylvania*, London, 1839

Pálóczy-Horváth, G., *In Darkest Hungary*, London, 1944

Pápai Párisz, Ferenc, *Pax Corporis*, Koloszvár, 1747

Parker, G., *Europe in Crisis*, New York, 1980

Pázmány, Péter, *Sermons*, Pozsony, 1636

Penrose, Valentine, *La Comtesse Sanglante*, Paris, 1957

Périsset, Maurice, *La Comtesse de Sang, Erzsébet Báthory*, Paris, 1975

Péter, Katalin, *A Csejtei Várúrnö Báthory Erzsébet*, Budapest, 1985

——, 'The later Ottoman Period and Royal Hungary', *A History of Hungary* (ed. Péter F. Sugár et al.), London & New York, 1979

Pictures from the Past of the Healing Arts, Budapest, 1993

Pizarnik, Alejandra, 'The Bloody Countess', *Other Fires*, A. Manguel (ed.), London, 1986

Pócs, Éva, *Fairies and Witches at the Boundary of South-Eastern and Central Europe*, Helsinki, 1989

Purchas, his Pilgrimes, London, 1625

Radford, Ken, *Fire Burn*, London, 1989

Radvánszky, Béla, 'Foglalkozás, Idötöltés, Játék a XVI es XVII Században', *Századok*, Budapest, 1887

Radvánszky, Béla, 'Lakodalmak a XVI és XVII Században', *Századok*, Budapest, 1883

——, *Régi Magyar Szakácskönyvek*, Budapest, 1893

Ranft, Michael, *De Masticatione Mortuorum in Tumuli*, Leipzig, 1728

Raskó, Gabrielle, *A Nöi Bünözsés*, Budapest, 1978

Revický, Bartolomej, *Báthory Erzsébet*, Piešt'ány, 1903

Ronay, Gabriel, *The Truth about Dracula*, London, 1972

Bibliography

Schram, Ferenc, *Magyarországi Boszorkányperek 1529–1768*, Budapest, 1970, 1982

Seabrook, William, 'World Champion Lady Vampire of All Time', *Witchcraft, Its Power in the World Today*, New York, 1940

Sheridan le Fanu, Joseph, 'Carmilla', *Dark Blue* magazine, London, 1871

Sinor, Denis, *History of Hungary*, London, 1959

Szádeczky-Kardoss, Irma, *Báthory Erzsébet-Igazsága*, Budapest, 1993

Szepsi Laczkó, Máté, *Emlékezetül Hagyott Írások*, 1983

Takats, Sándor, *Régi Magyar Asszonyok*, Budapest, 1982

Thaly Kálmán, 'Gyógyítások Ráolvasás és Babonaság Által', *Századok*, Budapest, 1883

Tóth, Béla, *A Magyar Anekdotakincs*, Budapest, 1899–1904

——, *Mendemondák. A Világtörténet Furcsaságai*, Budapest, 1896

Túróczi, László, *Ungaria Suis cum Regibus Compendio Data*, Tyrnava, 1744

Vándor, Kálman, *Báthory Erzsébet*, Budapest, 1941

Várkonyi, Ágnes R., *Connections between the Cessation of Witch Trials and the Transformation of Social Structure Related to Hygiene*, Budapest, 1991

Wagner, Michael, *Beyträge zur Philosophischen Anthropologie und den Damit Werwandten Wissenschaft*, Vienna, 1794

Wéber, Samuel, and Szádeczky, Lajos, 'Adalékok a Babona és a Hiedelmek Történetéhez', *Századok*, 1882

Werbőczy, Istvan, *Opus Tripartitum Juris Consuetudinarii Hungariae*, Buda, 1514

Zsigmond, Móricz, *Tündérkert*, Budapest, 1921

Filmography

Ceremonia Sangrienta, dir. Jorge Grau, X Films/Luis Films, Spain/Italy, 1972

Contes Immoraux, dir. Walerian Borowczyk, Argos Films, France, 1974

Countess Dracula, dir. Peter Sasdy, Hammer Films, GB, 1970

Le Rouge aux Lèvres, dir. Harry Kümel, Showking/Cinevog/Maya Films/Roxy Films, Belgium/France/West Germany, 1971

Index

Index

Index

Picture acknowledgements

The publishers would like to thank the following for permission to reproduce their works: the Hungarian National Museum, Fotomas Index, Mary Evans Picture Library and the British Library. The publishers would also like to thank Gérécor, Erzsébet Baerveldt, Douglas Adams of Tooley Adams, Matrix Cartography and Tony Thorne.